Praise

"This story will pull at your heartstrings as Rachael wrestles with the truths within her marriage. Bonus Phish fandom for all music lovers! I couldn't put it down! Very relatable."
MELISA PETERSON LEWIS, AUTHOR OF THE LAZARUS CITY SERIES

"An instantly relatable story that takes the reader through an emotional roller coaster. All of the Phish content is a bonus, but the real win is following Rachael's tale about uncertainty, confusion, adventure, and of course, love."
BRIAN WEINSTEIN, HOST OF ATTENDANCE BIAS PODCAST

"Perfectly captures what many of us are confronted with at midlife: questioning who we have been and the choices we have made. Placing that questioning inside the colorful, rich Phish universe helps the story come to life in a way that is engaging and unique. A great read for dedicated phans and those to whom this world remains a mystery."
MEGAN GLIONNA, WRITER, PODCASTER, TEACHER, PHISH PHAN

About the Author

Rachael's first concert was Paula Abdul. Since then, she's seen over 1,000 shows. A proud former East Coaster, she now calls Denver home, where she's spoiled by its thriving music scene. If she's not at a show, she can be found hiking, with her nose in a book, or ogling all the doggies. She's thankful every day for second chances and is always trying to make meaning in those signs from the universe.

rachaelwesley.com

Second
Set
Chances

RACHAEL WESLEY

ℳ

www.vineleavespress.com

To all the phans who found their place in this crazy world within Phish's raucous and welcoming circus of light. Cause this is your book too.

Author's Note

I love Phish and all that the band encompasses: the music, Jon, Mike, Page, and Trey, the people and places I've been led to, and the community we've created. My life, yours too, I'm certain, has been saved in one way or another, by this rock and roll. Being a Phish fan has been a significant part of my identity for over half of my existence. My first show was on January 2, 2003, planting me at the very beginning of the short, sweet, and sour 2.0 era of the band.

Second Set Chances captures six months in 2013, when I had less than thirty shows under my ears. By this book's publication, my show count will hover above 130. Much has changed in between these two points, but when writing this book, I tried to best depict my thoughts and opinions toward the band and our community as I felt then. Over a decade later, many of them remain the same (try to guess which ones). This is a memoir. All events and people are real, proving that fact can be stranger than fiction. Characters' names have been changed. Some identities have been combined and certain events have been merged for the sake of a more engaging and smoother-flowing narrative.

Chapter 1

Should I stay or should I go?

My feet straddle the bedroom's threshold as I contemplate what to do. Right foot points to the door, left aims at our bed and Jason's prone figure. I need to leave. I should have left already. But I can't without speaking to my husband first.

Yesterday may have been Independence Day, but today I celebrate my freedom. For months, my daily routine repeated on an endless loop of contradiction, see-sawing between banality and uncertainty. Wake up. Eat breakfast. Job search. Workout. Then what? The plentiful downtime trapped me in my head too often, causing me to believe I was stuck, doomed to live the rest of my life on its current path. And at thirty-one years old, I couldn't think of anything worse.

My trajectory righted itself in the past month. Checking things off my big-girl to-do list (a job offered and accepted, an apartment rented, and a moving date scheduled) released me from all that plaguing stress and uncertainty. As a bonus, for the next seventy-two hours, I'll be liberated of the disappointing dullness that can accompany day-to-day adulting.

I'm ready to get this show on the road and trying not to be selfish. Today marks a big day for Jason too. He's approaching the end of a long process and has reached the final step. I feel obliged to linger and exchange words of encouragement, but he's sleeping. It's his favorite thing to do. Meanwhile, some of my favorite things await me.

I compromise, the key to a successful marriage as the ubiquitous *they* advise.

"Jason," I say, touching his shoulder gently. He remains motionless. I apply more pressure. "Jay, wake up."

His eyes open. "You leaving?"

"Yeah. Kylie's waiting for me. I'll see you on Monday."

His eyes close. "Okay."

I kiss him, lips to cheek instead of lips to lips. "See you in a few days. Good luck with your test. It's almost done. You made it!" I deepen my voice like I'm a sports announcer and he's made a winning play, but I can't tell if he hears me. He gives no response and may be back asleep.

Grabbing my backpack, I walk out the door. A gentle breeze touches my skin, offering a stark contrast to the humidity building in my tiny house. Our new place comes with air conditioning to combat the dry desert heat. I'm on the brink of getting out of my hometown in north-eastern Pennsylvania.

Again.

This time, I won't be returning. It's surreal, and this weekend away serves as the cherry on top.

I drive to Kylie's and find my friend a quiet and sallow version of herself. While I only overindulged on the ribs my father grilled, Kylie used the holiday to practice drinking. Even ashen, she's beautiful. Wearing a sheer tunic over a long white dress, the red flowers dancing on the outer layer complement her dark features and make the vibrant tattoos covering her arms pop.

She groans and perspires while we pack her CRV with our camping supplies. Though the music we listen to is calm and soothing, the soulful Americana of the Wood Brothers does nothing to alleviate Kylie's pain. The cooler is the last thing to heave up and into the trunk, but she needs a breather first.

"Kylie! Nooooo!" I wail like a toddler on the verge of a tantrum, teasing her with my affected fuss, but I do want her in tip-top shape. "Hungover you is not allowed. Will hair of the dog help?" I open the Coleman to grab her a beer.

"No. None of that. Not now. I can't." She throws some drama in, too, and covers her mouth with both hands.

"A nap then? I'll drive," I suggest. We have over a three-hour drive from Scranton, Pennsylvania, to Saratoga Springs, New York. Enough for her to recover, but she shakes her head. I'll have to threaten her. "I have no problem busting a move alone because you're too hungover to go to the show."

This works. She hugs and kisses me in acceptance of my offer. I climb into the driver's seat and adjust the seat and mirrors to accommodate my five feet of height and search for appropriate driving music in a thick binder of choices. Obeying my rule to never listen to the band's music on a show day, I skip over the plethora of Phish CDs. With three nights of the jam band ahead, I opt for *Led Zeppelin III*.

We stop at Burger King for breakfast. Kylie satisfies her sour belly with a meal of carbs and grease. She wolfs down her egg, sausage, and cheese sandwich and passes out as soon as we reach the interstate.

♫

"What's going on with you and Jason? Are you guys happy, or did you get married so he could get his Green Card?" Kylie's voice cuts through the acoustic guitar strumming of *Tangerine*.

"What?" My John Bonham-like drumming on the steering wheel in slow traffic stops as I grapple with her unexpected question.

Five minutes ago, she'd been napping. I sneak a quick look her way and note how her brown eyes sparkle. The snooze proved a success. And this is how she repays my favor, by examining the state of my marriage?

Kylie's bluntness doesn't surprise me. It's her words that throw me off and cause my stomach to tighten. I've not voiced my marriage apathy to anyone, not even my husband. There was no point in expressing my discontent, in stirring up trouble or giving cause for unnecessary concern, not when Jason and I are on the verge of breaking through our malaise. Kylie is intuitive and possesses high emotional intelligence. Perhaps she is the only one who has noticed?

"Your husband, Rachael. Does he love you or is your marriage one of convenience?" she asks.

My marriage is one of the three things I don't want to discuss this weekend (the other two being my new job and the move). So much is riding on this trifecta of potential, and they'll become my focus when this music vacation ends. For now, I want to keep my brain pressure-free for my return to Phish, on my first set of shows since I moved back to the US. Live music acts as my antidepressant, and I've not had my medicine in a year and a half.

I am, however, impressed with the timing of Kylie's question. Though she's aware Jason hovers in the final stages of gaining US citizenship, she doesn't know the exact timeline. Plus, I'd like to get to the root of her interrogation. So instead of shutting down the conversation, I elbow her across the console and open it up. "Your question is ridiculous, but there is money to be made with your mind-reading skills."

She howls. "You know I'm down, though I don't know what you're talking about."

"His civics test is on Monday. It's the last thing he needs to do before he becomes a citizen."

"Woman! Why aren't you with him?" She pivots from her original message to scold me.

"No, no. no, no. It's not like that. It's a test, that's it. I would never miss his citizenship ceremony. No fucking way. But why are you asking me about my marriage, anyway?"

"I can't remember the last time I saw him." Kylie turns the music off and I no longer hear Robert Plant telling us this is the way things ought to stay. "He never does anything with you. Happy couples do things together. Would he be here if he didn't have that test? Probably not."

She is serious. I consider what she says. Once upon a time, in the spirit of being a good sport, Jay joined me for a few Phish shows. Three to be exact. He traded his everyday uniform of jeans and a button-down for a pair of khaki shorts and an old concert tee of mine to blend in with the other fans, as if he wouldn't stick out among the mostly white crowd. He earnestly tried to get into the music while I took responsibility for making sure he enjoyed himself, asking him constant questions.

"Are you hungry?"

"Do you need to go to the bathroom?"

"What do you think of this song?"

Despite our best efforts, Phish didn't become his earworm of choice. I felt more relief than anything else. Such vigilant babysitting took away from my best time ever. Out of a sense of obligation, I did continue to ask him to join me.

But not this time. This Phish holiday belongs to me.

"Can you imagine Jay camping for three nights? The man hates skipping showers," I say. "Besides, I wouldn't enjoy myself nearly as much. I'd be too worried about him."

"That's fair."

"Besides, Kylie, this trip is about the estrogen. You and I need to fit in as much quality time as possible before I move." I slap her knee lightly.

"And this is precisely why I asked about your marriage. It'll be you and him alone in a new city and you two seem off. Something is different."

"It's the ebbs and flows of a relationship, that's all. This move will be good for us. I think we need to 'be' in a place for a while. We've been going back and forth between Seoul and Pennsylvania for our entire relationship. It's exhausting." I keep my voice light as I mildly experiment with speaking some truth aloud.

A hint of the old "us" resurfaced on a recent vacation to Vietnam. Linking hands to stroll the moped-packed streets of Saigon. Talking incessantly about what we'd seen and done that day over freshly caught seafood dinners. Delighting in boat rides on the Mekong River, taxi services on the backs of scooters, and rickety trains linking us to our destinations. Those two weeks of traveling together proved to me that we still work; we've just gone a bit dormant.

I honestly believe this upcoming move will reverse any damage we created throughout our six years as a couple. Jason and I have always been strongest during times of discovery and exploration. Our relocation to the southwest, to Las Vegas, will not only ground us, it'll also provide the necessary adventures suitable for a relationship revival.

Kylie digests this. "I accept your answer. But I'm keeping my eyes on you from afar. Gotta make sure my girl is happy."

"Don't worry. We're going to be fine. Everything is going to be fine." I manifest with this mantra, hoping my assertions will become my reality.

We stop for gas and Kylie takes over as captain to finish our drive to Saratoga Springs. I relax beside her, comfortable in my traveling attire. A tight cream tank top hugs my torso while brown genie pants balloon over my legs until gathering tightly at my ankles. My long dark hair hangs in a low ponytail and gives center stage to my wooden hoop earrings.

I finger the fourth ring on my left hand out of habit as I gaze out the window. When Jason and I capriciously became engaged, I chose a cubic zirconia over a shiny diamond and paired it with a simple silver wedding ring, his name inscribed on the inside in Korean Hangul, Hwang Ji Soo.

My wedding band stands alone in proclaiming my marital status. I rang in 2013 by losing my engagement ring at a Korean spa back in January. I'd gone to the jimjilbang to decompress and spent the Sunday afternoon naked with dozens of other women, alternating between hot tubs of varying temperatures and wet and dry saunas. The ring disappeared while I soaked in the lavender and green tea scented tubs. The soothing scents of the purple and green-tinged waters calmed me to such a relaxed state that I didn't notice my ring missing until I had showered and dressed. I've yet to replace the inexpensive cubic zirconia.

We don't have many miles to go until I'm immersed in my former life, and I plan to go big. What I suggest next to Kylie slips out of my mouth as soon as the thought appears. It absolutely contradicts what I said about my marriage, but paradox permeates the human condition.

"No more Jason or marriage talk, please. We're moving in a month, and it'll be just like starting over, which makes this weekend my final chance to really boogie down stress-free. So, let's have some extra fun. I'm going to pretend I'm single and flirt with the handsome men of Phish."

I pull the thin band from my finger and place it in the cupholder between us. Flirting is innocent; it's only words. Sticks and stones may break my bones, but words will never hurt my relationship. I am and have always been attracted to ponytails and beards. We're headed to the mecca of such men. Jason couldn't grow a beard if he stopped shaving for a month. I can pretend for three days and then return to the real world. To start fresh in another city with my short-haired, smooth-faced spouse.

Chapter 2

We reach Adventure Bound Camping Resort by midafternoon. Kylie finds our reserved camping spot and we survey our home turf while stretching our limbs.

She assesses the other campers setting up their sites that line the perimeter of the tree-framed field. "I'm seeing a lot of cargo shorts and mandalas. They must be here for Phish."

"Swimming pools, showers, and flushable toilets. My butthole is already thanking me! And all these fellow fans. YES!" I was originally disheartened when I booked the spot, the only campground with availability, because of its distance (over thirty minutes' driving) from the venue. I'm stoked it's brimming with this load of unanticipated amenities.

I text Jason and my mom to let them know we had safely arrived. My mother's response (*Good. Have fun and be careful. Tell Kylie I said hello. Love you.*) reads lengthier than Jason's standard *okay*. He's most comfortable communicating in his second language in-person. I get it, but his reticence for interactions via phone call or text message drives me crazy. Come on, dude, talk with me.

However, this reluctance may serve me this weekend. Out of sight and out of touch, our lack of contact means he'll take up less space in my head. If he's satisfied with such brief exchanges, so am I. Perhaps it'll help me feel less guilt should I get a hug from a handsome scruffy stranger or three.

Kylie and I unpack the car to grant access to the cooler. She grabs one handle, I grasp the other, and we heave the overloaded red Coleman out of the hatch. The ice rattles against the beer bottles inside when it hits the ground. I open two Sierra Nevada pale ales, hand one to an eager, hair-of-the-dog-unnecessary Kylie, and we get to work.

We assemble camp in record time, experts due to years of attending shows and festivals. At the inaugural Bonnaroo in 2002—the first festival I ever attended—my friends and I arrived in Tennessee equipped with a single tent, sleeping bags, and a cooler full of beer. We possessed nothing to shield us from the strong southern sunshine, not even a tarp, but troubleshooting such a fatal problem proved easy. We immediately made friends with our neighbors, who had wisely brought a large canopy. They granted us refuge beneath it whenever we needed, and we hung out with them throughout the entire festival.

It's still essential to befriend camping neighbors. It's become more for enrichment than survival.

Now, with a pop-up canopy blocking the overhead sun and thin tapestries hanging from its four sides to keep angled rays of light off our skin, we open another beer and turn to meet the three men camped beside us. Something in the grass sidetracks us.

"Oh, look! Is that five dollars?"

Kylie moves toward the bill. Just as it's within her grasp, it snakes away, drifting out of her reach on a path so perfectly straight that it couldn't possibly be the breeze moving it.

The roars and howls coming from the adjoining camp furthers my suspicion. Our neighbor, the blond one, confirms. He holds up a fishing pole and line from which, instead of a lure, the five-dollar bill dangles.

"Ha! Fooled you!" He's triumphant. As he should be. This may possibly be the best way I've ever met someone. It's certainly the most entertaining.

I double over, grabbing my belly to contain my giggles. "That was good!"

We shake hands, clink beer bottles together, and exchange names. Jack, Ian, and Bill. Though friendly and possessing a sharp sense of humor, none of our neighbors have long hair or beards. They receive another strike when they tell us they're on the casual end of the Phish fandom spectrum. I won't waste my flirting on them. If I'm feigning singledom it'll be with someone opposite my husband.

Kylie appraises the half-full trash bag and beer bottles littering their camping table. "You guys wanna ride with us to the show?"

"That would be awesome."

Fifteen minutes later, we pile into Kylie's CRV. Claiming the front passenger seat, I watch the other campers scrambling to leave through the windshield and glance at my reflection in the rearview mirror, looking anywhere but at the cupholder. I'm not going to peek inside, to think about what's in there. It's safe and will go back on my finger as soon as the weekend is through.

The men climb into the back, sitting knee to knee with broad shoulders touching. We listen to Ween on the drive. The chorus of "Voodoo Lady" adds a complementary touch to our "*weees*" as Kylie navigates through three roundabouts, my arms rising, almost involuntarily, as if I'm riding a roller coaster.

Halfway there, Jack, the prankster, shouts up front to me and Kylie, "Can you find me mushrooms?"

I turn down the music. "Are you afraid you'll get arrested if you try to buy them? Look for the undercovers in their jeans and aggressively tie-dyed Dave Matthews band T-shirts and walk in the opposite direction." There's some truth to my joke; many years ago, a friend was busted for underage drinking on Lot by similarly dressed police.

"You two know what you're doing here. I don't."

"Ha! Okay, glad I can use my expertise," I tell him.

Acquiring drugs, any drug, on The Lot shouldn't be a problem.

Phish and weed go together like tie-dye and Birkenstocks. As ubiquitous as Bud Light at a Kenny Chesney concert, marijuana exists as the bastion of altered states among fans. Endless clusters of smokers contribute continuously to the clouds that hang seemingly permanently above the audience's heads during a show, leaving a lingering scent of sprayed skunk.

Pot is far from the only substance consumed. There's booze, of course, but that's entry-level—and legal—compared to the smorgasbord available and ingested: ecstasy, molly, and MDMA in all its forms, psychedelics like LSD and mushrooms, cocaine, pills, and opioids. People use drugs for various reasons and base their substance use on the desired effect. Most provide energy and can enhance euphoria, increase the merriment, and help one tap into their spiritual side.

"Cool, cool. Thank you. I haven't done 'shrooms in years," he replies.

I haven't either. I experimented with drugs regularly during my late teens through my mid-twenties and had a blast doing so. Hours of nonstop hilarity, chain-smoking menthols throughout stream-of-conscious ramblings, these altered states of consciousness causing nights to blend into mornings. I used drugs for my own amusement and quest for transcendence. Wisdom has taught me that they aren't tantamount to a guaranteed blast. At thirty-one, the blackouts, hangovers, and retrospective "how did I survive that wild ride," produce more angst than entertainment.

Most of the time.

I occasionally dabble with psychedelics and MDMA, once or twice a year instead of at every show, and never while living in Seoul. Future, forty-year-old Rachael will develop a preference for quasi-California sobriety, sipping on beers, taking intermittent hits of weed, and floating into a natural music-induced high. This more mature version of myself remembers entire concerts, wakes up ready for another show, and experiences little of the racing heart and gloomy thoughts accompanying the anxiety of a hangover.

Many have evolved to this lifestyle; sober fans comprise a large segment of the scene.

But I'm not there yet. Not in 2013, so recently returned from South Korea, open and suggestible to the promise of an elevated bacchanal.

Chapter 3

The venue, Saratoga Performance Arts Center, or SPAC as it's referred to, is nestled in the middle of a massive state park. It's teeming with concert traffic. We pass several full parking lots before entering one with spots open. Kylie parks and the five of us exit her packed clown car.

I stand, my sandaled (but not Birkenstock sandaled) feet planted on the concrete, united with one of the best parts about going to a show. Hanging on The Lot.

People cluster around the backs of vehicles in small groups, sipping on cans and bottles and cocktails mixed inside red cups. Music blasts from speakers and joints pass around in circles. Such space allows people to converse and drum up excitement for the main event. I over-hear some chatter in nearby clusters of fans.

"What do you think they'll open with?"

"I don't care what we hear, as long as they play a sick '2001.'"

"Oh man, what I wouldn't give for 'Split Open and Melt.'"

Essentially, we're tailgating, but I never want to hear someone call it that. No. Should someone utter that word, I'd suspect them of being a narc. A veteran fan knows better. The jam band community refers to this pre-show revelry as hanging on The Lot.

Many choose not to linger car side for too long. Adventures await and tasks to lead you away from your vehicle, such as the mission Jack gave us. With beers poured into red plastic cups, the five of us traipse across the parking lots on the hunt for his requested psychedelic mushrooms.

"Whose got my 'shrooms," I repeatedly shout in hopes a purveyor of fungus will hear me.

Alas, though many hear my request, no one delivers the goods. We wander through The Lot without any success and stumble to the venue's entrance. Here, people mill about everywhere: waiting in the security line, standing at will call, or finishing their drinks before heading inside.

I drain the last of my beer as we pause to catch our bearings. The dregs of warm pale ale linger. The bitter aftertaste should vanish with a menthol. I puff my cigarette and take in the madness circling outside the venue. Thousands of voices merge to create a cacophony of undecipherable sound, but it's my eyes that experience the most stimulation.

Fashion has a way of revealing one's identity. A Phish show, where most attendees are welcoming and open-minded, presents the greatest of opportunities to unfurl the real you. For several shows in a row, I encountered a bearded man who donned various bedazzled prom gowns. A buddy of mine once encased his slender body in a skintight electric green onesie. "I feel silly," he said, pointing down at his shoes as we walked toward the venue. The soles lit up upon contact with the ground and he worried others would find the lights distracting.

I'd changed earlier. Hot pink flowers dot my strapless blue dress. The flowy skirt permits the evening breeze entrance up to my stomach and enables my arms and legs to move unconstricted. It's perfect for dancing, though relatively tame compared to others here.

Bright colors and bold patterns splash all clothing surfaces. Wigs of tight purple curls or yellow bobs hide boring browns and blonds. A tight-bodied young woman glides by in a thong and bikini top under a sheer dress (she'll be cold later). White-people dreadlocks appear in all forms, from thick knots embellished with beads and hemp that hang to the waist to shoulder-length locks tied back in a basic red bandana. Several shirtless men swathed in long, gauzy skirts mosey through the crowds. I own several of the same style, found at Goodwill, a score of a purchase with panels of colors sewn together and jingly bells attached to the drawstring waist.

I believe it's one of the skirted men who helps me score. One walks by as I take a final drag of my cigarette. He's cute enough to spend some of my flirting on, with sun-streaked brown hair pushed back by sunglasses and a wiry upper body, but I need to get rid of my finished menthol. I bend to extinguish it, holding my red cup so the rim faces up while my head faces down, and, when I rise, the cup is no longer empty. Inside lies a plastic sandwich bag.

Thanks for using me as a trash can, sir. I like your skirt.

Except he didn't garbage me. He gifted me. This bag isn't bare. Maybe the handsome stranger wanted to flirt with me too.

I pull it out and examine the contents. Thin, grayish-white sticks extend out to a bulbous end. Wait, these are no sticks. These are mushrooms! Jerry Garcia's ghost must be with me, ensuring we will have a real good time.

"Holy shit," I gasp, shocked at what literally fell into my lap, er, cup. Looks like my "expertise" did prevail.

I hand Jack the bag and explain my good fortune. He chomps on the psilocybin fungus until all that remains is a corner pocket of dried remnants, and offers the rest to me and Kylie, pouring the flakes into our open palms.

I wash my share down with a sip of Kylie's beer and think nothing of it. What could a tablespoon of shake do? It's not enough to make me trip.

Chapter 4

Kylie and I venture toward the amphitheater, leaving our three buddies behind to finish their drinks. The line to get inside the venue extends long. Security searches bags and pats down bodies to ensure no contraband gets through, but there are ways to get around prodding hands and eyes. Sports bras and underboobs conceal joints, pills, and powders and underpants tuck around beers and flasks.

I purposely slipped on a pair of granny panties for the occasion and shove two Sierra Nevadas snug against nature's pocket while waiting in line. My thighs squeeze together to keep the bottles from clinking. The security guard wishes me a good evening as she waves me past.

Despite the thousands of fans loitering out front, it's packed inside. The pavilion, with its coveted assigned seats and pit, fits one-fifth of the venue's 25,000 capacity. The structure obstructs much of the view for those in general admission on the lawn. Though these general admission tickets are easy to procure, decent space on this expansive swath of grass is not.

Kylie and I search for and successfully locate a spot at the edge of the walkway that halves the lawn. Here, the ground's tilt gives way to a more leveled earth and my legs thank me for having less gravity to contend with.

I lounge on the soft grass and open one of my secret crotch beers, wearing a smile that nothing and no one can rip from my face. Other than the "welcome home" embraces of Mom and Dad I received upon my return from Seoul, I feel more comfortable, safe, and present now than I have at any other moment since moving back to the US in March.

Tonight marks the twenty-seventh time I've witnessed the band taking the stage. I've friends who've checked off dozens upon dozens of shows, and acquaintances surpassing the two hundred mark. My stats suffer from teaching abroad and the band's five-year breakup. Give me more opportunities combined with permanent US living and I know I'll hit over one hundred shows.

Why would anyone see the same band so much? It's easy! Phish's catalog extends into hundreds of songs. The uninitiated may not know this, but many of their songs are composed, complete with lyrics I occasionally sing along softly with or mouth the words to as I move my body to beats and tempo changes that I anticipate because almost every version of the song resembles the other.

It's only the jam vehicles, the songs that sound like "noodling" to virgin ears, that veer off into a creative explosion of improv. Sure, there is a bit of that noodling as the musicians play various notes and chords, searching for a groove, an unexplored territory in the vast musical universe. Once one of the members find it, whether it's a bass slap provided by Mike (Gordon) to change the song's entire tone, or (Jon) Fishman supplying an off-rhythm drum beat to inspire an innovative chord progression in Trey (Anastasio), or a melodic pattern keyed upon Page (McConnell's) grand piano, the other three lock in, their instruments supplying layers of sound, and a new jam, a song within a song, is born. The jam vehicle songs almost always begin the same way, but eventually deviate from the structure into the improvised jam. No two versions of the song will ever sound the same, no matter how many times Phish has played them.

My favorite, most fans' favorites, are when the jams stretch on, extending over twenty, thirty, even, if we're lucky, forty minutes long, morphing from one discrete melody into another. My sense of perception alters; I get lost in these minutes. "What song is this?" but remain laser-eared focused, not wanting to miss any nuance.

Between their massive catalog of music and the amount of improvisation, every show is enormously different and is one of the reasons such a ravenous following form around jam bands. This Friday's show at SPAC is the first of three and most of us here tonight will attend all of them. I warn that this music isn't for everyone, but for those that "get" it, it becomes a passion. Hence, the high show count.

Noise erupts from the pavilion. This can only mean one thing and I shoot to my feet. "Kylie, it's happening!"

My eyes fix on the stage, but I can't see the four members assuming their positions behind their instruments. I stand on my tiptoes, as if this could help me see through the pavilion's obstructed view any better. Thankfully, giant screens project the stage action in a panorama from stage right to left.

Though they look exactly as they did when I last saw them a year and a half ago, their appearances have matured through the decades. Page's thinning curls frame a receding bald spot, while Trey's red hair glows less bright, and Mike gels his former mop into a stylish gray pompadour. Their fashion sense has evolved as well, with ratty and worn T-shirts replaced by fitted button-downs, flannels, and structured jackets.

Two constants remain: Fishman's mumu, covered in red circles with holes in the middle among a blue backdrop and worn at every performance, and their music. Rooted in rock and heavily influenced by masters such as Frank Zappa, The Talking Heads, and Jimi Hendrix, the band's sound covers the spectrum, from punk to bluegrass to classical, and all vibrations in between. Something for everyone, provided you don't mind your music oozes with all that jam.

The first riffs of "Kill Devil Falls" spring from Trey's guitar. The bluesy pleas circling off his instrument transition to the song's main rhythm chasing a one, two thump of Fishman's drums, and my feet, knees, hips, shoulders, arms, and hands get to work.

The arena rock-style song ends in its usual guitar-led jam punctuated with Page's playful key work. The song serves as a warm-up, as an opening song should. We've two sets of music awaiting us, and my physical body and emotional being sometimes need to be eased in, especially following a long absence.

"Moma Dance" comes next. Page rises to his clavinet, and I prepare to get down. Any frenzy of funk calls for larger, more precise turns of the hips and sharper glides from the shoulder. Joints properly lubricated, I oblige.

Dancing is my soul's response to the music. My movements belong to me, but thousands of people join in, sharing and moving to the same groove. In my peripheral vision, I glimpse the woman on my right. She's taken dance lessons at the same school as me; she looks to be matching my every move. I ground my feet to better twirl my hips and elbows to the harpsichord sounds emitting from Page's keyboards. She does the same. When Trey takes over with a twirling, swirling guitar solo, my heels lift to emphasize my groove. My pal turns her dancing dial up too.

Maybe we all dance like this.

An ethereal yet palpable force threads the collective mass of fans together. For us, a Phish show is as spiritual as Easter Sunday mass is for Christians and I have come ready to receive my communion. The bliss produced while enmeshed in the music is a natural high and we keep chasing it, needing more.

It's not hyperbole when I call live music one of my antidepressants (there are several). I suck in the energy of the music and the upbeat vibes permeating the crowd as if I'm a hippie vampire. These intangible sensations fill my physical being and my essence absorbs them. A tree in reverse: I exhale my negative and pull back positive, transforming my anxieties and fears to be present here.

Out: I have to start all over in a new city. Again.

In: Wow, I'm finally back!

Out: Do I need to list topics of conversation so Jason and I have things to talk about?

In: Oh my, that mother dancing with her little one. Cuteness overload!

Out: How am I going to make friends as an adult?

In: Oh, that breeze feels so cool on my sweaty body.

With arms bent at ninety-degree angles, I roll my shoulders in exaggerated movements, keeping rhythm with the band. Elaine from *Seinfeld* throws down better moves than me, but while I'm grooving to live music, I'm a master class choreographer.

The band plays "Sample in a Jar" too soon in set one. Many of the band's songs fall outside the formulas of rock music, but this one sounds as close to standard rock as Phish gets. The short (for Phish) tune has long become my bathroom song, but it's only the third song in and I'm already dancing my way toward the grand prize on *Dancing with the Stars.*

I forfeit the toilet break and pretend to be nineteen years old, cruising south on Interstate 81 at the end of a workday and hearing this song for the first time. In the present day, optimism washes through me as it did on that Friday evening when I cranked the volume up on the newly borrowed CD.

Then, I was filled with hope for what the weekend would bring me, finally feeling good about myself and having plans I delighted in. Now, I'm awash with the simple joy of my return, of knowing I have this back in my orbit.

I move imaginary plates with my hands, twirling my arms in zigs and zags below my hips with extra oomph through several songs. The crowd around me is in heavy competition for my dancing trophy, moving with their own stellar motions.

The composed chaos of the grand piano signals "Bathtub Gin." Fingers move in furious control, as if Page is sipping from a martini glass full of the prohibition-era booze.

A skinny dude, his tan face contrasting with the white baseball cap on his head, stops directly in front of me on the walkway in anticipation, I guess, of what's to come. Sure enough, as Trey sings into the mic about us all being in this thing together, the man lifts his right hand into the air, pumping it. We all do, shouting the proceeding line. Proclaiming our love for taking a bath.

As our universal connection grows more robust, I twirl around.

And my world shifts.

Not in a good way.

While choking back the thimbleful of mushroom shake earlier, I thought I hadn't ingested enough to feel anything. The mushrooms have different plans for me. My beer buzz alters as the lightness leaves my head and upper body. A bolt of nervous energy claps me like I'm in the throes of a caffeine-induced panic attack. The beautiful buzz pulsating from the audience has entered the top of my head. It shoots through my veins and arteries, into my fingertips and toes, and fires back out into the world.

I'm not prepared for any of this.

A pinched scowl replaces my perma-grin. My heart pounds at the speed of a hummingbird as it transports blood throughout my body, dispersing more and more energy. My hands and feet tingle with pulses of life.

Though I'm no longer paying attention to the music, I need to move. And so I do, and it helps. I'm not so cognizant of my pounding heart or tingling limbs while in motion through some reggae pop, a sweet, slow tune, and the frenetic tempo of the next three songs. Though completely different in rhythm and mood, each soothes me in their own way.

But then comes a Talking Heads cover: "Cities." The lyrics, how I relate so closely to them, taunt me. Go find yourself a city to call home. I'm about to do that exact thing and have been questioning the decision since making it, but to myself, silently and in the hidden compartments of my mind, and only when I let my guard down.

The mushrooms have removed the protective barriers of my subconscious. The anxieties and uncertainties pour in, infiltrating my brain and forcing me to stop moving. I'm trapped in my head on a doomsday scroll of thoughts of my own making.

What the fuck am I doing, taking off my wedding ring? What kind of wife does that? I could have kept it on and still had a good time. Flirting is no big deal, except I had to go to the extreme. But if I was a good wife, would I even be here? Why didn't I go with Jason? I know he's just taking a test, but any other wife would have gone in support. Right? But wouldn't he have asked me to go with him? Is Kylie right? Did he marry me for his Green Card? And now we're moving to Vegas by ourselves. I'm going to be all alone except for him.

What am I doing?

The images of my cracked marriage should have consumed me, but I'm rescued by my tremendous body buzz. I'm hyperfocused on the energy coursing through my body. It causes greater anxiety than my headspace does and needs to be expended. And fast.

I turn my attention back to the music and my body picks up the rhythm. Arms flow, hips swing, feet swivel. My grimace loosens and the panic trickles out of my body.

Too soon, Fishman's sticks hit the high-hat introduction of frequent set closer, "David Bowie," indicating I will soon be without this musical release. Struggling to exorcise my mushroom-induced vigor, I've no choice but to surrender to what's left of the music. For the final ten minutes, I bust into a calisthenic burst of moves. It's after midnight somewhere and I'm letting it all hang out.

"Bowie" finishes, set one ends and my body demands more movement. I turn to my show partner. Kylie revels in the blissful afterburn with closed eyes. She drank two beers to my four but consumed equal amounts of mushrooms and I wonder if they affected her similarly. To rid my dark thoughts faster, I hide them from her.

Kylie suggests we head to the bathroom. The women's room steams with humidity and dampness, a product of sink splashing to cool the sweat of bodies in motion. I contribute to the wet mess by splashing water on my heated skin.

"You're fine, Rachael. You're fine," I say, repeating the simple mantra for assurance. This mushroom trip isn't all that bad. I am not a terrible person. My marriage is fine, just like I am. "You're fine. You're fine. You're fine."

I leave the bathroom feeling somewhat revitalized and request we find a different location to dispel any lingering anxieties. As we scout out lawn space, I hear my name.

"Hey, Rachael."

Unsure if it is directed at me or someone else, I look around. A man is looking directly at me, but I'm not registering his face. He tries again.

"Rachael, it's Faris."

Faris?

It's not a common name, but I once knew a Faris. In fact, my college buddy randomly popped into my thoughts while I was visiting an aunt and uncle a few weeks ago.

I stare back at the man standing ten feet away. Though thinner than when I'd last laid eyes on him, I finally recognize the person behind the voice. While not an exact instant karma, the universe appears to have answered my naked ring finger in delivering him, and in my most sacred of places too.

Is this really happening?

I scream, run up, and wrap my arms around him.

Chapter 5

I met him while buying a bag of weed.

It was an early summer night in 2003, the endless weekend between my junior and senior years at Penn State. I spent the latter end of my evening drinking skunky Heineken ponies in the dingy, cement-floored Rathskeller.

I hated the 'Skeller, with its bare walls that held the perpetual stink of spoiled beer. Though it was one of many basement-dwelling drinking establishments in the university town, it had gone the least out of its way to appear unique. The bar attracted a clientele as dull as the bar itself, drunk frat boys who only spoke of Penn State football, screaming over blaring top forty hits. I sucked down my miniature, eight-ounce green bottles of beer hunched in the back room, avoiding the crowds and music.

The outing had begun at another underground bar, yet Zeno's, with its worldly collection of brews, was my favorite place to frequent. My good time was interrupted when my roommate received a phone call from a friend she hadn't seen in months. He pleaded for us to join him around the corner. We abandoned our tasty drinking selection to meet him. At least the 'Stellar wasn't crowded with its usual Greek life clientele, a massive perk of staying through the offseason in a college town.

I loved State College summers. Most Penn State students went home at the semester's end. The town became ghost-like between early May through late August, consisting primarily of locals and the few students who opted to stick around. Hordes of undergrads didn't inundate the college town's streets, bars, and restaurants. Hiking trails weren't crowded. Lakes and swimming holes held plenty of space to splash in. The biggest problem with State College summers was our go-to pot connection also left for the season.

My roommate's friend made up for his suggestion to meet at the Rathskeller. "I know where we can buy a bag."

We piled into his car and drove away from the two main streets and into a residential area populated more by townies than college students. A large yard connected the two matching houses in the middle of the property. In the darkness of the after-hours sky, I caught sight of bright orange feathers moving slowly.

"Is that a chicken?"

"A rooster. There's two of them." Our chauffeur had clearly been here before.

We walked into the closest house. They were expecting us, but the three guys in the dimly lit living room didn't move off their couch. They offered beers and smiles. I settled on the carpeted floor, having consumed too many ponies of Heineken to worry about the filth woven within the fibers. Engaging the three roommates in conversation, I was stunned to find out they hailed from northeast Pennsylvania as well. We grew up less than ten miles from one another, yet were strangers.

This wasn't surprising. In high school, I hadn't ventured far outside the realms of friendships made with my fellow students of Pittston Area Senior High. My graduating class consisted of one African American, one Chinese American, and two hundred and forty-eight white kids. Other than what I read in books, I lacked knowledge of societies and cultures outside the typical melting pot of European immigration that painted northeastern Pennsylvania in various shades of white. It was while I was in college, surrounded by people from all parts of the world, that I started to lose my ignorance.

A fourth roommate soon joined us, a tall dude with a round, easygoing face, and hair in a ponytail that, when pulled free, hung past his shoulders. He wore a zipped-up hoodie with a familiar yellow emblem sewn into the top right corner, a leaping antelope mid-flight, its long antlers poised high in the air. His sweatshirt automatically cemented us into friendship. I jumped to my feet, needing to know who this guy was.

"Hey, I'm Rachael," I stuck out my hand.

He shook my hand in return. "I'm Faris."

"Faris? Like, Bueller? Bueller? Bueller?" I cracked up at my horrible joke and was the only one laughing.

"No, Faris as in Faris." He repeated his name, pronouncing it in an accent I didn't recognize, giving the "r" a slight roll.

"What kind of name is that?" Ouch. Despite my newfound exposures, I had much to learn about other cultures.

"It's Arabic. My dad's Kuwaiti. I grew up there."

He shortly learned about my obsession with Phish and forgave me for my lack of tact.

♪

Unbelievable.

I'm afraid he'll disappear if I let go, but an embrace is no way to rage the second set of a Phish show. I extricate myself from our hug and am relieved when he stays put.

I study him. Several people around us display attire with the same yellow antelope emblem that connected us years ago, but Faris isn't one of them. He's clad in blue jeans and a navy T-shirt bearing a geometric skull. A blue baseball cap is perched backward over his large head. Looks like he's not grown his hair long again; he chopped off his signature ponytail once we'd graduated for a more professional appearance. His massive hands hold a can of beer and a plastic cup of wine.

His shoulders stretch open confidently, no longer rounded in a college-era hunch. He's lost his baby-faced appearance; angles cut his stubble-flecked cheeks and chin. These are subtle differences; he looks almost identical to the Faris of eight years ago.

Faris raises his eyebrows and opens his mouth in a mock grin as his blue eyes dance at me. The same expression that would greet me on a

Friday night in State College, spreading warmth through my body and causing my insides to quiver.

I reiterate confounded thoughts from moments earlier. *Is this really happening?*

"Holy shit," I shout, unable to control the volume of my voice. "What are you doing here?"

He sips his beer and answers. "My younger sister lives here. Perfect opportunity for a family visit."

"No better fucking time," I agree. So, he's here with his sister? Anyone else? A wife? Girlfriend?

Kylie sticks out her hand. "Hey, I'm Kylie."

Faris holds the plastic cup of wine in his teeth and shakes her hand.

"Oh shit, I'm sorry. Where are my manners? Kylie, this is Faris. We're old college buddies."

"Crazy running into you like this. What brings you here?" He must be shocked as well, asking such a silly question. Faris, so logical and level-headed, would never ask things with obvious and reasonable answers.

"For the Foreigner show. I can't wait to hear 'I Want to Know What Love Is.'" I attempt to be witty. Damn all those quick people. Why can't I be more like them?

But Faris chuckles. "Me too. Is it the two of you? Come join Maryam and me."

Ah, so it is only him and his sister. I shoot Kylie a glance. *Say yes!* There's no reason for her not to.

She doesn't disappoint. "Lead the way, Faris."

He obliges and he takes us through the crowd. My eyes zero in on his broad back, inches in front of me, determined not to let him vanish from my sight. People happen upon old friends at shows frequently, but I never would have expected this. I'd occasionally run into Faris's former college roommates in northeast Pennsylvania, and we'd always inquire of the other "have you heard from Faris?" to which the other would answer "haven't talked to him in years." He had disappeared.

Shocked at our encounter, and processing the last five minutes, I'm rendered speechless. Faris takes the conversational lead.

"You know, this is the first time seeing them since they got back together." He turns and looks down at me.

I received the worst present ever when, in May 2004, a day before my birthday and right around college graduation, Trey released a letter announcing that Phish was breaking up at the conclusion of their summer tour.

I sat at my computer, stunned and frozen, sure that what I had read was a joke. This revelation devastated the fanbase. We thought our band was done; an integral part of our lives gone forever. What do you do when part of your core no longer exists? I sunk my sorrows by seeking adventure in Asia, replacing part of my missing identity with expat living.

But we, and Phish, would have our second chance. In 2009, Jon, Mike, Page, and Trey revealed they were getting back together. I jumped back into the show going with gusto (at least when I was Stateside). Four years have passed since their return. What's taken Faris so long?

"For real?" I don't believe him. "I don't think you're allowed to call yourself a fan anymore."

"Well, I've become somewhat of a workaholic. Plus, I've lost touch with a lot of my show friends. Like you."

"And now you're reuniting with the band and old show friends simultaneously. What crazy and magical timing." I leap at the word "magical," hoping I look like a cute hippie fairy.

"And I'm only here because my sister lives here."

"So, what do you think?"

"Of my sister? She's okay, I guess," he jokes.

"Just okay?! That must make for an awkward visit." I play along. "I hope the music helps."

"Actually, the first thing I thought is how healthy Trey looks."

"Your first thought was Trey and not the music? That's quite the man crush."

"The music was great, but man crush or not, Trey looks great. Like a completely different man." He stops and peers into the crowd slanting below, scanning for his sister, I assume.

Phish's frontman offered several reasons for their 2004 split, but the leading cause wasn't revealed until he was several years into his recovery. Trey was an addict and musician life was killing him. He needed to stop touring to get clean.

The breakup didn't initially help Trey sober up; a 2006 arrest for DWI and possession, not too far from where we stood now, did. Trey was to have his second chance as well. The man has been clean and sober since his arrest.

"Yeah, no more worrying about him possibly collapsing onstage," I agree.

In the months preceding their breakup, it was uncomfortable watching him perform; he looked as if he was about to keel over dead at any moment. Now, he looks better than ever. Ashen skin gone, his eyes sparkle behind his glasses, and his face looks to be permanently upturned in a brag of happiness.

Faris takes us deep into the lower lawn of stage left. The ground inclines steeper here but offers more spread-out dancing space. A woman sits in the grass beside a backpack.

"Maryam, this is Rachael and Kylie. And this is my sister, Maryam." Faris possesses better manners than I do.

We shake hands with the younger Al Bakar. Resemblance runs strong in this family. She has the same fair skin and blue eyes as her brother, his easy laugh too. She chuckles when she hears of my astounded confusion running across Faris.

"He is pretty forgettable," she says, punching him lightly in the shoulder as she teases him.

"You're getting your next drink." He rolls his eyes.

Our groups doubled, we four chat as if we're old touring buddies from the '90s. It's at this moment I realize I no longer feel the effects of the mushrooms. All the dark, penetrating thoughts, the coursing energy. Gone.

It's possible I hadn't even been tripping. My anxiety creeps in at inopportune moments and mine and Kylie's road trip conversation offered enough fodder to trigger it. My panic causes the obsessive thoughts of doom, out-of-body vision, and jumping-out-of-the-skin energy I experienced during the first set. If the 'shrooms had any influence on my head and body, I'd certainly still be feeling them.

But now, I am relaxed, content, and ready for another set of music.

Chapter 6

Kylie thrusts a cup of convenience store coffee in my face as I emerge from our tent in the morning.

"Thank you! Where did this come from?" I take a cautious sip.

Even with our combined camping experience and my coffee addiction, neither of us had brought any beans, instant packets, or cooking methods to provide us with magic morning juice.

"The camp store."

"Hell yeah. This may be the greatest wake-up surprise ever. I'll cook us breakfast once I'm caffeinated." Cooking ranks low on my list of hobbies, but I make a passable chef and will trade the coffee-upon-rising for kitchen duties.

We sit in our camp chairs, drinking coffee in comfortable silence, allowing the caffeine to do its job. My brain floats in the serenity of the morning, white noise humming in my head while I drink my way to alertness. My gaze stares into the field, at the campsites, at the fans also content with a slow and lazy start to the morning, and lands on my camping companion.

Kylie entered my realm with perfect timing, as if sent by my guardian angel. I graduated high school in June 2000, a depressed and anxiety-ridden eighteen-year-old struggling with an identity crisis. Serendipity struck a month later when I randomly attended a Phil Lesh and Friends show. Equally enraptured by the music The Grateful Dead's bassist played and by the vibrantly dressed and twirling crowd, this concert experience revealed a lifestyle I was eager to explore.

My shift began in the following months. I traded my trendy khaki pants, dyed red bob, and three pounds of pancake makeup for patchwork, hemp necklaces, long hair, and a fresh face. I expanded my social circle to befriend other "hippies," leading me to Phish. A new friend recommended, nay insisted, I give them a listen. Her suggestion changed, and perhaps saved, my life.

Around the same time, I began working at a call center, The Order People, where several of my new coworkers' appearances resembled my own, including Kylie's. I admired her from afar for several months, fascinated by this gregarious, loud, brash, and beautiful woman who sang Grateful Dead songs to herself in between customer service calls for Coach Handbags.

Her smooth skin and long, dark hair turned heads, but I was drawn to her style. She wore flowy, fringed dresses and pants with broad panels of patchworked corduroy running the length of each leg. I wanted to be her, but that was impossible. I could, instead, be like her. Maybe I could even be her friend.

Though also outgoing, I was awash with self-doubt from high school bullying. Bullying is weird. I wasn't a loner. I had plenty of friends. But I was a target, an invisible "kick me" sign taped to my back the instant I walked in on day one of my freshman year. An upperclassman took an immediate dislike to me during a study hall later that week.

"You're so ugly. I can't stand looking at your fucking face," she cursed at me every Thursday for an entire year. Three years older than me and twice my size, I had little recourse other than to sit there quietly and take her abuse, her words seeping through and burrowing into my psyche.

That spring, a slam book circulated between the girls in my class. Under my name, someone had written "she's too happy-go-lucky." I never thought my positive outlook to be a bad thing. Apparently, it was.

Sophomore year brought a different bully. He sat behind me in homeroom, forcing me to interact with him daily. I faced similar insults about my looks, but he took his torments a step farther. He accosted me in the lunchroom one day, grabbing me from behind and smacking my ass in front of my entire class while saying repeatedly, "You have such a big ass. I've never seen such a gigantic butt."

I fled the cafeteria in tears and refused to eat lunch inside for weeks following the incident.

I encountered standard high school insults as well, the kind every teenager receives at some point. It doesn't sting any less. Comments about my clothes, my makeup, my personality. One of my best friends didn't pick me up on a Friday because she needed room in her car for a more popular girl. Another time I threw a small party at my house and, other than my core circle of friends, no one showed up on account of another gathering at a classmate's house to which I wasn't invited to.

The shittiest thing about bullying is how it scars. My peers' remarks and actions caused craters of lingering insecurities I still occasionally obsess over. In 2001, so freshly removed from these experiences, they haunted me. I worried I would face the same ordeals. I second-guessed everything and thought through my every move while trying to find my place in this novel hippie world.

The hours spent in my head overcome with these concerns proved unnecessary. When I showed up at that Phil and Friends show, the music enthralled me, but the environment sealed my interest. The crowd of nonstop twirlers smiled and beckoned me to move with them and I obliged. I danced like no one was watching—and no one was because they either had their eyes closed or were too intent on the music to bother—and even if they were watching, it didn't matter. No one made fun of me.

It was the same with Kylie and the other crunchy, groovy folk at The Order People. Conversations bounced back and forth were filled with compliments, generosity, and positivity.

"Oh, I like your dress. Where did you buy it? Can I borrow it?"

"Oh this? I found this patchwork dress at Goodwill. Isn't it a score?" I would have been afraid to wear the long, color blocked corduroy smock in high school for the snide comments such a piece of fashion would bring.

"Rachael, your nose is beautiful. It fits your face so well."

"My nose? Oh, thank you!" My roman nose had been a frequent target for abuse, and I disliked it with a passion.

"My friend is having a party Saturday night. Want to go? Maybe we can go hiking too. Oh, and there's a show at The Jazz Club next month."

"I would love to. Thank you!" Hikes, parties, and shows at our local music venue were always filled with cackles of laughter. No one dismissed my effervescence, a core part of my personality that I had tried so hard to change in high school. They encouraged it.

At nineteen, what I wanted and needed most was an inclusive community I could depend upon. And here it was.

I had found my place.

Mine and Kylie's friendship exemplifies the strange synchronicities that strike within the universe. I doubt I'd be sitting here right now, twelve years later, swallowing the most disgusting yet delicious cup of joe, if I hadn't worked at The Order People right after that Phil and Friends show, when the appeal of this bohemian counterculture was so fresh, right when I needed it most.

Kylie breaks the silence. "Rachael, I have to tell you woman, that scream! That banshee yell you screamed when you saw Faris. It embarrassed me." Her words sound harsh but are spoken playfully and with a wide grin.

"Embarrassed you?"

"Yeah, I was ashamed to be seen near you. You sounded like those young girls who yell out whenever they see one another." Her voice pitches high and shrill in imitation. "Oh my god, Becky, it's been days since I've seen you. Why has it been so long? I've missed you!"

I know she's teasing me, but I still defend myself. "Get out of here, Kylie. It's just that I haven't seen him in almost ten years. I never expected to see him again, let alone run into him at set break. My long-lost college crush."

"Well, what happened with him?"

"You know what happened. This is all we talked about when we got back last night."

"Yeah, I know, but it's so fucking exciting that I want to talk about it some more. In fact, I may want to talk about this all weekend. So talk, bitch." She claps her hands at the end of each word.

"I don't know what else there is to say that I didn't already tell you."

Kylie frowns, furrowing her brows and shaking her fist in my direction.

"Okay, okay. I used to buy my weed from him, but we ended up hanging out a lot. It makes sense, right? His roommates were from northeast Pennsylvania, too—you graduated with half of them—and he's a Phish fan. So yeah, we went to the same parties. The same bars. The same shows."

"And you had a crush on him?"

"It was inevitable. Smart, witty, cute, Phish fan."

"Checks every box."

"And kind. Don't forget about that one. He didn't make fun of me. Ever. Teased me, yes. But never to be mean."

"So why didn't you date?"

"That's all on him. I made my feelings obvious, but he never reciprocated." I repeat everything I told her last night, but Kylie continues to listen with keen interest.

"The man doesn't know what he was missing." She shakes her head. "So why did you guys stop taking?"

"I don't know. Nothing happened. We stopped living in the same city and lost touch."

I shake my head in disbelief. So many things necessary for our unplanned reunion had aligned precisely so. Kylie and I chose to attend these SPAC shows when we could have easily gone to the three concerts in Maryland next week. Faris planned to visit his sister for this exact weekend, and she happens to live in Saratoga Springs. To stumble upon each other in the middle of over twenty thousand people. And for him to recognize me, with the passage of eight years' time.

Do coincidences like that happen without divine intervention? I'm not sure.

I hope yesterday wasn't our only chance to hang out.

I compulsively check my phone all morning and into the afternoon. I press buttons, any button, throughout cooking and eating breakfast, so the screen glows. Nothing. Keep my eyes glued to it, drinking a second cup of camp store coffee. Silence. Before and after putting my swimsuit on to take advantage of the camping resort's pool. Still waiting.

I fulfill my wifely obligation and call Jason while walking to the pool. Despite telling myself I wouldn't feel guilty about any innocuous flirting, I do. Hearing his voice may assuage some of this, except he doesn't answer.

When our swim is over, I reach for my phone. It indicates I missed a call and not from my husband. My guilt lifts. Jason hasn't bothered to reach out at all today, but someone else did.

I ring him back immediately, my heart fluttering, waiting for him to answer. Faris picks up during the second ring.

Hallelujah!

I smile into the phone. "Hey. How's it going?"

"Maryam and I are fixing to head to The Lot now. Want to meet us?"

It's exactly as I had wished. Thank you, universe! "Give us an hour. We've been swimming and need to wash the stink of chlorine off first."

"Text me when you're on your way. And then you can drop a pin when you arrive."

"Drop a pin?"

"On your phone. It'll send me your location."

Smartphones abound and I've yet to upgrade my phone. I tell Faris this.

"Well, have Kylie do it from her phone," he says.

We catch a ride to the venue with our neighbors. They bring a cooler full of beer and stay close to their car today. Kylie tries to drop a pin, but her phone refuses to reveal our location. A quick call to Faris fixes this. We agree to meet in the heart of town.

Shakedown Street.

Named after the disco-funk Grateful Dead song, it's the heart of The Lot. A circus-like market that moves with each show, this is where fans gather for the buying and selling of goods, both legal and illicit. Its parking lot location changes with each venue, but many of the vendors remain the same. Walking through a ten-foot radius in the chaos of Shakedown, one could purchase a witty T-shirt or hat, a pendulous labradorite pendant, a gooey cheesesteak topped with mac and cheese, and a ten strip of acid.

The marketplace screams sensory overload. In the same ten-foot radius, scents of toasting bread for grilled cheese, the earthlike greenery of lit joints and bowls, and the BO of too many showers eschewed combine at the nostrils in an olfactory assault. Nitrous tanks hiss as children's party balloons fill with the laughing gas. Those that don't peddle their wares from tables do so from backpacks and pockets. Scroungy lot rats covered in do-it-yourself prison tattoos whisper "doses" or "molly," but I highly recommend buying your drugs from a more trustworthy source.

Too many people bump into shoulders and step on the backs of sneakers. Shakedown is not for the claustrophobic.

I love it.

We find the market two lots over, where the revelry is bursting in full swing. Vendors blast music from their makeshift stores. A small circle gathers behind the main row of customers, dancing to the Donna Summer disco beat pouring from the speakers of a makeshift bar. Kylie joins in on the pop-up discotheque. I would, too, but my phone buzzes, and I rush to answer it. Priorities.

"Rachael, hey, where are you?" My right ear barely makes out Faris's shouting.

It's hard to pinpoint our exact location. If only one of us could drop a pin. Kylie, back from faux Studio 54, and I hang off the main street of Shakedown, but even the outskirts overflow with people milling about, meeting up with friends, slamming beers, celebrating. I'm dwarfed by average-sized and tall people and see nothing distinct to separate our location from the rest of the packed parking lot. Stymied, I'm silent.

"Hold on, stay where you are," Faris advises me. "We're coming."

The siblings appear two minutes later. Faris wears a triumphant grin. Maryam, a more casual fan herself, observes the overstimulation of sights, smells, and sounds of the black market with wide eyes. She hands us each a water bottle in greeting and takes a sip of her water as a bead of sweat rolls down my forehead. Good idea. I open my bottle and slug half of it.

"Thanks, Maryam! I needed that. How did you two find us so quickly?" I ask.

Faris points to the speakers blaring disco. "We were over there. I heard the sound coming from your phone."

As much as I love the chaos of Shakedown, it's not conducive to conversation. I suggest we take a stroll and Faris and I use it for a proper catch up.

I tell him about my decision to teach in South Korea. That I returned to Pennsylvania in March at the completion of a third and final year in Seoul and am a month shy of moving to Las Vegas to begin my teaching career in America. He looks surprised when I tell him I'm married.

He has a Facebook page. We'd reconnected briefly years ago via the social media app. I was ecstatic when I found him on the site and wrote a long message, hoping our correspondence would be a continuous volley of questions, answers, and reconnections. His reply, no more than two sentences long and dead-ended, stalled my enthusiasm. Since his reticence didn't leave much opportunity for conversation, I left him alone.

As most newlyweds would, I plastered my wedding pictures and changed my relationship status—but most certainly not my last name—to married on my Facebook page. He must not be the stalking type, otherwise, he would know.

His social media reluctance means I'm uninformed of his life as well. He first tells me he's single and a father to a hound named Reba. Phish song titles, characters, and the members themselves inspire pet and children's names. Julius. Caspian. Leo. Big Red. Wilson. I've personally known two Piper pups, named for the red, red worm, a bulldog called Icculus, and now, with one degree of separation, a Reba.

He resides in Fort Worth and spent his twenties working his ass off across the Lone Star State: Houston, Corpus Christie, in tiny west and south Texas towns.

"Holy shit, engineering!" I exclaim. His college endeavors differed greatly from my English studies.

"What does that mean?" He scrunches his eyebrows in confusion.

"You told me last night that it was your first Phish show back because you're a workaholic. At first, I thought that was hyperbole, but now, you're telling me that you spent the last ten years moving all over Texas. My math skills are awful, but even if they weren't, I'd never want to be an engineer. It sounds like such a sacrifice."

I thought I had given up a lot when I moved to Seoul. I yearned to find my way and place in the world and, in doing so, went years without seeing my parents, brother, or other loved ones. I missed out on weddings, funerals, new babies, and so much live music.

But man, did I enjoy myself. I traveled to places many people will never visit, and I met interesting people from all over the world. My sacrifice seems nothing compared to Faris's.

"Yeah, but it wasn't that bad. It's satisfying to work with my hands. And I learned a lot." He looks around. "But I'm back. I missed this part of my life. And I can't wait to see Foreigner. They better play 'I Want to Know What Love Is.'"

He remembers my corny joke from yesterday. As if cued, we burst into the song's lyrics, the ones we know, the exact words to the title. We stumble to the venue entrance and decide to head inside to snag lawn spaces closer to the pavilion.

Kylie insists on grabbing evidence of the overdue reunion and pushes the two of us together for a photo before we get in the security line.

I wedge myself under Faris's shoulder. He towers over a foot above me. Phish hat perched backward on his head and sunglasses pushed up on his forehead. His blue eyes squint in the sun, and his gigantic palm settles on my right shoulder. His face is flecked with stubble. I wear a pair of oversized maroon sunglasses. A weekender pack of Marlboro Menthols is tucked into the top of my red dress. It's another breezy sundress, one I purchased on holiday in Thailand last summer. We expose our teeth below outstretched upper lips, a testimony of our joy in being at a Phish show and the auspiciousness of our random run-in.

Chapter 7

All things must pass, but why do dreadful moments crawl at a snail's pace while cherished ones rush by at warp speed aboard the Millennium Falcon?

Monday morning arrives to signal the party's end, and I'm grateful we have the afternoon to revel in. At the conclusion of last night's show, we asked Faris and Maryam if they wanted to come back to our campsite. Maryam never consumed more than two drinks in a sitting and wore the exhausted look of someone craving nothing but their bed. Faris pondered our invitation but wanted to get his sister safely home. In parting, we conspired on a plan for today, procrastinating our inevitable goodbye. No one had to work. Let's wander the quaint downtown of Saratoga Springs as tourists.

As Kylie and I break down camp, I fantasize about what could have happened had Faris joined us. I did the same thing as I drifted off to sleep last night, visualizing him and me sitting in adjacent camp chairs around a lantern (open campfires not permitted), Kylie long gone to bed.

"Are you sleepy?" Faris turns to me.

"Nope." I take a swig from my beer. "You?"

"I'm feeling pretty invigorated."

I smile. "Oh yeah. I guess I am too. What are we going to do with all this energy?"

"I have an idea." He leans in closer.

"I do too." I match his move until our faces are inches apart. (The hubris I possess in my fantasy astounds me.)

48

Faris closes the space between us and clamps his lips on mine. I knock his backward cap off and twine my hands in his short thick hair. His hands wrap tightly around my waist, our tongues greedily explore one another's mouths while his hands venture down my waist to ...

Wait, should he touch me like that, or is that move going too far?

I show restraint in my imagination, even though only I can see inside my head. The guilt won't allow me to move my invented hookup past first base. It's much more innocent than my risqué imagination from college, where I would masturbate to thoughts of Faris and me involved in various naked acts.

I'm in trouble. It ferments in my belly. Dozens of hummingbirds arrive unsolicited. They fly freely inside my abdomen, fluttering their wings and flying in the pattern of a Ferris wheel. My insides float topsy-turvy whenever his name is mentioned, either aloud or in my head. *Faris.* I've had small crushes on other men since I married Jason, but none ever elicited such a physical response.

The first hummingbird presented itself on Saturday, during "Tweezer."

While many showgoers smuggle illicit substances into the venues, some fans opt to sneak in packs of dayglow plastic, hoping the band will play one of their songs known to provoke an infamous glow stick war. "Tweezer" is one of them. Once the song's beat drops, a deluge of sticks will synchronously fly into the air from all sections of the crowd. Even if you are anti-glow stick (they produce an enormous amount of waste) you cannot deny the delight in the unified explosion of Day-Glo color.

The glow sticks flew in a mad torrent during Saturday's "Tweezer," and Maryam radiated as she took in the eye feast. She collected the ones that fell at our feet and arranged them in her hair to resemble Lady Liberty's crown.

I appreciated the splash of fluorescence flying by, but I don't give a fuck about the glow sticks. I don't toss them. I don't pick up discarded ones. Not when the music is playing.

Long regaled as a fan favorite, "Tweezer" may contain Phish's most ridiculous lyrics (something about stepping into freezers with those pleasing tweezers) but it's given birth to some of the longest and most experimental jams. The composed segment, Trey's bluesy riffs repeated over a rollicking piano, lasts only about five minutes until Uncle Ebenezer (more absurd lyrics) sends us to space with a distorted slam of the freezer door (throw those glow sticks). From there, the jam emerges. Whether it's ten minutes or forty, you don't want to miss a note. And since one never knows what to expect where a jam will go, it's best to keep your attention on the song.

Faris broke his spell with the music to contribute to his sister's efforts. He continually retrieved abandoned sticks from the grass and handed them to his sister to add to her thick bun, alight with a child's play of luminescence.

I broke my own gaze off the stage to watch this silent interaction between the siblings. What seemed a simple act of kindness unpacks into so much more in the life of a Phish fan. It's a good thing this "Tweezer" didn't grow past the ten-minute mark. We didn't miss too much.

But it sent that initial hummingbird zipping.

I ignored it, denying a re-emergence of the feelings I used to possess for this man long ago. The idea was absurd. I crushed on him long and hard in college, and, up until Friday evening, he had been nothing but a pleasant memory. How can I have feelings for him again? And I'm married! Preposterous!

Perhaps my possible crush was a part of my Phish trance, an extra oomph to make my return to Phish so much more special.

Or maybe it was my brain's subconscious way of dealing with the future. So hyped up on all the emotions, preparing to say farewell to my family and friends in Pennsylvania and acclimating to the idea of starting over in Las Vegas with Jason, that I needed a momentary interruption. A schoolgirl crush may be what any good doctor would order.

So, I acquiesce to the bliss of a brand new (or is it old?) crush, and it rolls over me. A kaleidoscope of birds swoops unrestrained in my stomach; I feel as if I'm twenty-one again and I get to enrich my newfound youthfulness all day today on account of Maryam and the best idea ever.

"None of us has work tomorrow. Let me show you around downtown," she had suggested when we were parting ways last night.

Now, with camp packed up, Kylie drives us to Maryam's. The siblings greet us with conspiratorial grins at the front door. They rose early to prepare for another Al Bakar visitor who arrives tomorrow. Faris holds up a sign. Blown up on a large twenty-four- by eighteen-inch piece of cardstock and attached to a yardstick is a picture of a woman I assume is their mother. It's candid. A metal pasta strainer lies on top of her head like her son wears his backward baseball cap. It's apparent Faris and Maryam inherited her light eyes and fair skin.

"We're going to meet her at the airport with this," he says and a staccato chuckle bursts from his belly. He's pleased with his creation. His laugh, the pride he takes, the humor in it, causes my stomach to flip.

"The airport is so tiny that my mother would never miss us, but he insisted we make it," Maryam says.

Kylie and I heard many stories of their family. They sound like a spirited group, the kind of people I like to spend holidays and vacations with. Forever eager to expand my social circle, I was bummed when I learned how tiny Jason's family was. An only child, Jason's father passed away when he was a teen, and his mother has resided in Japan for nearly two decades. I hadn't added many in-laws to my family when we married.

The four of us leave the house on foot. We spend hours perusing the main street of Saratoga Springs before our stomachs rumble in annoyance. Maryam leads us to an Asian restaurant. I order kung pao chicken and turn my attention toward my three friends. Maryam manipulates the conversation to focus on her brother's love life.

"Weren't you dating someone in your office?" she inquires. "You two would go to shows together?"

"We went to one show together," he says.

"What happened? How come you didn't go out anymore?"

He seems reluctant to talk. "I don't know. It wasn't me. I liked her. I don't think she was comfortable with the idea of dating someone from work."

Another rumble pangs in my stomach. It's not hunger, and it isn't a hummingbird. This twinge hits below my sternum. The ache demonstrates another signal of my reemerging feelings. Jealousy. I angle my head down in case my nonexistent poker face gives me away.

Maryam continues with the conversation. "I want to be an aunt! You need to meet someone so you can have kids."

"I'm not planning on having any kids."

She slams her hand on the table in contrived exaggeration and scolds him like a parent. "You have to have at least one kid."

"I don't want kids," he says firmly while shaking his head.

I concentrate on my water. With the speed I finish those sixteen ounces, people must think I'm an athlete. My feelings threaten to reveal themselves with a red face or downturned lips, exacerbated by thoughts my brain rudely won't stop transmitting. They carry me to the tiny two-hundred-square-foot apartment me and Jason shared last year in Seoul.

We'd just returned from his grandmother's house, a visit we took most Saturdays. In our early days of dating, Jason mentioned how close he was to his grandmother. Such relationships vital to my core, my heart surged at his revelation. The weekly trip across the city to see *Halmoni* became routine once we married.

Korean grandmothers are like American grandmothers, like any grandmother. They want to feed you and shove money in your pockets so you can eat more later. They also question about babies. Jason's grandma would put her hands to her chest and grab her elbows with opposite hands as if cradling a baby and say "*aggi, aggi?*" curiously. *When are you going to give me some grandbabies?* I'd respond with a smile and shrug and attempt to steer the conversation elsewhere, a difficult task when only one of us three spoke both languages used.

Jason and I married the year I turned twenty-six. Then, I'd noncommittally thought I wanted kids. I imagine many young women automatically assume *"I'll have kids one day"* due to family and societal norms. It's abstract, an idea existing because, ostensibly, it's what all couples, regardless of their country and culture of origin, do. The order of adulting, you get married, you have children.

As a newlywed, baby cravings panged at me intermittently. Fleeting yearnings, they disappeared within three months, coinciding with an accidental pregnancy I wasn't ready for. I terminated the pregnancy. I expected that want, a need for a baby, to return as we settled into the routines of marriage. We'd start our family then. Except that biological drive exited my womb with the abortion and never returned.

After the accidental pregnancy, I questioned this expectation of all women, wondering what a child would add. A deep examination of what I personally valued (my identity and mental health, among many other facets) showed nothing but a decrease in my quality of life and I realized I didn't yearn for motherhood.

We hadn't discussed parenthood desires while dating, a result of my generic thoughts of "I'll have children someday" and Jason knowing it's the obligation of all couples to do so. But when those two pink lines on a positive pregnancy test attempted a coup on my world, he voiced no objections in my choice to terminate. In the months and years following, he never mentioned starting a family, and I didn't bother to bring it up.

But that visit with his grandmother shook me. The pleading in her voice, *"baby, baby,"* haunted me on our trip home. *Please give me a great grandbaby.* She was always kind and loving to me, yet I was never going to make her a great-grandmother.

I had to come clean with my husband. It was time we communicated. *Halmoni's* most recent pleadings for "*aggi, aggi*" enabled me to work up the ovaries for such a conversation. I initiated it as soon as we entered our third-floor walk-up studio.

Jason took off his sneakers without unlacing them. He left them on the floor of the recessed entranceway and immediately collapsed on the bed. It was his habit. I placed my shoes in the cubby. No need to clutter the space we lived in. A queen-sized bed, placed precisely in the middle of the almost perfect square, dominated the room. The remaining space held a college dorm-sized fridge and a two-burner stove, a square plastic table for two, and a twelve square cubby in which I had placed tchotchkes and pictures of loved ones to make it feel like home. There was enough floor space to do burpees and push-ups, or for a quad of people to enjoy a meal.

Our minuscule studio provided opportunity for intimate conversations among couples, a possibility for learning to understand each other at a deeper level. But for us, such intimacy never happened. This style of communication is a foreign language for us; we're flawed in how we do, or don't, speak with one another.

We could partially place blame on the language barriers and Jason's not-quite-fluent English. Despite his extensive vocabulary, he struggles to think of words to best communicate, especially when overcome with emotions, and I avoid uncomfortable conversations with him. Sometimes it's best to prevent them.

But I couldn't avoid this dreaded baby conversation anymore. It wasn't fair to either of us. Jason lay at the edge of the bed with his legs dangling over the side, and his upper body cushioned on the mattress. I wedged between his legs and cuddled upon his chest, affecting the closeness married couples should have.

"Jason," I said.

"Yes, my honey?"

"I … I don't think I want to have kids."

He patted my shoulder. "Ah, you may think this now, but there is time for us to have kids."

"But Jason," I protested. "I don't think I'm going to change my mind. I don't want kids."

"Ah, it's okay, Rae. We don't have to talk about this now."

Here I present communication problem number two. When one of us attempts a frank conversation about any of the many things couples should talk about, the other deflects. "Let's talk about this later," or "not now." Jason repelled then, but I'm guilty of this maneuver as well. It fits with our inability to have uncomfortable conversations. If one of us tries, the other isn't prepared. Things are pushed into the shoe cubby, out of sight and out of mind.

We've yet to revisit the baby discussion.

"Hey Rachael, watch out."

I snap out of my reverie. It isn't my husband talking, but my former crush. Our food has arrived. My eyes meet Faris's as I unwrap my pair of wooden chopsticks. I wouldn't have to attempt such a difficult conversation with Faris. I would simply say, "I don't want kids," he'd reply, "I don't either," and there would be no further discussion. We could high-five one another when encountering difficult children in restaurants or at the airport, an unspoken cheer for our decision.

But who am I kidding? None of this will ever happen. Faris will find a partner who doesn't want children, and they will be the ones exchanging high fives while I have yet to finish this conversation with the man I'm married to.

Once lunch is finished, Kylie suggests we get on the road. The moment for the dreaded farewell has come. Do we have to say goodbye and not see one another for another eight years? Maybe not ever? I want the opposite, with Faris back in my life.

My brain schemes how to see him again. Fortunately, I have the perfect occasion to spring upon him, something I hatched last night.

Sunday's first set delivered an early "Divided Sky," my cousin Anna's first favorite Phish song. As soon as I heard that sunny day opening of lilting guitar meets bunny hopping piano allegro, I was transported to a July 2003 show in Camden, New Jersey, as I am every time I hear the song, where Anna and I arrived separately with full intentions to meet up. Except neither of us could get our shit together and we spent the show within our different Phish crews on opposing ends of the lawn.

In an ode to the rain that dumped throughout that show, Phish played "Divided Sky," a mostly instrumental melodic masterpiece, and Anna texted me in the middle of it.

I'm so sad we're not together. I love you.

Since then, one of us always texts the other when it's played.

Sure enough, by the time Trey's searing outro chased away any remnants of figurative rain to close out the song on Sunday, I had received a message from my cousin, who must have been checking the setlist posted live on Phish's website ...

Divided Sky!!! I love you. Can't wait to see you!

… giving me an idea.

"What are you doing Labor Day weekend?" I now ask Faris.

"I don't think I'm doing anything."

"Would you want to see Phish in Denver?"

"Possibly." He hesitates. I need to give him more information.

"So, my cousin got married last month. Anna! You met her at that Spectrum show in Philly back in college. You'll remember her when you see her. Anyway, we're having a bachelorette party in Denver over Labor Day for Phish. Actually, it's a post-wedding bachelor party. She's already married. With Selena and Demaris. I mean, she's not married to Selena and Demaris. They're joining us for the party. You know them too!" I'm rambling, anything but succinct, as I spit the plans at him. I want to get them all out so he can say yes.

"I do?"

"Yeah, from college. You'll remember. Wait until you see them. Demaris lives in Denver, so we're all going to stay with her. Want to join us?" I've not asked my friends yet if it's okay for this not-so-random stranger to join our festivities and I don't care.

"Umm, sure. Yeah. I can probably do that."

I hug Faris for the joy in the haphazard plans we just made. I hope my friends don't kill me for inviting him. I doubt they will. The more the merrier, right? At least, that's my motto. Especially with how merry this more makes me!

I give Maryam a tight squeeze. I enjoyed our weekend together and would have become friends with her even if she wasn't Faris's sister. I wonder if she likes me or if we'd ever get the chance to hang out in the future.

I squeeze Faris in a final hug, lingering with my arms around his waist. It's like that first unexpected reunion hug and reluctant with-drawal during a Phish set break on SPAC lawn. Was that only three days ago?

Crossing paths with him was such an unforeseen extra to an already guarantee of fabulousness, like a three-song encore when one tune was anticipated. I should have felt ecstatic our meeting had happened. But I feel such a loss as we part ways. My spontaneous invite lessens the blow, but it's a hard goodbye.

Until we meet again, old friend.

Chapter 8

Our drive home hums silently as Kylie and I deal with the lows following such highs. These blues are inevitable. Something we looked forward to for so long is now over. With our Saratoga Springs Phish run come and gone, I set my sights, and my mind, on the near future and what I anticipate in the coming weeks. A big move, a new job, a marriage readjustment.

My chest weighs heavy with the very same things. I stare at my thin silver wedding band, back in its place, safe around my finger.

I know I'm not exactly happy, but that's temporary. All my unease will disappear once we chase the sun west, right? It's just these damn hummingbirds flying around my diaphragm are causing complications.

Faris.

The manic vibrations buzz in my belly with the memory of our hours together. Of his face. His humor. His gigantic palm resting on my shoulder. And because Kylie and I remain quiet, lost in our own musings, I can think of nothing but Faris.

How have I developed feelings for another man? And so quickly? What does this say about me? About my marriage?

I'm loaded with questions for myself, but, like the difficult conversations I avoid with Jason, I force these thoughts from my head. It's in my best interest to curb any confusion. I'm weeks away from a cross-country move and a fresh start with my husband. No need to muddle what will already be a necessary but difficult change with things that have nothing to do with my reset in Las Vegas.

Back at Kylie's house, we unpack her car, I give her a hug, and I take off. My drive is short. It never takes long to get from point A to point B in northeast Pennsylvania. These points are limiting in choice. A bar, a church, a big box store or franchise, your house, a friend's house. Head to the Mohegan Sun casino for a big night out.

Moving back here had never been my choice. I never desired a permanent residence in my hometown. I needed distance, and lots of it, between my physical self and the emotional baggage permanently packed in the square mileage of my hometown.

I couldn't let all that bullying I withstood in high school go. If by chance I crossed paths with a former classmate or stepped inside a popular high school hangout, I time-traveled back to the late '90s. Whatever confidence I'd grown shriveled. I became a fifteen-year-old crying outside the cafeteria doors, terrified of going inside, not knowing what kind of abuse would be hurled my way when I did.

Plus, in my mind, moving away meant I had made it. I had gotten away and was better than those that stayed behind. Those hometown losers. You peaked in high school, but look at me now. I got away.

Seven thousand miles away.

And I enjoyed my role as an expat English teacher. So much so that, when I returned to Pennsylvania in June 2009 with my brand-new husband at the end of a second, yearlong contract, our intention was to spend six months in the States and then head back to Seoul.

My parents offered us my grandmother's tiny, 350 square-foot house, which lay vacant in their backyard since she'd passed, seven years prior. I accepted this living situation without a problem. It was temporary and Jason and I were used to cramped living arrangements. I endearingly dubbed our humble abode The Wesley Hwang Wee House.

My husband, unbeknownst to me, devised a different scheme, revealed two months into our arrival in the States. We'd opened a calendar to plan our return to Korea and Jason, rightfully so, saw his opening.

"Rae," he began, "I was thinking of applying for that table games class. I want to learn how to deal blackjack."

The class he referred to was linked to the Mohegan Sun. Jason worked there in the employee dining area. I recently started as a teacher's aide in an elementary classroom. They were jobs, not careers. Something to keep us busy and pay us a barely livable income during our stay in the US. Thank goodness, and thank you, Mom and Dad, for our free rent.

"What's the point?" I asked him. "The class is three months long, right? We'd be heading back to Korea right after that."

"I changed my mind," he said.

"About what?"

"I decided I want to get my US citizenship instead of a Green Card."

"Okay, that's fine." I didn't realize what this change meant to our plans.

"If I apply for my citizenship, Rae, it means we stay here." Jason reminded me of the process. He could officially apply for this citizenship once we'd been married for three years. During the period, he couldn't be out of the country for more than six months at a time.

"But what about going back to Korea?" I asked.

"We're not going back," he told me matter of fact.

"But what are we going to do?"

"I'm going to go to this school, my honey. And we can stay here."

"But I don't want to stay here," I said. "This isn't what we planned."

It didn't matter what I wanted or what we had planned. Add this to our list of communication problems. One of us makes a decision that affects both of us, but the other has no say. Jason stated what he wanted to do, and he wasn't changing his mind. Married ten months, I didn't want to do or say anything that might cause strife so early in our marriage, even if that meant my own unhappiness. I knew marriage meant compromise, but I conceded without getting anything in return.

We stayed in Pennsylvania. In the Wee House. Feet from my childhood bedroom.

To distract me from what I felt like a giant step backward, I enrolled in a licensure program to certify me as an official teacher. At least I'd gain a career out of my regression. Living next door to Mom and Dad provided us the opportunity to make up for lost family bonding.

I visited friends in other cities, sometimes with Jason, but mostly by myself: DC, Detroit, Fort Lauderdale.

I saw music. Lots of music. Phish, of course, but other bands, and many not jam. Sigur Ros. Huey Lewis and the News. The Dead Weather and The Kills to cheer on my favorite rockstar, Alison Mosshart.

All these things, how I loved them and could experience none if I stayed in Asia. Hometown living wasn't the death trap my brain turned it into, but I couldn't escape the self-imposed notion that I was a failure if I settled there.

"You're a loser, Rachael. A hometown loser," my head told me. My ego had turned into a high school bully.

My insecurity explosion exacerbated the other thing that bothered me. Only recently, I'd relished in my chic, cosmopolitan phase as an expat in one of the world's biggest cities. If I wasn't traipsing through Seoul's various neighborhoods in my free time, I was camping in one-room cabins raised high on stilts on the shores of the Yellow Sea. Marching through endless rows of green tea fields. Hiking mountain peaks in temperate forests in the middle of the city. Vacations passed climbing the ruins at Angkor Wat or water taxiing from one Thai island to another on a quest for psilocybin shakes. Pennsylvania brought none of these escapades.

I had to get out. Become a winner again. Reclaim my sense of adventure. The best way I thought about doing that was to return to Seoul. Once I completed my licensure program in 2012, I signed a contract for one more year in South Korea.

Instead of consulting Jason, I told him what our future step was without considering his wants or needs. I didn't care. He'd done the same to me. Payback, baby!

I signed a one-year contract at a *hagwon*, or private school, in Gangnam, one of the most affluent of all places in Seoul. I referenced the song "Gangnam Style" when I told folks back home where I lived.

A different pop culture icon was used when speaking of my hometown to my friends and colleagues in Korea. "I'm from Scranton. Yes, the same place where *The Office* is. It's an even bigger shithole than the show depicts."

Jason flew back to the States at the halfway mark, spending a month with my parents to continue the citizenship process without a relapse. He took accounting classes while in Korea, quite different from his law school aspirations when we first met.

That contract, my final one, finished in February. We'd been floundering back in the Wee House, debating our future moves, waiting for our opportunity to get out for good, since.

And now that's three weeks away.

I pull my dented hooptie in front of my childhood house. Both my parents' cars are parked in the driveway. I'm tempted to poke my head in their house to say hello before going home, but Jason's car is also stationed in its usual spot, home from his day trip to Philadelphia. Finally on the verge of his US citizenship, his civics test today should have concluded the last step until taking his Naturalization Oath of Allegiance to the United States of America.

I walk through the yard we share with my parents. The tiny house stands at the bottom of the slanting side yard. A concrete porch meets the blacktopped patio where my family hangs out in decent weather. Dad and I drink coffee most mornings on the maroon Adirondack chairs pushed against the porch. Mom and I use the same chairs for happy hour beers or cocktails. As much as I anticipate getting out of here for good, I'll miss the occasions meant to be spent with family.

I swing the cheap screen door open. The early evening sun hangs high in the sky and the ceiling fan turned to full speed does little to break the heat and humidity of summer. Jason sits at the heavy wooden kitchen table behind his computer. The light from the screen shines on his handsome face.

It was his sculpted cheekbones, high and angular, that had attracted me first. That, and his thick black hair, which has endured many incarnations in our six years together. He first sported a natural black mop with short bangs, but then fancied it shaved and bleached blonde. His current hairstyle is a shag, dyed to an indecent red that doesn't complement his olive skin. A six-hour mustache grows above his full lips, but he's unable to produce more facial hair than that.

His dark eyes hide behind the glare of his oversized black plastic frames. They look up from the screen when I walk in. He beams, showing both upper and lower teeth in its magnitude, and picks up a miniature American flag lying in front of the computer. It's the kind you see six-year-olds waving during 4th of July parades. He waves it like a six-year-old.

"My honey, you're home!" he exclaims.

"How did the last step go? Did you get any hard questions? Did you have to name the thirteen original states?" With palms open, I spread my arms in excitement to hear the details.

"Guess what?"

"What?" For all the questions I ask, I'm never good at guessing games.

"I'm a US citizen!" He whips the flag even more vigorously.

"Wait ... what?" I freeze in confusion. He was supposed to take the civics test today, nothing more than that. I ask him that very thing.

"I took the test," he says. "And then they told me they were having a ceremony right after and I could join if I wanted to. So, I did."

As boring and depressing as the Immigration Office was, I wanted to see him sworn in as a US citizen. A huge moment for him that was long awaited for, the result of our, of my, sacrifice.

What the fuck? I missed it? Fuck!

I pull back my lips and force cheerfulness. "Oh my god, that's fucking awesome! Congratulations!" I throw my arms around my now-American husband and give him a quick peck on the lips. "How was it? How do you feel? You're an American citizen!"

"Yes, I'm an American citizen, my honey." He twirls that damn flag in the air again.

He asks about my trip, but I barely bust into my adventures before Jason turns back to his computer, indicating our conversation is over. He must be chatting with friends back home via an instant messenger and looking at his stocks back in Seoul, where it's already Tuesday morning.

That fucking computer. It's become a barrier between us. At one point, the machine endeared me to my husband. We'd sit side-by-side in front of the screen, Jason showing me various regions of South Korea he wanted to take me to, or the two of us googling various places to check out.

One winter weekend's end in 2009, he brandished its technological power in a wizard-like fashion to completely capture my heart. Hit hard by Sunday scaries, my back-to-work woes came accompanied by an extra dose of homesick sadness. The end of my second teaching contract stretched out five months into the future and I longed to hug my mother and stay up late watching a movie with my father. It would be ages until I could do either.

"Here, let me show you something," Jason said as he grabbed his laptop and brought up Google. "I have an idea that may help. What's your parents' address?"

He typed it into the keyboard and turned the computer to face me head-on.

"What am I looking at?" I moved closer to the screen, staring at the image that materialized on the computer.

He pointed at a house with one hand and squeezed the top of my shoulder with the other. "There. That should be your parents' house."

He was right. There, inches from my face, was my house. I stared at the screen for a quarter of an hour, marveling at how clearly the image captured everything: the brick façade flanked by the classic siding of most northeast PA homes, the manicured green yard, both cars parked in the driveway. Those fifteen minutes of staring at the screen flooded me with everything I missed about my home country. Physically, I may have been lying on my bed in Seoul, but mentally I was eating my grandmother's spaghetti. Dancing at a show. Driving my car. My homesickness temporarily alleviated, all because Jason had so thoughtfully shown me the magic of Google Maps.

It's been ages since his use of the computer has thrilled me, but I use the moment to escape to Mom's and Dad's. Soon I'll be back to relying on the internet's power to see my parents' house and I need to get my fill.

Chapter 9

I dread the monumental task of moving and I've not even started packing. My Tuesday starts eager to get that step out of the way and my anxiety drives my motivation to complete most of the project by day's end.

It's a tangible goal. In dividing our lives between two continents, we've not accumulated many possessions and it's made even more achievable by our plan to purchase our furniture in Vegas. New items for our fresh start. Besides, most of what we own is second- or third-hand and will cost three times its value to get to Nevada.

Jason is working. I tackle the task single-handedly, sorting all items inside the Wee Wesley Hwang House into one of four categories: what we can squeeze inside of Jason's tiny Kia, what will be shipped to our address in Henderson via snail mail, donatable goods, and trash.

The purge forces my brain to focus on the move.

Jason and I moved back to the States in March, aware our sojourn in northeast Pennsylvania would be brief. Jason, sick of the locals assuming he was from China, finally acquiesced to my pleas to permanently move out of Pennsylvania and he tasked me with finding us a city to live in. He didn't care where we moved to, he simply requested we settle in a place with a sizable Korean population (practically nonexistent in Scranton). I craved large city living and thought it essential to know at least one person already there to fill my socializing needs.

I researched. What school districts were hiring teachers? Were they in cities I pictured myself living in? Some were. Denver beckoned loudest with its mountains, live music scene, and Demaris. Fort Lauderdale competed with its beaches, warm weather, and Anna. I applied to districts in both cities and added Austin for the hell of it, but Jason did little more than murmur "Okay, my honey," when I spoke of completed job applications and phone interviews. His indifference didn't matter. None of the schools I spoke with reached out afterward.

The stress set in. What if we were stuck in northeast Pennsylvania, in the Wee House, because no one would hire me? Was I doomed to teach in my former school district where I was currently substituting? The temporary teaching jobs caused my insecurities to rage daily, reporting to schools where so many familiar faces from high school worked.

Sin City seeds were planted when a friend, Molly, enrolled in nursing school at the University of Nevada Las Vegas and further nourished when we factored in the job opportunities for both me and Jason. Clark County School District, with its hundreds of elementary schools, is the fifth largest school district in the country, and casinos galore awaited Jason's skills in dealing blackjack.

Only then did Jason begin googling information. He sprawled across his side of our bed, face up with his computer resting atop his midsection, engaged with Google Maps, examining the Korean restaurants and churches spread throughout Clark County.

"Check this out, my honey," he said, tapping my shoulder, sometimes every five minutes, to point out another Korean establishment. Karaoke. A spa. Three Grocery stores. All on the same block! He was warming more and more to calling this city home, and, once Jesse Martin Elementary offered me a position (my very first job in an American public school!), we made our decision.

But I can't help but be plagued with misgivings, mulling over how this move will affect every area of my life. I'm stoked about starting anew with Jason, forming new friendships, meeting my second-grade class, and creating a home in the desert, yet fretting it will amount to the worst decision I ever made. Settling in a novel city on the other side of the country while the thrive button is paused on my marriage is almost tantamount to partners who have a baby to revive their relationship.

Like these couples, I believe such a decision will save us.

I divert my thoughts by spending hours deciding the fate of various household items. It gives me something else to agonize over, as what seemed like inconsequential possessions causes monumental turmoil. My library bursts from the shelves of the entertainment unit I use as a bookshelf. A devoted bookworm from the time I could read, my collection of books dates from early elementary school to the present day and displays my reading evolution from the teen horror of Christopher Pike to the literary fiction of Barbara Kingsolver.

I bought these books, and read these books, and made sure these books somehow stayed with me through all my moves. I transported many while living in Seoul, wedging paperbacks in between packs of Korean teas and artwork shipped to my parents. This maneuver won't get my collection to Vegas. It won't fit in the car and to mail it would cost more than I can spend at this juncture.

A mint green cover on top of a stack of paperbacks catches my eye. *Easy Korean Cooking.* The cookbook was a present for me and Jason from my aunt. Though I've searched its pages to help me prepare dozens of meals, I open it, flipping through the recipes we've relied upon to deliver Jason a taste of home anytime we had the required ingredients. I land on a red-stained, much-loved, much-used recipe for *ddukbokki*, spicy Korean rice cakes.

When we were first gifted the book, Jason birthed an idea to cook a Korean feast for my family.

"Oh, I love that idea," I'd said. "What should we cook?"

"Definitely *ddukbokki.* Your father loves rice noodles."

We took our "pop up" seriously, taking a few days to determine our menu (a spicy scallion salad, rice, and *samgyupsal*, grilled pork belly, in addition to the *ddukbokki*), and road tripped to Philly to procure the necessary ingredients at the closest Korean grocery store. Dinner preparations began twenty-four hours beforehand and involved lots of chopping. Garlic. Green onions. Garlic. More garlic. Jason and I stood parallel one another at our kitchen table with knives and cutting boards.

"I'm never going to get this smell off my hands," I complained.

"Why don't you go take a bath and I can finish here," Jason said.

"Are you sure? There're still a million garlic cloves to chop."

"I got it, my honey." He waved me off.

He did have it. An hour later, I emerged from the bathroom to a cleaned kitchen and a refrigerator full of marinating meats and vegetables. Dinner was a hit, with Chef Jason grilling the pork, then demonstrating how to build a proper Korean barbequed lettuce wrap. It was the first of many meals we'd host for family and friends, never out of a love for cooking but an eagerness to socialize and share delicious food.

While Vegas offers a plethora of Korean restaurants to dine in, it also has several Asian grocery stores. We'll still find much use in *Easy Korean Cooking*. It must come with us.

How about the rest of my books?

My cell phone beeps as I pace in front of the shelves, contemplating how my beloved library will follow me. My phone displays a picture, but because my flip phone lacks intelligence, large pixels blur the image. I make out a fuzzy green lawn accompanied by a picnic basket and camp chairs. The message buzzes through next.

Looks a lot different from the weekend.

It's Faris.

I plan to reach out to him later in the week to finalize our plans for Phish in Denver, but he beat me in the communication game.

What is it? I text back.

It's SPAC. I'm at the ballet with my mom and sister.

How is it? Three nights of Phish proceeded by the ballet, oh, the dichotomy.

Faris replies with a similar thought. *So lame! We were at a Phish show two days ago and now I'm watching people in tights prance around on stage.*

Five days ago, Faris had been a distant college memory. Now, we're joking about ballet.

Our banter entertains me, but I'm still without a solution to my library dilemma. I am, however, able to make a choice concerning books I won't find on these shelves: The *Berenstain Bears*, my first big literary love. My personal career mission is to lead my second-grade students to the joys of reading. No better way to accomplish part of this goal than by sharing my original *Berenstain Bears* books with them and I know exactly where to find the series.

Chapter 10

Barefoot, I head to my parents' house. I don't knock before I step inside. The cool linoleum floor and blast of arctic air from the air conditioner offer sweet relief from summer's intensity.

"Hello," I shout into the house.

"Hello," comes the reply from within.

My father. I follow his voice to the kitchen. He hovers over the coffeemaker.

Jason picked up his old job dealing cards at Mohegan Sun and works all weekend. I spend much of my free time with my parents. I prefer lounging here and in their company, even if my nose is in a book, than to chilling by myself at the Wee House.

Mom, Dad, and I do get out. Dinners at family-owned Italian restaurants, occasional road trips on a Sunday, driving an hour to Allentown for a decent bowl of pho while listening to classic rock. The casino draws us in. We visit Jason, waving from afar if people sit at his table. My parents gamble at the slot machines. They encourage me, push a twenty in my hand to take my chances, and I do, but I curse the machines, the silliness of the rote pressing of a button.

I'll call the city that birthed gambling in America home in under a month. Less than thirty nights left to soak up my family, the diversions they offer, and I'm counting each one down as they pass all too quickly.

"Hey, Rae." Dad pours a quarter cup of creamer into his instant cup of coffee. "Want one?"

I sure do. I pause my book hunt to sit in the living room with my father, mugs in our hands. When he lights a cigarette, I immediately open one of the many windows. Secondhand smoke bothers me unless I am sucking down a weekender menthol.

"Hey," he protests. "You're letting the cold air out."

"I'm sorry, but I don't want to smell like smoke," I say. I'm a hypocrite, but, for years now, a weekend warrior and no longer a pack-a-day smoker. I'm practically a quitter. "Though I wish I could join you and calm my nerves a bit."

I'm frazzled (and perhaps I've ingested too much coffee) from my brain's morning sabotage. My anxiety, all the overthinking, steals my logic. I ramp potential problems up to worst-case scenario, visualizing foul outcomes that leave me battered, bitter, and alone. An ultimate loser. Hours of obsessive thinking and I've reached that level.

I've not spoken these fears aloud to anyone. I was the master planner of this new stage. I can't let my guard down, expose its flaws, disclose how terrified I am. But perhaps Dad can help me think things through more sensibly, provided I'm willing to reveal some of my insecurities. It's weird. Normally, I've no problem voicing my thoughts, opinions, or feelings to anyone. I seem to only shut down over matters falling under the umbrella of Jason, perhaps a side effect of my conflict-avoidant marriage.

"You're nervous about your move." He's not asking me.

Dad executed the perfect opening. Might as well follow through. "Yeah, it's starting to become real. Like, this is happening. I'm going to be in charge of my own classroom in a month. I came over here to grab my old *Berenstain Bears* books so I can share them with my students, but what if they hate them? What if they hate reading?" I rub the tops of my thighs while speaking. "I don't know how to teach in America. I'm worried I'm going to have no idea what I'm doing. That I'm going to be the worst teacher ever."

Dad takes a drag from his cigarette and lets the smoke trail out slowly. "Well, Rae, anyone would be nervous, at least anyone who cares. But look at it this way. You love reading and that will rub off on your students. You're going to make it exciting for any student in your classroom. And you won't be the worst teacher. You have experience;

you're not brand new. Geez, you taught four-year-olds in a language they didn't understand yet. That's incredible."

"I guess any new teacher would be nervous. And you're right. I'm not green." I nod, the immediacy of relief flooding my senses.

Okay, I'm glad I opened up to Dad. Might as well continue. I stop my rant momentarily to sip the coffee I obviously don't need and move on to my next crisis, one any extrovert would highlight. My litany of questions and declarations, a ramble of thoughts I'm famous for among my family and friends, particularly when my anxiety is present, come out stream-of-conscious style.

"And Vegas wasn't my first choice to move to. You know this. I'm worried I'm not going to meet people. Or, what if I can't meet people I have anything in common with? They're going to want to go shopping and clubbing and I don't want to do that. I want to explore the desert, but Jason hates hiking and I'm afraid I'll get lost so I can't go by myself. And I don't want to go by myself, anyway. I want to go with people I can talk with, my new friends, but they'd rather grind on strangers in the club wearing tube tops they bought shopping that day."

Dad meets my questions with his own blathering of answers. Genetics runs strong in my family. "Rae, you've always worried about making friends, always, but you've never had any trouble with that. Even in high school, even with all that shit you dealt with, you still had lots of friends. Moving across the country is nothing! You'll meet plenty of people who want to hike with you. And so what if you make friends with people who like to go to the club. You don't have to do that. You can do other things with them. You moved to Korea by yourself and that was across the world and look at all the people you met there."

"Yeah, but Korea was like college. It was so easy to meet people. I hung out with dozens of other foreigners who were doing the teaching thing, and everyone was looking to make friends. Plus, it wasn't permanent. Now I'm moving to a city where I don't really know anyone and it's hard to make friends as an adult. And this isn't temporary, it's for good."

"You won't be alone. You have Jason."

I spilled out anything that had crossed my mind over the past few hours to Dad. Everything except for that. I dare not speak these fears, these worries that carry the largest consequence, to him. There's no point in vocalizing any apprehensions I have about Jason or our marriage now. I've accepted a job, signed a contract and a lease for an apartment. Jason's citizenship is less than twenty-four hours old. It's too late to do anything but move forward with the plan.

Besides, everything with us is going to be okay. We'll get over this rough patch once we settle in Las Vegas.

Instead, I say, "Yeah, and I have Molly too. She and I were good buddies in Korea."

"See, you have a friend there already. You're outgoing. You'll make lots of friends. And you'll meet people at work. I know it's a change. I know it's hard not to be nervous but give yourself time to adjust and know that your mother and I are a plane ride away. And you can visit your brother in LA whenever you want to."

Dad infuses me with enough sense to halt my disaster reel. He's right. I'm not alone. I have Molly, my partner in crime during my last year in Seoul. We hiked, biked, partied, and explored together almost every weekend. I assume we'll continue our antics in Nevada. Why wouldn't we?

We finish our coffee. He is off to work, and I'm back in pursuit of my *Berenstain Bears* books. I enter my childhood bedroom, now the designated guest room. My mother redecorated it to reflect her aesthetics and it now includes an antique sewing machine, made of dark wood, with a heavy, wrought-iron bottom. It's decorative over functional, and the drawers aren't filled with sewing materials. Their contents belong to me.

Numerous student loan statements litter the top drawer. I pay my monthly bill online, but a pointless paper version never fails to arrive at my parents' house. No matter where I've dwelled, Sunrise Road has always been my permanent address. This changes next month. There will be no more student loans sent here. I remove those to toss in the garbage on my way out.

Junk mail out of the way, I spot the picture books, pressed flat by two picture frames on top. I grab one in each hand. A tiny green flowered frame contains an image of me and an old college friend from a long ago Phish summer tour.

The other picture shows another college-era memory.

"Holy shit." The words pour out automatically.

My left hand grasps a picture of Faris and me, taken during a 70s theme party. We stand side-by-side, my arm around his waist, his fingers barely gripping the sparkly pink hat on my head. I wear a pink polyester dress covered with flamboyant blue flowers and clutch a painted wine glass filled with red wine. Faris's hair is pulled back in his standard ponytail, and he holds a blue Solo cup.

I think back to that bash. My three roommates and I were known for our parties and that fest, thrown in July 2004, may have been the best we ever hosted. Our vintage, heavily wooded console television projected a VHS copy of *Saturday Night Fever* on a constant loop. When it ended, one of us rewound it and pressed play, again and again, all night long. A giant plastic tub held a concoction of 150-proof grain alcohol hidden within a mixture of cheap high fructose fruit juices. We laid out a long rectangular mirror on the coffee table and dumped half a bag of baking flour on it. Cut up straws and rolled dollar bills placed in and around the pound of white powder offered a realistic effect.

Faris and his roommates strolled in more than fashionably late. Our eyes met and he beelined my way. I coveted his attention, lusting for this man throughout our year of friendship, and, watching us, one would think he echoed my feelings. Gravity drew us close whenever in one another's presence. We passed hours at parties and bars like a couple, engrossed in conversation, him bending down to me, me on tiptoes leaning in, heads together conspiring strategies playing beer pong, displaying all but the physical aspects of a romantic relationship.

I can't fault myself. I didn't hide my crush from him. When he communicated his need to focus on school and had no bandwidth for a relationship, I decided I would be fine with a casual hookup. I unabashedly tried to seduce him with zero success in the wee hours of a Sunday morning. We'd spent that Saturday at a party and when that wound down, a small group of us continued on at my house. Five of us clustered in my tiny bedroom, drinking beer and smoking cigarettes interspersed with weed for hours. One by one, my friends left until the only two people in my smoke-filled room were me and Faris.

"Is that the birds chirping? It's morning already?" I'd said as he opened another beer.

"Oh shit, should I not have opened this? Do you want me to go?" He asked.

"No, dude, it's all good. I was gonna have another one anyway," I said aloud while silently telling him to never leave. Telekinesis. I was so high I thought my wordless transmissions would work.

Standing beside my bed, Faris told a story about his father shaking a giant key ring at a toddler. "He thought he was funny, but the kid didn't even smile."

I laughed louder than the anecdote warranted. The art of seduction.

"Hey, it's late. Rather, it's very early," I said to him once he finished his story. "Why don't you stay here?"

"I kinda want to pass out in my own bed."

"Well, I was thinking we could get in bed, but we wouldn't get all that much sleep."

"I don't think that's a good idea, Rachael."

"Oh, come on Faris. It'll be fun." I smiled up at him, hoping I could charm him into changing his mind. Inside, I was scowling. Was he turning me down? I didn't get it. How could a twenty-two-year-old, straight, American—okay half-American man—turn down sex with a woman?

"It's not a good idea," he repeated. "What if things got weird between us after?"

That fucking logical brain of his. While Faris possessed a wicked sense of humor and loved to cut loose (we'd spent several other nights greeting the rising sun together), I'd never known a more rational person. Maybe Faris really wasn't rejecting me. Maybe he was trying to preserve the endearing friendship we had formed.

Thankfully, my blatant but bombed bedding attempt didn't skew our relationship, and we hung out often in the months leading up to the '70s theme party. By then, I'd begrudgingly accepted that I was stuck in the friend zone.

"What took you guys so long?" I asked him once he was standing in front of me. He'd detoured to the keg first and was holding a rare blue (not red) Solo cup.

He gave an exaggerated groan. "My roommates took fucking forever to get their shit together."

I looked at him, took his outfit in. "You sure it wasn't you? Your shirt is the perfect kind of ugly for this. It must have taken you a while to put your outfit together."

"I found this at the Goodwill last week." He grabbed the bottom of his shirttail and then touched my hat. "You should talk. This hat is god-awful."

"It matches my outfit. Come on. Let's get our picture taken before I forget to."

That moment captured forever. Nine years later, I hold it in my hand like an old Nancy Drew mystery. *The Secret in the Sewing Machine.*

It's as if I've recovered a long-lost family heirloom. I presume my discovery to be a sign from the universe, that my random run-in five days ago with the man in this very picture was meant to be. It reassures me our friendship will endure this second chance.

I scoop the two dozen *Berenstain Bears* books and the cheap frame in my arms and head back to the Wee House. I place the frame in the center of the kitchen table and take the best picture possible with the pixelated camera on my phone and send it to Faris.

Look what I found!

What am I wearing?

It was from the seventies party we had. Remember that?

Ah, that makes sense.

What a great picture, huh?

Are there any other pictures?

Just this one.

That's a bummer.

Those three words provoke a strong enough reaction to wake up my dormant hummingbirds. I secure *Easy Korean Cooking* and the *Berenstain Bears* books inside a reconstructed cardboard box and place the newspaper-wrapped frame on top, and seal the box with shipping tape. This box wins a coveted spot in the car.

Chapter 11

We crest a hill in darkness. At the peak, the valley opens and reveals itself to us; the black sky suddenly glows with the unnatural wattage of millions of lights shooting out their full potential. It's as if a bedroom light is switched on in the middle of the night. This lack of subtlety paves the most appropriate way to introduce my husband to his new city.

We absorb this gigantic electrical grid in the middle of the desert silently. With wonder. The lights emanate from the plethora of houses and apartments, restaurants, casinos, and shops, stretching out like a limitless sea. We can identify where they begin but not where they end.

Jason sits behind the wheel. One final push to Vegas, we've been taking turns driving since a late lunch in Albuquerque. At almost nine hours, it's a haul, but we're weary and ready to be done. Though we've road tripped throughout New England and the mid-Atlantic on dozens of escapades together, this drive, spanning almost the entire length of the country, is the farthest we've ever gone.

The longest distance covered prior to this had been to Michigan when we'd traveled to Detroit to visit a dear friend over Labor Day in 2009. Those eight hours passed quickly. Like now, we took turns behind the wheel while the passenger played DJ with my binder of CDs and helped navigate. My brand-new husband was animated and verbose during the drive. He spoke of his various road adventures in Korea and peppered me with questions about my own history of car travels, all while absorbing the rust belt's landscape with curious eyes.

His eagerness and curiosity set the tone for that weekend. Upon our arrival at my friend's, he accepted and drank a bottle of beer handed to him and this mood of "yes" stayed with him for the three days of our trip.

"Want to go to this strip club near Nine Mile where Eminem grew up?" My friend's husband asked him. "The food is great. We can eat lamb chops."

"Sounds great."

"Jason, that dress looked great on Rachael. You should buy it for her," my friend insisted.

"I'd love to, and get the other one too, my honey."

"Want a bong rip, Jason?" I held it out to him.

"Yeah, sure," he said and accepted it.

A salsa band played during dinner in a Cuban restaurant. As our dishes were cleared away Jason stood up and reached his hand toward me. "Dance with me."

Ready to boogie, I accepted his hand. He led me to the dance floor, where he was able to copy the moves of the dancers around us flawlessly. I was not able to mimic so well but laughed through my blunders. Jason laughed with me and grabbed my hips to help me keep the rhythm of the music.

Afterward, the four of us headed to the MGM casino. We didn't gamble. We sat in a lounge listening to a three-piece band bust out classic rhythm and blues. My husband, mesmerized, watched intently, his mouth ajar in wonderment, occasionally muttering a quiet "wow."

Back at the house, Jason accepted the bong when it came his way. Earlier, when he smoked from it as a bong virgin, he inhaled a baby hit. A tiny stratus cloud came out with his exhale. With take two, he went all in, resulting in coughs and cumulonimbus clouds. The hit wrecked him.

We retired to bed where, with his arms and legs wrapped tightly around me, he proclaimed repeatedly through fits of giggles, "Rae, I can't feel my legs."

I cracked up each time he said this. We took our clothes off and made love, except Jason couldn't feel his body functions either and we ended up conceiving a potential baby. I terminated the accidental pregnancy two months later, but then we were clueless about the consequences. When we finished, we fell asleep cuddled up tightly together.

Aside from the getting knocked up part, I want that relationship back and I plan to reclaim it here in the desert. Except our four days of driving across the land of the brave and free droned mostly quiet, save for the road trip soundtrack of CDs I curated for our journey (the St. Vincent and David Byrne collaboration *Love This Giant* repeated the most frequently). What little conversation we did have, however, displayed Jason's once-constant magnetic charm, which stopped its steady shine shortly after our Michigan vacation. Perhaps this was a small sign of its re-emergence.

"Eww, look, another giant cross! They're practically everywhere here," I pointed out while traversing southern Illinois.

"I was thinking of building one in front of our apartment," Jason teased me.

"Man, Oklahoma is so flat. I don't know if scenery has ever made me feel as depressed as I do now," I groaned two states over.

"But if we lived here, we could have ones of those things. What are they called? Those spinning chicken things on top of the houses."

"A weathervane?"

"Yes, a weathervane. I like them, my honey. They're cute, aren't they? Can you picture me climbing a roof to put one on?"

Though ecstatic for this easy and silly banter with my husband, I fixated over why there wasn't more. Why our limited conversations stayed surface-level. Why we didn't speak much of our anticipated plans for Nevada. The apprehension that flooded me during the acute preparations for this move haunted me throughout the endless miles of our drive.

But this boisterous poltergeist of unease dimmed the closer we approached our destination. Manifest destiny, we moved out west to make our lives better. While I'm incapable of compartmentalizing my feelings among the vast spectrum of emotions, I can force the positive to the forefront and focus on that. I blame much of Jason's diminished charisma because of what he—and we—lacked in Pennsylvania. In the southwest, opportunities hover around us so thick we can reach out and grab them.

I break our silence to hear his impression. Please, please, please, let it be an upbeat one. "There it is! All those lights. That's Vegas! What do you think?"

His reply disappoints. It's short. Simple. Vague. "It looks very big."

I refuse to concede. *Come on babe, tell me more!* I press him with more questions.

"We should definitely get a Korean dinner tomorrow. Do you have a specific place in mind where you really want to eat?"

We struggled with food, something so simple yet essential to culture, in Pennsylvania. Scranton offered a generic *teppanyaki* buffet we frequented regularly. The closest Korean restaurant was in Philly. A monthly date, we drove the ninety miles so Jason could taste his home-land in a midday meal and then we'd fill the car's backseat with goodies purchased from HMart: *Naengmyeon* (cold, spicy noodles), *shin ramyun* ("fancy" ramen noodles), *mandu* (dumplings), and meats sliced specifi-cally for Korean barbecue.

I understood such needs. No matter how delicious the grilled meats of Korean barbecue are—covered in rice, raw garlic, and spicy *gochu-jang* and wrapped in a lettuce leaf—when I lived abroad, I would get intense hankerings for sandwiches containing thinly sliced meats and held within bread that was perfectly so, crusty on the outside but soft on the inside. I wasn't even an avid sub eater. I just craved a taste of home. Though I never succeeded in finding such a perfect sandwich in Asia, a single bite of mediocrity could temporarily transport me back to America and soften my homesickness.

Jason considers my question. "I'm almost positive there's a restaurant close to our apartment. Why don't we go there?"

"I'm down with that. Are you craving anything?"

"Rae, I want to eat everything."

"So, we'll order the entire menu!"

"Yes, let's do that. I'm so hungry, I can eat a horse," Jason says, using his favorite adage. The man loves his food.

"Have you thought much more about meeting other Koreans? The quicker you make friends, the quicker we'll get home-cooked Korean food and we won't have to settle for my subpar cooking." While Jason has the patience to soak and cook a perfect pot of sticky rice, I possess slightly better kitchen skills and prepare most of our decent but rarely spectacular meals.

Jason may have formed friendships with my hometown pals in Pennsylvania, but he longed for companions he shared more connections with. He did meet several Korean exchange students at the University of Scranton in 2010. Unfortunately, those relationships ended when semesters did, and his friends returned to Korea. Jason needn't rely on exchange students for temporary friendships here. He'll meet fellow expats with whom he shares culture, language, and possibly lived experiences.

"I know you laugh at my plan, but I'm going to go to a Korean church."

"I think it's funny." Neither of us were religious. "But I get it. It's the perfect way to meet a large group of people."

"Will you come with me?"

"Of course I will. When do you want to go?"

"Maybe in a couple of weeks. Let's focus on getting settled."

"How about checking out The Strip? Maybe we'll have enough done and we'll be able to go out by this weekend."

Our Scranton dates as banal as our Asian food options. They consisted of a weekly dinner and a movie outing, though I once surprised him with a trip to the shooting range and he relived his revered era as a Korean soldier. Here, a trip to the firing range will not be our most highlighted outing. We can investigate a myriad of casinos, take in a show, and trek along desert trails, all within a single day if we choose to.

"Yes, I want to check The Strip out as soon as we can. Let's try to go this weekend, my honey."

I'm buoyant by Jason's optimism, how he mimics my enthusiasm. Like he'd shown interest when searching for Korean-owned Vegas establishments on Google Maps, he voices the possibilities without hesitation, speaking of his, of our, plans with a smile to his tone. He seems dazzled by it all, pleased by what could be.

I know I'm ready for it. The power and potential behind a momentous change.

Chapter 12

In 2006, I was two years out of college and floundering, finally ready to begin the career I'd postponed since graduation, but in what, I didn't know. My English degree was earned out of a love of books and writing and an interest in the publishing industry, but I used my privilege in higher education to sharpen my partying skills rather than mastering my talents. I worked as an administrative assistant and learned that sitting behind a desk for eight hours bored me as much as any economics class.

What was I going to do with my life?

That answer came on my computer on a frigid Wednesday in early December. My inbox held an intriguing email.

We want you to teach English at our school in Seoul, South Korea.

I knew such opportunities existed, but had never thought about doing it myself. With the offer explicitly extended to me, was it something I wanted to do? My bookworm ways developed an appeal for adventure and formed a curiosity for other cultures from an early age. Within the pages of a novel, I could journey across the country or, better yet, continents. The world opened even more through my fascination of Anthony Bourdain's *No Reservations* (discovered upon reading his *Kitchen Confidential*), deepening my yearning for such worldly experiences. But I didn't know how to make this my reality. I had never ventured west of the Mississippi.

It turned out, moving to Seoul to teach English was an effortless choice to make.

I arrived in the Land of Morning Calm six months later. I shadowed an American colleague in her classroom for a single day. The very next morning, I, a twenty-five-year-old with zero teaching or babysitting experience, faced a classroom of four-year-olds who didn't speak English. As cute as my students—practically toddlers—were, they were anything but calm. A visitor could enter my room and step into a scene straight out of *Kindergarten Cop*.

"Did you pinch my bottom?" I asked Dorothy, my class clown, daily. She'd giggle, hands up to her mouth, face scrunched up, eyes shining behind her wire-rimmed glasses.

"Hey guys, let's not swing on our locker doors," I repeated mornings and afternoons to my three usual suspects hanging from the green wooden cubbies that held their street shoes (we all wore slippers or socks while inside). They grunted like monkeys when I tickled their underarms to loosen their grip.

Those beginning months caused me professional stress, but I loved my expat exploits. I'd never resided in a major city, and Seoul was a megapolis, almost the size of New York City. Giant, modern skyscrapers towered over newer districts, and, in older parts, closely built squat brick buildings topped by sloping roofs skirted the crumbling streets. Each neighborhood offered something unique, and for an American on her maiden voyage outside of the US, provided an adventure no matter which direction my feet stepped.

I regarded my world with the excitement that a four-year-old, like my students, looked at theirs. Trying Korean BBQ with hollow silver chopsticks, so different from the disposable wooden ones I'd always used, exploring a Buddhist temple barefoot, drinking Cass beer and singing in a *noraebang* (a private karaoke room) for hours on a Friday, belting out Oasis's "Wonderwall" and Lionel Richie's "All Night Long" along with a gaggle of fellow expats.

To further heighten my pleasures, I was surrounded by handsome men from all parts of the world. When I received a random message on Myspace from a mysterious yet young and attractive Korean man, curiosity reigned. The message explained that he, Jason, was looking for English-speaking friends to practice the language with. A thorough perusal of his profile revealed a man posing for a selfie with a kangaroo and hanging on an Australian beach with swim trunks pulled up to his nipples and his head covered in a hot pink bathing cap.

Because I'm always a sucker for a sense of humor and a handsome face, Jason captivated me. If he wanted an English-speaking buddy, I was available—and looking for a Korean boyfriend.

We met in early November, at a subway station in the middle of Seoul under the pretense of a casual English lesson. I immediately forgave him for running late when he presented me with a beautiful smile, his eyes crinkling to reveal tiny crow's feet, and a baby bottle of *soju*.

"This is for you," he said, handing me the four-ounce green bottle.

Though I avoided drinking the ubiquitous rice liquor for the gut rot it caused me, the present, and that smile, charmed me. "This is great! Thank you!" I gushed as if he'd handed me a bright bouquet of peonies and dahlias.

We ventured to Itaewon, an older, foreigner-focused neighborhood containing dozens of steep and narrow alleyways that wound toward hidden restaurants, bars, and shops. This region is the place for authentic pasta, cheesy moussaka, or a green curry, without the omnipresent side of kimchi that would accompany an "ethnic" meal in any other place of the city.

I visited Itaewon often. Eating. Shopping. Partying. Daylight visits always included What the Book, a used bookstore specializing in English texts, while Saturday evening trips extended late to take advantage of bar specials aimed at women.

Except it was a Sunday. I had just met this internet friend in-person, and I was not looking to get drunk. I suggested we grab lunch at a tiny Egyptian restaurant known for its shawarma. Over sandwiches and hummus, we started the act of getting to know each other.

We communicated without too much trouble, though I occasionally had to ask him to repeat himself on account of his thick accent. He appeared easy-going, complaining more than once about the unspoken Korean rule of working oneself to death. His brain attracted me; I presumed anyone with law school aspirations, as he communicated on that first date, and an almost bilingual fluency possessed some smarts.

"When I started to get serious about learning English, I watched a lot of *Friends.* Do you know that television show?" he asked when our conversation landed on television and movie interests.

I nodded. Of course I did. What American hasn't watched at least one episode of *Friends?* "Why *Friends?* Why not another show?"

"It's so funny. Joey is ridiculous. That episode with the turkey on his head."

Jason put his head down and laughed at the memory. I laughed too. I hadn't watched the show in years, but the Thanksgiving episode he was talking about had made me laugh my ass off.

He paused to take a bite of his gyro and continued. "And there's so many episodes to watch. I watched *Forrest Gump* a lot too. Forrest talks slowly, so it's easy for me to follow along."

I'd learned quickly that I needed to slow my rapid-fire cadence when teaching my little ones and talking to English-speaking Koreans. Jason's comment was a good reminder to talk with him just as deliberately.

"So, is that how you learned to speak English so well?" I'd been curious about this answer since we sat down.

"No, I lived in Australia for a few years."

"Oh, that explains your pictures! How were you able to get a selfie with a kangaroo?"

"I put my face up to his and ran away before he wanted to box with me." He punched his fists out in a mock sparring.

We finished lunch and sauntered to a tropical-themed bar. En route, we crossed a busy street. Jason weaved his body from one side of me to the other, starting on my left side and switching over to my right halfway across the road. It took me a moment to grasp what he was doing. This unfamiliar friend ensured my safety and placed his body most directly in line with upcoming traffic. Oh, the chivalry!

Our destination, The Bungalow, transported its patrons to paradise and provided an ambient setting for an English lesson, aka first date. Sand blanketed one floor and wooden swings suspended from the ceiling of another. Two swings hung empty in a darkened corner of that room. No one denies such a vibe. We sat.

Due to an alcohol allergy, Jason doesn't drink. His body absolutely rejects it. Downing a single beer causes his body to flame in red splotches. This "Alcohol Flush" instantly buzzes his brain and sleep comes quickly.

He did not divulge his allergy on date one and drank two beers. In hindsight, he did a remarkable job of hiding his alcohol intolerance. My own drinks settled me into a pleasant buzz. He must have been wasted.

While he used the bathroom, I plotted how I would get this adorable man to kiss me. I needn't have wasted the energy. He returned, plopped on his swing, and swung closer, clamping his lips on mine. Like two teenage make out masters, we locked lips for what seemed hours in the middle of the faux Thai beach. We pulled away from one another long enough for me to invite him to my place and for him to accept.

We flagged a taxi down and, back at my apartment, made out in my bed without taking it any further. Drunken Rachael is always up for a good time, and I hadn't shaved my legs on purpose to avoid any sexual intimacy. I wanted to bang, bang, bang, bang, but was ashamed by my hairy legs, prickly enough to slice a man.

When we parted ways in the morning, I was smitten. He must have been too because he came back the next night, and the night after that, and perhaps the next one. He took the bus. Public transportation turned a thirty-minute taxi ride into a ninety-minute journey. I shaved my legs.

Now, six years later, the hours spent together aren't nearly as exciting. But tonight is different. Tonight, we begin again.

Chapter 13

We can't move into our apartment at this late of an hour. Molly, my sole friend in Nevada, offers us her spare bedroom to crash in. We sleep hard and awaken early in the morning to go home.

I usher Jason to the passenger side of the Kia. "I'm driving, Jay. Sit, relax, and look. Check everything out in the sunlight."

The thirty-minute drive from Molly's in Summerlin to our apartment in Henderson crosses a diagonal path from the northwest end of the city to the southeast and offers more views of the purple-tinged mountains that ring the valley and the massiveness of The Strip. Vegas's most invasive species, the strip mall, appears in twos and threes on every block. Housing developments built in tracks blend together. The matching red stucco of the roofs line up like a red carpet and makes it difficult to discern one house from the next. All around, the brown of the desert stretches out until the soil, rocks, and flora meet the bottom of the craggy mountains surrounding the town.

As enchanting as a mirage, the Las Vegas Strip bisects the repetition. It extends for an unsuspecting four miles to our left, a spectacle to behold even in the daylight without the neon lights setting it aglow. Skyscrapers don't rule the skies here. The casinos do. The behemoths hog blocks and blocks of prime real estate and dwarf any buildings with the audacity to stand alongside them.

My inaugural trip to Vegas in 2010, taken with women who were mostly acquaintances, left me with a bad first impression. We traipsed Las Vegas Boulevard by daylight, wandering in various casinos for a drink and the random push of a slot machine button. The three nights duplicated one another: an expensive yet unexceptional dinner and dancing to awful house music in clubs where women in tight clothing would grind and twerk on men with overly gelled hair. No, this city was not for me.

A recent Vegas vacation taken with my father six weeks ago showed a different side. I traveled here to secure an apartment and complete the paperwork necessary to receive my Nevada teaching license. Jason refused to take work off and Dad didn't want me going solo. These three days of father–daughter bonding revealed things I didn't know existed in Las Vegas and filled me with an excitement for what was to come.

The mountains caught my attention that very first morning. I eyed them from my hotel room window as I drank my coffee. They surrounded the desert, making a bowl out of the city.

"Hiking will be much different here than in Pennsylvania," Dad observed.

"I think I understand what the song means about purple mountain majesty," I said.

We ventured out into the dry desert heat to explore the other treasures the city offered. Downtown, Old Vegas, offered more fun than on The Strip. The bars burst with character and the food and drinks come at a cheaper price.

We stumbled across Spring Mountain Road on a random scouting mission. Vegas's Chinatown stretches for dozens of blocks and is lined with restaurants and grocery stores sure to mentally teleport Jason back to Korea.

On our final day, I signed the lease to my new apartment. Dad and I celebrated by lounging at our hotel's pool.

"Rae, your place comes with a pool. That's gonna be really nice," he said.

I started to revel in the idea of living in a desert climate. Las Vegas grants a longer pool season and year-round hiking. Can't beat that! Yes, let's make Las Vegas home.

And it's off to a good start. I feel well rested. The sun is shining. And our surroundings have sucked Jason in. He "oohs" and "ahhs" every few seconds.

"In a quarter mile, turn right." My archaic GPS suctioned to the windshield directs me to Arabella Apartments. To the pool. To easy access to authentic Korean cuisine. To the adventures awaiting on the trails.

"You have arrived," the feminine robot tells me and Jason.

Our property manager waits for us outside the office building positioned in the center of the property. The structure matches the brown stucco of most residences in the valley. Inside, we sign the last of the paperwork and are declared official tenants.

The grounds are pretty. The semi-detached buildings each house four apartments and are spread across a lawn covered by clusters of trees. Charcoal grilling spaces with picnic tables disperse throughout. In the middle of it all, a fenced area contains a large pool and a hot tub. We're led past the swimming area and over to the adjacent building, to the apartment on the lower right side.

"You guys are lucky," our property manager says. "This unit opened up last week."

Talk about auspicious! How lucky are we to have a bottom-floor apartment that opens right up to the pool! I turn the key and swing the door open. Directly over the threshold, as if waiting to greet newlyweds as the husband carries his bride through the door, is a thoughtful greeting. "Welcome Home" is vacuumed into the carpet. The phrase adorns a design of palm trees. This simple gesture warms me.

Cognizant of the stencil below, the three of us take wide steps to enter the apartment. The door opens to a beige carpeted living room, and an island separates the rectangle room from the narrow galley kitchen and dining cubby.

I wander into a small square hallway. Our bathroom hangs to the left, the bedroom to the right. It includes a walk-in closet. I can display my entire wardrobe without keeping offseason clothes in storage bins. A simple pleasure. It's something I've never been able to do.

It's the largest place Jason and I have ever lived in together. These seven hundred square feet of space will grant us advantages that three hundred square feet could not. A bed is not our single option for chilling and our couch will be full-sized, not a love seat like we had at the Wee House. It'll provide space for us both. I'll no longer look up from reading in bed and be able to see him chilling on the living room floor. We can escape the tension of a fight in different rooms and have separate spots to relax in without being in one another's space.

"All right, Jay, you ready to work?" I ask my husband.

He exposes his teeth in a contrived grin and nods.

I mailed six boxes to our updated address weeks ago and they beat us to our destination. They're stacked in the empty dining room. We get to it, unpacking and finding places for the things packed inside the car and from these boxes.

We break for lunch at a Korean restaurant, so close to us that we walk. Jason doesn't order the entire menu. He's content with squid fried rice and *japchae*, a chewy glass noodle dish. I get *bibimbap*, a classic rice and vegetable dish topped with ground beef.

With our bellies full, we go shopping. Our highest priority, we test out and choose a mattress. It's delivered a few hours later and we sleep soundly on it, covered in the green ferned comforter we also bought.

Life plays on repeat the next day. More unpacking, more organizing, more shopping. Our second biggest priority, we test sit and choose a couch, though that won't be delivered until tomorrow. To close out Thursday, we visit a consignment shop for accent furniture and décor, unique pieces to separate our aesthetics from Pottery Barn's.

"Oh my god, would you look at that!" I shout and stop, absorbing the cheer of my dream patio furniture set in front of me. Surely, there's no other like it in the world.

The bright yellow tabletop is cut to resemble a flower. The legs are green stems. The two chairs match the table, one is painted bright pink and the other periwinkle. It must have been built for a beloved daughter or granddaughter for her tenth birthday.

"Jay, I need this."

"Rae, are you sure? It looks like it was built for a doll. No one else is going to be able to sit on it."

"You'll fit on the chairs too. We're getting it!"

I place it on the patio, my refuge, where I plan to spend countless hours sitting. The views of the pool and the lush green grassed grounds of the property make for the best place to decompress in. I can begin Saturday and Sunday mornings here, drinking cups of coffee and soaking up the delicious warmth of southwest sunshine.

Nope, not a bad start at all.

Chapter 14

By Friday, we've purchased and found places for our home's essential components. We invite Molly and her boyfriend over for dinner. I compile a physical list of pizza fixings to buy at Trader Joe's and look over at Jason. He's sprawled on the living room floor with his eyes closed. On my way out the door, I stop at his motionless figure. There remains one final unfinished thing from my massive to-do list that's plagued my thoughts all week.

My husband and I'd just embarked on a cross-country adventure together, a trip I was hoping would add spice back to our sex life. After six years, it's as troublesome as our conversational skills. Though I envisioned us getting down and dirty in every state we spent the night in, we ended up unwinding from our long drives in front of the TV, lying beside one another, a few feet apart, not touching. There were no bedtime or early morning cuddles either.

Jason feels more like my roommate than my husband. I miss the hugs, kisses, and cuddles. Our inside jokes.

I'm not horny. I don't particularly feel like having sex with my husband, but maybe my libido will awaken once we do. I'm encouraged by the shift I've seen over the past few days. How we're communicating, talking about what we need to do, planning for the coming weeks. How we're flirting. And Jason's upturned body looks ready to receive a revival.

I lower my body and straddle my husband's pelvis. He opens his eyes wide. Bending over, I kiss his neck, his lips. He likes this move. It's worked in the past, and it works now. We christen the apartment on the living room floor, already Jason's favorite area to unwind.

I feel no closer to my husband than I did before our afternoon delight. My orgasm fails to open a gate between my clitoris and brain; as I climax, my body doesn't surge with love or tenderness. But oh, how I wish it had. To have that yearning back. The desire to have him inside me. The need to be as physically close to this other human being as possible.

Maybe we need more of this. Our infrequent sex has caused our emotional connection to lag. Perhaps if the former happens with more regularity, the latter will emerge, long awaited for and better than ever.

But I don't linger in my husband's arms. I stand up. I have errands to run.

♫

Our guests arrive a few hours later.

Molly and I taught together in Seoul last year. We're recently made but close friends. Living as expats facilitated a fast friendship. Forever my weekend buddy for almost fifty-two of them in South Korea, I'm thrilled we can continue to do so here.

Molly disproves these objectives with her first words to me.

"*Anyeoung Chingu*," she says and envelopes me in a hug at my door-step. *Hello friend.* "It's wonderful living in the same city as you again. I wish we could hang out like this every week."

My stomach flips. Not in an "I have a crush, and it's the best" soaring, but with a sinking of "how is this going to ruin my plans?" flop. Molly's friendship in Korea provided me with the conversation, support, and understanding we turn to our female friends for. She made up for what my husband was unable to give me.

My vision for a satisfied Vegas life includes the two of us socializing here as much as we had in Seoul, helping one another transition into this next stage. I romanticized meeting other people with her by my side, widening our group of friends together because it's easier than going at it solo. Her words cause me to think about revising such a campaign.

"Well, we only live a half hour from one another. Why can't we?" I ask.

"I have this part-time job at a juice shop on weekends and nursing school starts on Monday. I'm already nervous about how intense it's going to be. I'm going to have no life."

"Adulting. Meh. We have no choice but to do it." I force a smile to give lightness to my words. "That's a bummer for both of us. I was looking forward to a redux of our Seoul adventures here. Now who am I going to get into trouble with?"

"Well, you can always help me study, but what fun is that? I'm sorry."

"School is why you're here. Don't apologize," I say and wave my hand as if it's no big deal. "Besides, I start work next week too. I'll make friends there. Look at us! We worked together, and here we are, continuing our friendship from across the world."

"We'll still get to hang out, but not as much as we did in Korea."

"We don't need to worry about that yet. You're here now. Let's enjoy our first Vegas Friday together." I hand her a stemless wine glass.

When we're finished with dinner, Molly and I insist we head to The Strip. I'm eager for Jason to experience it. He lights up at the idea, though Molly's boyfriend, with an early morning shift at work, shows no enthusiasm. Our group divides. The boyfriend drives home, and the rest of us go to The Strip with Jason behind the wheel.

It's said the blue light beaming from the Luxor's pinnacle can be seen from space, like a ray blasting from an alien ship. Although hyperbole, the casino's lights radiate so brightly they fill the sky in a faux spread of electrified Northern Lights. The sky glows yellow with luminescence, announcing the casinos' presence miles before we can clearly see any of them. It fills me with excitement for the outing's possibilities. Jason will fall in love with The Strip, which will lead to a love for living here, and all will trickle down into a renewed passion for me.

But then the Kia turns onto Las Vegas Boulevard, and we're bombarded with douchery. Giant faces of unctuous Vegas celebrity chefs and entertainment stars adorn casino walls and ramparts. They outnumber the lights. Tiesto's fifty-foot expression of smugness scars the east side of the MGM Grand. Pop country music debases the legacy of Dolly Parton and Willy Nelson, but I would rock a Kenny Chesney album on repeat instead of Tiesto's electronic house music.

Then one must contend with the Bellagio fountain. My own personal eighth layer of hell. Crowds observant of the water show swell to such oversized thickness that escape can seem impossible, depending on the hour. Trapped, you're stuck watching the synchronized water dance to Frank Sinatra's "My Way" for the thirty-sixth time while tourists clap their approval.

We avoid this by heading straight to New York, New York. No fountains, no Bobby Flay, only a giant red roller coaster. I can handle that. Just don't make me ride it.

Jason parks in the casino garage. He radiates high spirits as we walk toward the casino, rubbing his palms together and announcing, "I'm going to win a lot of money!"

"Are you going to play some slots, Ji Soo?" Molly pronounces his name with a perfect Korean accent.

She uses Jason's real name instead of his chosen moniker. It's typical for English-speaking Koreans, and those learning the language, to go by a Western name. I alternate calling my husband Ji Soo and Jason— the name he selected for himself—depending on whom I am speaking with.

He makes a face. "No, the slots are shit."

"What are you going to play then, *chingu*?" she speaks the Korean word for friend, her accent impeccable. I sound like an idiot when speaking the few Korean phrases I know, but Molly handles the tonal language with the ease of a gifted linguist.

"Blackjack," Jason tells her with the confidence of Kenny Rogers and repeats, "I'm going to win a lot of money."

I worry that Jason doesn't have the experience of Mr. Rogers and won't know when to walk away, but I don't voice my concerns. Though we have to be careful with our funds until Jason finds work, I know he's been looking forward to gambling. Blackjack will give Jason the best introduction to Las Vegas and is part of my grand plan to get him to fall in love with all our new city has to offer.

Molly looks at me. "Are you going to gamble?"

"Hell no." I furiously shake my head. "I'd much rather people watch with a drink in hand."

"I'll join you," she says. "No point in gambling. I'm a poor college student."

We descend the escalator into the main casino. New York, New York's interior is meant to look like the streets of Manhattan. It may fool the inexperienced, but to this former East Coaster, it looks like an ironic façade. The center hub is lined with a fake cobblestone street. A mediocre pizza restaurant stands adjacent to a jam-packed piano bar.

Still, it's one of my favorite casinos. Maybe it's the dim interior or the approximation of the giant metropolis? Maybe I like how it's such a caricature of what New York actually is? Maybe it reminds me of home? West Coast living means New York City is no longer a two-hour bus ride away, but at least I can be in Faux York in fifteen minutes.

I gawk at the enormous line of people waiting to order pizza and listen to drunks singing along with the pianist. How many versions of "Piano Man" is sung every weekend? Jason searches for an ATM while Molly and I grab drinks. We sip our overpriced vodka sodas waiting on Jason. He returns, stuffing twenty-dollar bills into his wallet.

Jason spots a table with available chairs. With his cash traded for chips, he tries to win his first hand of twenty-one. Molly and I hover behind him like two escorts enticing the promise of good fortune, but we chase his Lady Luck away instead. He loses one hundred dollars in less time than it takes me to drain my fifteen-dollar cocktail.

Scowling, Jason gets up. "Ehh, this table is garbage. I'm going to find another one."

"Maybe Molly and I are bad luck? We'll go have another drink and leave you alone. That work?"

He nods and saunters off in search of a winning table. Molly and I return to the bar for another drink. When we finish that one, Molly yawns and looks at her watch. I know what's coming next.

"Uhh, *chingu*. I have to get going. I work at the juice shop in the morning."

"Almost time to make those donuts! I should find Jason and see how he's doing," I say.

I order a final vodka soda and escort Molly to the taxi, waiting with her until the car, its occupant in the back, slinks away, carrying off with my enthusiasm.

I'm not sure when I'll see her, when I'll be able to hang out with my only friend here. With both fingers crossed, I sure hope that among my soon-to-meet colleagues lies another Molly, one who isn't so boggled with responsibilities that she, he, or they (please let me make multiple friends) won't have any bandwidth for socializing, and that they, as my father promised, would be down for hiking and other non-Strip adventures.

My hour here has reaffirmed The Strip is not my preferred place to hang out, at least not in the confines of these great gambling halls where every action, every experience, is a lame repeat of the one before. Toss a chip down, flip a card, throw your hand, gather your winnings. Insert money, push a button, push a button, push a button.

Even the people watching has lost its appeal. The men swathed in the flaming skulls and tigers of Ed Hardy apparel high-five across tables and eyeball the young women who stumble by in high heels on their way to the clubs. The idiots waiting in line for a taste of anything but authentic New York pizza. The throngs of people inhabiting the piano bar as if Sir Elton John is tinkling the keys.

I'm over this meat market, New York, New York, and The Strip, but perhaps a relocation will shift my mood. I set off in search of Jason among the mass of slot machines and table games and find him looking for me.

"Rae, where were you? I've been trying to find you for the past fifteen minutes."

"Oh, sorry. I wanted to make sure Molly got in a cab safely."

"Ahh, okay. I'm ready to go." He makes a fist and points his thumb behind his shoulder.

"How did you do?"

"This place is stupid. I lost all my money."

"Oh, geez, I'm sorry. Did you enjoy yourself at least?" I say and touch his shoulder, but he brushes my hand off.

"No, not at all. I'm ready to leave. Come on, let's go." His fist opens and he hurriedly waves his hand.

"Okay, okay. I'm about ready to go too. Let me finish my drink first and then maybe we can go someplace else. How about that bar around the corner from our apartment?"

He eyeballs my glass. It's two-thirds of the way full, an expensive amount of liquid to leave behind, and I foolishly think some cheer will be found at the bottom of my glass once it's drained. The vodka holds the potential to change the course of my dispirited night, which, at ten o'clock, is still young.

"I want to go home. Come on, let's go."

I frown. A week of nonstop stress and movement makes me want to do nothing but unwind. Tomorrow will find me back to playing house. And I don't want our evening, one that I held such high expectations for, to end on such a depressing note for either of us.

"I'm not ready to go home. Let's go someplace else," I say firmly. Don't I get a say in this?

"No, I want to go to bed." He strolls off, leaving me standing there holding my drink.

I stand motionless, my decision-making stunted by the booze and the emotional rush to my body and my head. My fight-or-flight kicks in, accompanied by a heavy chest, racing heart, and frozen limbs. I've seen this side of Jason too often in our years together. His temper either flares and abates with the swiftness of a flambéed fire or lingers like a smokey odor snaking up through a blaze.

Jason is twenty feet ahead of me when I abandon my unfinished drink near an unoccupied slot machine and start following him, hoping the walk has initiated a quick cool down.

"Jason, wait for me!"

He ignores me and continues without slowing down, not looking behind him to see where I am. I run to catch up.

"Please slow down," I say.

He stops and stares at me. Glares. He wears an ugly mask of rage directed at me. "It's your fault."

"What's my fault?"

"That I lost all that money. That I don't have a job. I didn't want to move here, but you insisted."

Jason gaslights, but I don't rebut his lie; words will fan his rage. I trail him, acting the demure wife, to the parking garage and the car. I uncharacteristically keep my mouth shut. The date is already in the gutter, speaking will make it worse.

If only we could use our words proactively, discuss potential problems to curtail any bubbling pressure. But that's not our style. We tackle our issues in explosive exchanges of angry words.

Perhaps I could have prevented this. If I had discussed Jason's plan for gambling, proposed an acceptable amount he'd have been comfortable losing to help him decide when to walk away. But it's too late for that. On to damage control, starting with my zipped-up lip.

My entire body tightens with tension, and my shaking hands struggle to buckle my seat belt as I wrestle the urge to shout. If I hadn't been drinking, I would have insisted on driving. Though that wouldn't necessarily stop him from doing something stupid.

Three years ago, we celebrated my twenty-eighth birthday in a cabin in the Pennsylvania mountains. On Sunday, prior to heading home, we set out for a short hike. The day rose thick with overcast, and we couldn't find the trailhead in the gray drizzle. Lost, we pulled into a wooded, dirt parking lot. This middle-of-nowhere lot had a tire "shredder" at its entrance for some strange reason. A strip of metal teeth ran horizontally with the car. The "teeth" pointed at an angle, which was innocuous to drive over but promised instant tire death if reversed.

Unfamiliar with such a roadblock, Jason shifted the car in reverse to back out. I yelled for him to stop, and he erupted in rage over my shouted warnings, jumping out of the car and walking away. I hopped into the driver's side and followed with the car. It took twenty minutes of cajoling to get him back in. Rain-soaked and furious, he yelled at me for most of the drive home. While on the highway, as I drove sixty miles per hour, he opened his passenger side door, screaming he would jump out. When we arrived home, he apologized, and I accepted it without further discussion. Then we cuddled together and watched the series finale of *Lost*.

Jason doesn't fall in love with our new home. He drives fast, leaving the lights of The Strip behind, along with my remaining optimism for the night out, for everything I had planned.

Chapter 15

Jason stretches out on the couch with his computer in his lap. He turns his head and smiles in my direction when he hears me walk in the front door. We haven't spoken since our heated exchange in New York, New York. Our car ride filled with tense silence, he retreated to the bedroom as soon as we arrived home. I watched a home renovation show until I passed out on the couch and stumbled to bed once my bladder roused me awake.

I distanced myself from his sleeping form in our bed, staying well within my side of the imaginary line bisecting the firm mattress, and headed to the gym as soon as I woke up, tiptoeing around my apartment with the careful quietness new parents possess, careful not to wake my big cranky baby.

Jason hid this dark side from me at first. It didn't appear until we were married and living in Pennsylvania. Is twenty months the standard for the honeymoon stage of a relationship to wear off? That's how long it took for the friction to appear, a mere nine months of marriage.

I was first caught off guard by how Jason's temper flared seemingly over nothing, but I am long used to it by now. My passive silence on our ride back to the apartment was novel. Reactive by nature and anything but submissive, I allow my anger to rage back, shouting and standing my ground in rebuttal at anything Jason says.

Our move predicated around forging a stronger marriage, we can't continue to handle our marital discord through shouting matches. They don't work. We both lose while our relationship suffers the most.

My calm response to his behavior, as difficult as it was for me to mute myself, is key to us succeeding as a couple. Though last night I handled it with baby steps, my exercise-cleared-head validated this as a strong start. Now to get Jason involved. Get him to wield a positive influence on the power he has in our relationship.

Jason waves me over to the couch, his smile growing larger. He's forgotten our fight already, another bucket of water under the bridge. We've tossed so much down there that we're practically swimming. So, though I'd prefer a shower rather than rest my sweat-covered body on the upholstered couch, I oblige, wanting to remedy our latest tribulation through something else unique to us: a civilized conversation on how to treat one another.

I sit alongside him. He grips my knee briefly and rests his hand there, gesturing toward the computer with his other one. Yes, this is what I want. A husband who lights up in my presence. Who wants me in his company. Who wants to share things with me.

I look to see what he's proudly showing me, expecting a screen highlighted with a plethora of jobs he's applied for. Instead, it's his mother. Looks like our one-on-one conversation, what I hope to be a heart-to-heart, is to be a threesome.

Ahn, lovely as she is, intimidates me. A fiercely independent and successful businesswoman, I worry she's disappointed her only child married a foreign woman who cannot speak their language. That I'm not good enough. I suspect she shares *Halmoni*'s speculations on where those grandchildren were. She doesn't inquire directly like *Halmoni*, but perhaps she asks Jason. I wouldn't know. He's never mentioned it and I haven't asked.

The last time I saw Ahn, at her home in Tokyo, she insisted we visit the spa. Though I was terrified to strip down to my birthday suit in her presence, there was no denying her. I partially alleviated my discomfort by removing my nipple rings before leaving her apartment and wrapping my lower half in a small towel when moving from the tub to sauna at the spa. I feared my piercings and shaved lady bits would impress her with radical notions of her daughter-in-law, so I hid these parts of myself from her.

My soak in a personal teacup hot tub may have delighted me, but my nipple rings never found their way back to my breasts. Perhaps I left a piece of my Americanness, of my own fierce independence, in Japan, in Ahn's apartment, with my discarded body jewelry.

Ahn, fluent in both Korean and Japanese, knows four English phrases: "Hello," "goodbye," "I miss you," and "I love you." She uses these words whenever we speak. I know enough Korean to order food, ask for directions, and a variety of simple phrases.

I've attempted to learn Korean on several inspired occasions, but it's difficult and I lost my mojo quickly. The language is grammatically opposite of English with the verb spoken last. Plus, my accent is awful. I cannot manipulate my lips or tongue to speak the tonal language. For example, the Korean word for water is *mul*. Out for dinner in a restaurant, I would request more water by asking *"Mul chuseyo."* This statement was always met with a blank stare. Without inflecting my voice to pronounce certain words correctly, all meaning was lost even when the context was apparent. My attempts at learning Korean left me feeling more frustrated than accomplished and I gave up. I guess I didn't want to learn it badly enough.

Hello is a simple enough word. Koreans always knew what I meant when I said that.

"Ahnyeoung," I greet my mother-in-law. Her face lights up and I smile at her.

"Ahnyeoung," she says and smiles back. "Hello. I am missing you." She speaks the words slowly and with the cadence of practice. Her words sound artificial because of this.

"I miss you too," I say. A lie. I am relieved we are back on opposite continents. I'm nervous to even be speaking with her via a video call.

His mother now says something that is not "hello," "goodbye," "I miss you" and "I love you." I look to Jason for translation. His face betrays no animosity.

"She asked if you are enjoying Las Vegas."

I nod and keep my smile as I tell another lie. "Oh yes. It's very different from Scranton. It's very hot now though."

He translates for me, and the conversation remains in Korean. I zone out while Jason takes his mother on a "tour" of our apartment. He places the computer in front of me at its conclusion to say our "good-byes" and "I love yous" in English.

Finally, it is just the two of us. Time for a talk.

Judging by the way Jason's smile persists, he is content to brush off our fight, brush it right under the rug until one of us stumbles over it.

"She really likes our place, Rae. She wants to come visit soon." He looks delighted, like a little boy who has pleased his mother by using his manners correctly.

"That would be wonderful, Jay," I say. "Does she know when?"

"Not yet," he says and places the computer in his lap. He is done talking with me, but I'm not done talking with him.

"Jason." He looks at me, his dark eyes neutral behind his large plastic frames. *Please remain calm.* I shift next to him, and my body experiences an immediate physical change. My heart pounds within a chest weighed with bricks. "Last night, we were having a lot of fun in New York, New York. It felt so good to relax and get out of the house. But then, with the blackjack, you took your anger out on me."

"Yeah, okay. What's your point?" His eyes narrow.

"My point is you were an asshole to me."

Watch what you say, Rachael. Think about your words.

I pause and rephrase. "You were really mean, and you hurt my feelings and I didn't deserve any of it. It's not my fault that you lost money, but you acted like it was. Is that how you treat someone that you love?" I read that last line recently in an article about effectively resolving issues with a partner. *Remind your partner that they love you and that they should treat you with love.*

It doesn't work with him. He becomes defensive. "You should have stopped me. I didn't have to lose all that money."

"That's not the problem, Jason." I ignore his argument and speak slowly, keeping my voice level, but I hear its slight tremble. "The problem is you were aggressive and mean to me. And I don't want you, my husband, to treat me like that. It's not fair to me."

"It's not fair that I lost my money," he snarls.

"I am not trying to start another fight with you. It's the last thing I'm interested in doing."

"Then why are you bringing it up?"

"Because I don't want you treating me like that anymore. That's not how you treat someone you love."

"Then you shouldn't let people you love to lose so much money."

I sigh. "I'm bringing this up because I want us to get a fresh start here. I know it sounds cheesy, but it's true." I place my hand on top of his, but he shakes me off. "We love each other. Let's act like it. Please. We need to be kinder to one another. Both of us. I know I lose my temper too." Once, in a fit of rage, I swept my jewelry box off my dresser with an impulsive, open palm. Such madness forged nothing but wasted minutes spent untangling jewelry.

I continue speaking, "I think we should try to speak to each other as calmly as we can when we get angry. Maybe we can step away, take a walk or something, until we both calm down and can talk instead of yelling. I had some things I wanted to say to you last night, but I didn't. I knew my anger may have made me say some things I didn't mean. And I'm glad I didn't because today, now that I'm no longer angry, I don't feel those things anymore. Let's move on, but let's start doing things differently. We'll be in a better place."

He stares straight ahead, silent. If I continue to talk, he may explode. Baby steps. I said my part and I said it in a quiet and serene voice. I stand, feeling it's the right moment to retreat.

"Rae," he says, and his voice stops me. It's not angry or sad, but emotionless, like a robot. "I knew I was going to get my citizenship."

He catches me off guard. I can't process his words. "Huh?"

"When I got my citizenship last month in Philly. I knew before I went that I was getting it that day."

Several seconds pass. "Wait, you knew you were getting it that day? When you had your civics test? The weekend I went with Kylie to see Phish?"

"Yes. They told me that the ceremony would come after my civics test. They wanted me to invite family and friends."

"But you never told me. You didn't invite me." My heart pumps ice through my veins. The shock diffuses through my body, leaving me frozen in place. Nervous ticks zap down my arms and legs.

"I didn't tell anyone."

"Why not?"

"I don't know. I guess I didn't want you there."

This admission hits like an angry fist. My throat constricts and my lungs can't draw in enough air. These words, free of curses and slurs, are the harshest he has ever said to me. Lies can be lobbed back and forth when couples fight, insults exchanged to incite a reaction, but "I guess I didn't want you there," is an unequivocal truth.

He was aware of how badly I wanted to see him sworn in. I had pictured how joyous his ceremony would be, even in the sterileness of a cold government building. I'd cry happy tears. Jason's pride displayed in his open shoulders and chest, his strong voice repeating the oath, his determined steps silently announcing to all in witness that some great success had been reached.

I envisioned all this happening, knowing he and I had been moved to such intense emotions in other bland office environments. We got married in one.

Our wedding day was a gray and frigid Monday, four days past Christmas in 2008. My school granted me a rare day off so we could be united in wedded bliss through the signing and stamping of our marriage license. Koreans called this the "paper wedding." We would have a traditional wedding in Korea in the spring and another in the States in August (funny that a woman who never held grandiose aspirations for a dream wedding would have two celebrations), but our need to start Jason's immigration process hastened our marriage.

Our first stop was the US Embassy, where we procured the original license. We walked hand-in-hand across a wide street under a morning sky depressed with clouds to get the license signed and stamped at the Korean Embassy, then back to the US Embassy for the same procedure.

The American working the counter proclaimed an understated "Congratulations" as he stamped us legally wed. In the instant that stamp permanently marked our marriage license, I felt this love, humanity's very force, wash over me. A rush flowed through the entire length of my body and filled me with lightheaded giddiness. My affection for my new husband imbued me with an unnatural power that momentarily caused me to feel immortal. I could have walked out of that embassy and stopped cars and changed traffic lights with this intangible energy.

Now, this love force causes betrayal. I'm in a state of disbelief. He didn't want me present at his ceremony. Me. His wife. We're partners, meant to share a life, celebrate these momentous events that we worked for. We poured hours into researching the proper steps, filling out paperwork, traveling to embassies, and going to interviews.

I sacrificed so Jason could attain US citizenship because it's what he wanted and that's what partners do. You live in your hometown even though you don't want to because your partner wants to stay there. You work a shitty job because your husband wants to pursue a table game license. You move to Vegas even though you want to live in Denver because Vegas would be the best place for the two of you.

I made all these sacrifices for him, and he didn't even want me around.

Nervous energy pulsates through my fingers and toes. Pacing will help and I need to walk away from Jason before I do or say something I regret. I grab my phone and purse, put my shoes on, and walk out the door. Distractions necessary, I peruse my phone, looking for someone to call or text.

I spot an old message from Faris. I'd love to text him, but it's best not to as worked up as I am. Thinking of him does cause a pleasant disruption, a positive way to spin Jason's subterfuge. If he had told me about his citizenship ceremony, I most certainly would have attended that and skipped the SPAC Phish shows. Faris and I and would never have reunited.

I expected this move to bring about a momentous, powerful, and positive change. Sure, it's momentous. And yes, it's powerful. But, hearing Jason's confession, is it positive? I may have to find my silver lining in the unexpected.

Chapter 16

The entire Strip lies within my view. Looking past the rows of identical housing tracts and abundant palm trees, and sometimes through a thick cloud of mountain-meets-valley polluted haze, I take in the impressive panorama from the playground at Jesse Martin Elementary with wide eyes. The five hundred and fifty-foot Ferris wheel at The LINQ looms above the casinos in the middle of The Strip while the Stratosphere Tower rises high on the northern end.

I admire this view whenever I stand on the playground and marvel at this widely sought vacation destination. Here I am, a Las Vegas resident who works five days a week teaching second graders. My day-to-day repeats tediously while, ten miles away, thousands of people from all over the world gamble large sums of money, drink and take drugs, and sleep with strangers.

On a Tuesday.

The contrast is ludicrous.

Today marks the second Friday of the school year. I stand in my playground duty spot, on a soft cushion of grass with my gaze straight on The Strip, slugging coffee and waiting for the bell to signal the start of the day.

Two weeks of school and my energy is depleted. I arrive in the mornings an hour earlier than the start of my workday and work an additional two hours after school. My responsibilities endless, I call families, create lessons, grade assignments, look over data, and cry at my desk. Work eats up a few hours on Sundays too.

A horrible sleeper from birth, I now go to bed by 9:30 and sleep through the night, provided I don't wake up to pee. I kiss the end of my slumber when that happens, spending the witching hours listing my obligations until the alarm sounds.

The all-consuming life of a teacher comes with periods of pure delight. I love my students. Forming relationships with each and every one of my kids drew me to the profession and is what I love most about it. I give and get dozens of hugs and smiles, learn about their favorite colors, foods, and animals, their families, and what they like to do when not in school. They love to be around me and excitedly wave and yell my name when they see me outside the classroom.

Two weeks in and I know a group of my girls will find me on the playground for a before-school hang with their favorite teacher. Here they come now, five of the most darling little girls to ever grace my presence. They greet me with smiles and hugs and enthusiastic shouts of "Ms. Wesley!"

How could I not love this?

"Happy Friday, ladies." I squeeze each of them.

"What are you doing this weekend, Ms. Wesley?" I am asked with imploring blue eyes.

Oh, my heart, how thoughtful! These seven-year-olds are made to be loved, even when they are the cause of my constant stress and sixty-hour work weeks. "I am having some teacher friends over for dinner."

They answer with silence and eyes wide with shock. *Teachers do things outside of school? Teachers hang out together?*

Though I will be bonding with some of my closest people the following week in Denver for Phish, I need a Vegas group to call my own ASAP. Integral to this reboot in Vegas involves finding my people, and I'm making earnest attempts. Last Saturday, I participated in a hike organized through Meet Up. I surmised I could meet some cool peeps through this similarly interested online social group while simultaneously learning of desert trails worth exploring.

The hike itself, an extended traipse through an Arizonan canyon leading to a natural hot spring (warning of brain eating amoebas posted everywhere), exceeded my expectations. At one juncture, I had to leap from one twenty-foot-high ledge to another, tossing my back-pack across the chasm to a fellow hiker preceding my jump. Facing my sweat-inducing fear of heights had been exhilarating.

My fellow hikers proved less thrilling. Though together we comprised a diverse group of desert traversers, I was unable to engage anyone in easy or interesting rapport. One fit trekker self-righteously touted her homeopathic lifestyle for a third of our hike. Another hiker kept his ear buds in and head down for the entire ten miles, maybe to dissuade the homeopath from engaging with him. Halfway through, a woman striding alongside eyed me up and down and gave an unsolicited proc-lamation of my height, weight, and size.

Undeterred by the hiking failure, my efforts to find me some friends continue. Tomorrow, I'll focus on bonding with my colleagues. I already know none of them carry a fervent obsession with any band like I do on account of an ice breaker our principal presented us with during our first back-to-school staff meeting.

"What is your favorite place in the world?"

My answer combined two for a hypothetical response. "My favorite place in the world would be a Phish show anywhere in southeast Asia."

This earned scattered chuckles but didn't reveal any other Phish zealots. And no big deal. I've many friends who have nothing more than a basic interest in music. We interact in other ways.

I'm confident I'll find connections from which friendships can be built among my colleagues. We already share a profession and the altruisms of teaching. Perhaps I'll discover a hiking or book nerd buddy in one of them.

Problem is, I quickly detected an obstacle.

Adult mean girls.

Cliques run rampant among the grown ass teachers at Jesse Martin Elementary school. Adjacent to my classroom is the popular group's leader. They gather in her classroom before and after school. If I happen to cross paths with them, lock eyes with one as I pass by, I'm greeted with a pleasant "hello," but I'm rarely invited inside the threshold.

I hear them. Their conversations float the fifteen feet between our rooms and enter my classroom. They speak of the school day, but also of life outside, of socializing together: grabbing dinner and drinks, double dates with their partners, catching a show on The Strip. They don't go to the clubs, but they sure do like to shop.

I'm not interested in befriending any of these pretty, popular women. We've nothing in common and I typically avoid their go-to activities (they eat at chain restaurants), though it would boost my confidence to be a part of a group. Their banter heckles me. I'd love to be invited. To be included. To feel wanted. My self-doubt set aflame, it's a repeat of high school.

But the onboarding staff aren't corrupted; none of the teacher cliques have integrated them yet. I look forward to hosting them, and, lesson learned, I'll make sure not to follow dinner up with a visit to The Strip.

Saturday rises in dreariness. The short monsoon season arrived weeks ago, but chose today to show its full potential. I planned for a pre-dinner happy hour in the pool area, sitting around one of the pool-side wrought-iron tables exchanging stories in between sips of spar-kling brut wine. The paint-by-number yellow, orange, and pink colors of the setting sun will indicate when to go inside for dinner.

Instead, the singularly gray morning skies hold the look of an all day rain. No wine al fresco later; we will have to cram inside the apartment this evening. The weather also denies me my most simple morning pleasure of coffee and cigarettes at my flowered table.

Jason snoozes beside me. It's been several weeks since he confessed his citizenship ceremony omission, and we still haven't fully repaired things. The tension has died but I'm not comfortable with his physical touch, my favorite of the love languages. I keep my distance from him in bed and on the couch.

I glance at him, admiring how his full lips relax in his smooth and unlined face. Everyone deserves a second chance, and I owe it to my husband to try again. Sure, I've said this. A lot. I've acted on this tenet dozens of times. But if we are to have this fresh start in Vegas, I must let go of the past. And even with my recent misgivings about our future, I refuse to give up, to wave that white flag of defeat. Not after four weeks. Not after all our planning and sacrifices. Not when we've so much to settle into and figure out.

I press the metaphysical restart button by stroking his chest. He stirs. I press my lips to the side of his neck, and he rolls his head to the side, exposing more skin. My hand moves down slowly. Down. Down. Down. He opens his eyes a sliver.

"Ah, Rae, I'm sleepy. Maybe later?"

"Not later," I whine. "Now."

He turns over, away from me. "I'm sorry, Rae. Let me sleep."

Though I'm not in the mood either, the rejection stings. Trying to not feel incensed, I slip out of bed to indulge in coffee time instead of sexy time and then set about making my grandma's spaghetti sauce, which she taught me a few summers ago. We spent a Friday in my parent's kitchen browning pork ribs, country style, in a stockpot, rolling out meatballs, stirring the bubbling red sauce as it thickened over hours of cooking on the stovetop. I wrote down the recipe methodically. If I captured a step incorrectly, I'd grab a fresh sheet of looseleaf and start from the beginning instead of scratching out the mistake and rewriting below. A plastic sheet protector safely encases the finished version.

This traditional East Coast Italian American Sunday dinner, complete with a loaf of crusty bread and a tossed salad, is my most favorite feast in the world. If I find myself on death row, I will request this as my final meal. My Italian genes shine through my mediocre cooking and allow me to create a tasty version of my family's long revered and beloved recipe. I derive so much in bringing people together and am eager to share this special dinner with my work friends.

The smell of simmering sauce intensifies the longer it cooks. I clean the bathroom and dust. Jason washes the sink full of dishes and vacuums. He completes his half of the household chores without any reminders. He's not as good at keeping his promises of sex. We spend the afternoon hanging in the living room, not naked in our bedroom. I don't press for it. My libido remains low.

My dinner guests start arriving at six. Only one bears goodies to add to our meal. The other two enter empty-handed. I learned from my mother to never arrive at a dinner party without a contribution or thank you gift. They must not have received such a lesson.

We crowd around the dining room table, not spread around the pool, using a plush blue chair from the living room to accommodate the five of us. It's cramped but cozy. I pour four glasses of red wine, Jason sips on Dr. Pepper, and I set out a cheese and cracker plate for us to nibble on.

"Thanks for coming, everyone. This weather sucks. I really wanted to sit around the pool."

"On the bright side, no one will need to water their lawns today," Jenny says. "The cooler weather feels great too, doesn't it?"

Jenny is a veteran teacher new to Vegas. She's always quick to share her many learned tips and tricks acquired through years of being in the classroom. All teachers, I'll soon learn, aren't like this. Some are hell-bent on being "the best" in a profession where teamwork reigns key to one's success and sanity. I admire her way of seeing the bright side of everything and appreciate the tray of freshly baked brownies she made for dessert despite her self-proclaimed dislike of the kitchen. Oh, and I enjoy pouring her a second glass of wine, especially when everyone else asks for water after they finish their first glass. I want to be friends with her and hope this dinner will seal it.

"I don't mind," Mackenzie says. She's a recent college graduate from southern California who teaches kindergarten. "I had to wake up at 2 a.m. to watch my boyfriend's game, so the rain let me sleep in this morning."

"Do you watch a lot of his games?" I ask her.

"The ones on weekends," she tells me. "I can't do it during the week. I need a nap when it's finished."

Mackenzie's boyfriend pursued his dreams of playing basketball professionally by moving to the Philippines. I'm curious about how they make their relationship work, but Kelly chimes in, cutting off any further conversation about long-distance love and basketball.

"It was the perfect morning to get some work done, which is exactly what I did."

I dislike her authoritative tone. It suggests her opinion speaks the ultimate truth. *I got work done today. All of you should have done work today.*

"I figured out the best way to get my class to line up," she continues. "First graders can never get in a straight and quiet line."

No shit, Kelly. They're six.

"What is it?" Mackenzie asks.

"I'm going to give them each a number and put stickers on the ground labeled with each number to show where I want them to line up. I don't know what took me so long to think of it," she says.

"Oh," Mackenzie says. "I saw something similar to that online."

"Umm, yeah," Kelly's words emerge slowly. "I got the idea from a teacher's blog."

Kelly's open mouth reveals her arrogance. She brags about her teaching and acts as if the ideas she plucks from the internet are innovative and original. Her stories revolve around experiences she believes are novel. At the start of the school day last Monday, she regaled us with a long-winded story about recently eating her first bowl of pho, encouraging us all to try this delicious Vietnamese noodle soup. Worse, she habitually speaks about herself without any inquiries in your direction. Unlike Jenny, I don't want to solidify any type of relationship with Kelly outside of our professional one, but I couldn't leave her out of the "new teacher dinner" invite.

"So, you guys are all teachers?" Jason interrupts additional chatter from Kelly with a question he already knows the answer to. This habit helps him steer the conversation into a territory of language he feels comfortable in. I surmise he prefers to begin conversations anticipating the answers he'll receive.

Jenny's welcoming smile disarms her classroom full of hormonal fifth graders. She used it on me when we first met, and she now flashes it at my husband. "Yes, we are!"

Jason shows interest in each of them, asking basic but revealing questions while I finish preparing dinner. *What are you teaching? Where are you from? How did you end up in Vegas?* I smile as I strain two pounds of pasta in the sink, overhearing Jason's "oohs" of interest and attentive "hmms." His sincerity in getting to know people is endearing and I'm grateful he's here to diffuse my anxieties over entertaining these "friends."

I clear the table of our appetizer detritus and replace the dirty plates and napkins with clean ones while Jason brings over large bowls full of Italian goodness. We dig in. My guests gush compliments about my cooking, and I steer the conversation away from school. I spend more hours in my classroom than anywhere else, even my bed, and I want to forget about it for a few hours. My endeavors keep getting thwarted. "What's everyone's plan for tomorrow?"

Kelly answers right away. "Church. Then I'll have dinner with some family friends who go to the same church."

I have zero interest in church or giving Kelly the chance to tell us another story about her family friends, whom I've heard much about in the four weeks I've known her.

"I think I may go to school and work on some decorations." Mackenzie contrives a sad face, but I think she draws great pleasure in her classroom aesthetics. Her Kindergarten classroom rivals the best teacher blogs.

"What do you need to do?" Jenny asks with genuine concern. Though a distant memory, she hasn't forgotten how difficult and all-consuming the plight of a first-year teacher is.

"Oh, I want to make my door look like an apple tree."

"I think I'm in need of a lazy day." I bring the conversation back to tomorrow. "I need a day to do nothing. I'm so fucking tired. Today would have been the perfect lazy day."

Jenny nods in agreement. "I could use a movie day, too. What are you going to watch?"

"I want to read. I've hardly had any time to pick up a book this month," I lament.

"I reread *The First 100 Days of School* this month," Mackenzie volunteers.

"Oh, I have that book too," Kelly says.

No, not school again. No more fucking school talk. I jump up and begin to clear dirty dishes from the table. "I'm going to put on music. What does everyone want to listen to?"

"Country."

"House."

"Taylor Swift."

I scowl internally. No, no, and no. "How about some '80s?"

My suggestion wins approval. Who doesn't love '80s music? I turn my speaker to a random '80s Pandora channel and allow Daryl Hall and John Oates to be the only sounds for a moment while my food digests.

"Do you guys ever play music for your kids?"

Fuck you, Kelly.

I acquiesce. There's no escaping the school discussion. We were strangers to one another until four weeks ago. In this getting-to-know-you stage, school is our sole common bond. While Mackenzie and Kelly trade stories of their little students, Jenny listens and offers advice. Jason's attention wanders until I bring out Jenny's brownies. I offer coffee, but it's too late in the day. More wine? No, they have to drive home.

Mackenzie and Kelly leave almost as soon as dessert is finished. I don't care. I'm apathetic about their departure and don't want to talk about or listen to more stories about school. Jenny finishes her drink and takes off soon after our younger colleagues.

I sit at the table, silently drinking my wine and playing The Outfield's "Your Love" on repeat while Jason cleans our dinner dishes.

"Your friends are nice, Rae," he says.

I nod.

"And your food was really good."

I look down into my glass of red, debating whether to dump it out and put this night to bed. "Uh, huh. Thank you."

"What's wrong, Rae?"

"Ah, nothing, Jay. I'm tired."

My brain races wide awake, obsessing over how dinner didn't play out anything like I'd expected. I wanted to find a Kylie or Anna in one of them, someone who will be like family to me. I thought I would discover Mackenzie's freaky side or one of Kelly's likable traits. I wanted Jenny to hang out and drink wine with me until midnight.

Instead, our dinner acted as an extension of work. It played out similarly to how teacher cliques gather at the end of the school day to decompress and review the day's gossip. The only key difference between the two is that my hosted teachers' session was fueled by carbs and wine.

I'm defeated by another failed weekend, but, looking on the bright side, my fridge is filled with leftovers. That's never a bad thing.

And next week brings Labor Day. Dick's and a Phish homecoming will soon be mine.

Chapter 17

Denver. 6:15 p.m. Delayed.

I sit at my gate with a pathetic bowl of iceberg lettuce, thinking I'll have to inhale the airport salad so I can finish it before getting on my flight. Except, a glance at the boarding announcement shows it's delayed sixty minutes, pushing my Denver arrival to almost 9:00. The band will be well into their first set by the time the airplane even touches down.

Fuck!

I shipped a box of clothes and toiletries to Demaris last week and am fortunate I won't need to drop anything off at her apartment. Calculating a timeline in my head, if I run off the plane, through the terminal, and immediately jump in a cab, I can be there by set break.

But what if my plane is delayed even more? What if it gets canceled?

I think of nothing but the possibility of missing out on my long-anticipated trip to Colorado. I'm desperate to unite with my Phish family. Being surrounded by the love and acceptance of my people, with the excitement of Phish's music at the center, will temporarily relieve the disappointment of not just the failed dinner party, but the disastrous start to this new phase in Vegas. Those worst-case scenarios I'd ramped up during my day of packing the Wee Wesley Hwang House are possibly becoming my reality.

I enjoyed my life in Pennsylvania more.

Did I actually say that?

My heart and head have never needed anything like they need Dick's, Dick's, Dick's.

A reunion predicated on bachelorette festivities, we will not be celebrating with penis-shaped cakes and blow-up cocks. Instead, my cousin's marriage gala will include Dick's in our favorite fashion. Three Phish shows at a soccer stadium named for the sporting goods giant outside of Denver, Colorado. Referred to by fans as Phish Dick's, or, more simply, Dick's, the run of music is an annual event held over Labor Day weekend.

Adulthood responsibilities bring fewer chances to see friends and family united through music but disconnected due to miles. Opportunities galore present themselves when the band plays three shows in a row, especially when a Monday off work grants flexibility to travel. Many of the twenty-five thousand people in attendance use the holiday exactly as we plan to, as an occasion to reunite with your Phish family spread across the country.

Anna's decision for celebrations designed around a weekend of music isn't rare either. Apropos to include our favorite people, places, and things with our fondest moments, marriage proposals, honeymoons, even the weddings themselves, take place before, during, and after concerts. Birthday shows and those reaching milestone show counts are honored too, with pins, hats, and shirts proclaiming, "it's my birthday" or "it's my 100th show," soliciting cheers, high fives, and hugs from friends and strangers alike. Everyone wants in on the action, the love, and the feel-good vibes.

I'm so ready for it all.

The post-wedding bachelorette party consists of my original Phish crew of women and one infiltrating bachelor. When I arrived back from Saratoga Springs, I reached out to Anna, Selena, and Demaris separately, begging them to let my long-lost-and-now-found buddy to tag along.

"Faris. You know him from college," I said to Selena, another Penn State graduate and former college roommate of mine who now lives in Portland, Oregon. "He had roosters. And his house threw that mustache party. Remember?"

I repeated this to Demaris. She resided in State College while Faris, Selena, and me were students at the university.

To my cousin, I brought up a Phish show in Philadelphia we attended over ten years ago. "You met him at the Spectrum. My college friend? Ponytail? He almost slept on the floor of our hotel room."

My three friends denied any memory of the man, but it didn't take much cajoling for them to agree. Work provided the biggest barrier. I refused to bail on a workday so soon into a fresh school year and couldn't leave for Denver until after school today (Friday). Everyone else arrived earlier today or yesterday.

Faris landed in the Mile High City late this morning. I chatted with him on my drive to work as he was waiting for his flight at the Dallas airport. It was the first we had spoken since parting ways in New York, and hearing his voice sent tumbles throughout my abdomen.

"You sure it's okay for me to go over to Demaris's without you?" he asked.

"Yes, I told you a million times already. You all know each other!"

"But I don't remember them. Do they remember me?"

"Not yet, but they will. You all will. Wait until you see one another."

"What if they think I'm a serial killer?"

Any fears about the possibility of Faris being a serial killer were alleviated once he walked through Demaris's door. Familiar faces from the previous decade were recognized and triggered memories. I'd been reading text messages about their shenanigans throughout the day, and my impatience to arrive grows with each one received.

And now my flight is delayed. Fucking Spirit Airlines. Oh my god, this budget airline may cancel the flight and ruin my weekend. My month. The rest of the year. I stare at the flight updates over the gate, willing to change it with my nonexistent telekinetic powers. It still reads *Denver. 6:15. Delayed.*

I tap my feet, fidgeting in my cardboard-thin seat with bright fluorescent lighting illuminating the room in a headache-inducing glow.

I inform the group. Instead of texting my cousin or one of my friends, I message Faris. Of them all, I've been communicating with him the most lately. Not a day goes by that I don't hear the reassuring bing of a text alert. No matter how my day has unfolded, a simple line from him soothes me.

I text him a not-so-comforting message. *My fucking flight is delayed.*

He responds immediately. Reliable man, that Faris. He rarely leaves me waiting longer than ten minutes to reply.

Shit. How long?

An hour. I leave at 6:15 now.

I'm sorry. Keep us updated.

I look up at the flight update board. Nothing has changed since my last glance.

My phone buzzes again. It's Selena. *Your flight is delayed? Ugh. But you'll get here!* Her optimism shines, no matter the situation.

The hour passes with a heavy chest and skin that my skeleton is ready to jump through. My gratitude overflows when, at 5:45, an announcement is made. Our aircraft is ready to board. I finally step on the Airbus and thank the powers that be as I buckle up in my preferred aisle seat and remove a paperback from my multicolored backpack. I'd love to pass the flight with my nose in Michelle Moran's *The Heretic Queen*, but I don't think I can focus.

I text all four friends. *Ready to take-off!*

I don't receive a single response before we are told to put our phones in airplane mode, but I forgive the losers because … Phish Lot. In Denver, the party is in full swing. I'll feel less considerate if my phone remains blank upon landing.

I do try to read, but my anticipation doesn't permit my favorite pastime. My thoughts wander to my loved ones waiting for me in Denver. I saw my cousin last in early June, at her wedding in Fort Lauderdale.

Standing beside Anna as her maid of honor, I wore a cheerful yellow sundress with a large string of turquoise stones circling my neck. Pictures of the occasion show me beaming, so happy to be there honoring the joining of my cousin and her one-true-love.

My one-true-love had been absent from my cousin's nuptials. In true Jason form, he passed on attending the wedding. I understood he didn't want to use his PTO from the casino, but it wasn't like he was missing work to attend a concert. Using three days for an important family event shouldn't have been an issue.

Yet, I didn't argue with his decision. His absence hadn't ruined my fun. I spent the wedding festivities eating, drinking, and being among family.

But the celebration of love caused me to reflect on my marriage. He and I had a great visit to Fort Lauderdale a few years earlier, but at the wedding, I didn't long to have him lounging beside me on the beach, nor did I feel slighted posing for pictures without him.

Cognizant of my marriage's funk, I hoped those happy times together would reappear soon. I assumed they would reemerge when we settled into permanent American living. I interviewed for and accepted my teaching job here in Vegas the day after I arrived home from Florida and took it as a sign. Here was our chance!

Three months later, I remain obstinate to this idea, even with the obstacles our move intensified.

Even with Faris.

But I cannot, for all the good, bad, sickness, and health of my marriage, stop thinking about him. Even saying his name in my head, *Faris*, causes my stomach to loop around in circles. It's the main symptom of a classic crush.

I fantasize about him in bed at night. The thoughts and images provide instant gratification. My current life isn't providing me with such levels of joy, and I need to derive my happiness somewhere. I find it in these fantasies.

I base most on this weekend, about what, in a perfect world, could happen. Faris will reveal he has feelings for me, granting me permission to confess my crush on him. My fantasies become reality, but we move them from PG-13 to NC-17. Kisses on my mouth turn to kisses all over my body.

In this fictional reel, Faris and I don't speak of Jason. I never allow such a conversation to take place. No need to muddy such fantastical imagery with the dirtiness of real life.

When the images in my head come to the end of the weekend, I press rewind in my head and start it over from Friday.

I know none of this innocent fun will ever come to sinful fruition.

I also know, sitting on this flight bound for Denver, that I won't want to make the return trip come Monday.

Denver should be my permanent home. I spent the summer of 2006 in the Front Range, learning how to edit, market, and sell books while attending The University of Denver's Publishing Institute. With over three hundred days of sunshine, a seemingly endless choice of outdoor activity, and the best music scene for hundreds and hundreds of miles, I longed to stay in Denver at the conclusion of the program.

Unable to secure a position within the local writing and publishing market, I was forced to return to Pennsylvania. The opportunity to teach in Seoul came that December, but my desire for Colorado living always endured. As I was focused on finding a city for us to settle in, the siren song of the mountains sung loudly but couldn't compete with Jason's enthusiasm for Las Vegas.

This three-day weekend in Denver will provide me with more feelings of love, comfort, and belonging than the last month has. However, it's fleeting. On Monday morning we'll become a broken family as we disperse back to the physical locations of our permanent shelters.

Fuck, I don't want to have to return to Vegas.

I vow to stay present. To enjoy this escape. To not think about my Vegas life anymore, at least not until Monday morning.

Instead, even though it's not bedtime, I close my eyes and imagine Faris pouring his heart out.

Chapter 18

The Rocky Mountains rarely permit a smooth take-off or landing. My flight descends fast and rough, and I give a silent thank you to the pilot who got us to our destination in less than eighty minutes. Now, it's up to my legs and luck to make up for the rest once the passengers in the rows ahead of me deplane.

This is a true test of patience. I rarely stand in my seat until the row in front of me is on the move, but I send a text alerting everyone of my arrival, jump up, toss my backpack over my shoulders, and petulantly bounce in the nine inches of space around me. I stink-eye the families slowly ushering their whiny toddlers down the aisle and the idiots who forget their carry-on lodged three rows behind them.

Come on, I have a Phish show to get to. Let's go!

Finally, finally, it's my turn and I pop into the exit row even as the folks opposite me begin their departure. Sorry! I have more important places to be than you. Tucking your three-year-old in and reading a bedtime story can wait, but my plans cannot spare another moment! I speed walk on the jetway and break into a jog on the concourse.

I follow the signs to the main terminal and scan others directing where to grab a taxi. Slowing my jog to a fast walk in the crowded security and baggage area, I take an escalator to the floor below for pedestrian pickup.

The one thing separating me from that late summer cool Colorado air is an automatic glass door. I'm not the only one anticipating the awaiting freedom. A grinning young man prepares to exit. We stare at one another.

"You headed to Dick's?" he asks, looking me up and down and taking in my flowy purple pants and oversized lapis pendant.

I spot his Phish shirt. "Want to share a cab?"

For fans, the mutual love of the band can cement strangers into friendship. I automatically like this man, as I do with almost all Phish people, and I will until he proves otherwise. Lucky for me, our short ride doesn't present any drama, but absurdities have occurred because of this blind acceptance before.

During my first Phish shows in Hampton, Virginia in January 2003, my benevolent buddy invited his crusty, dirty hippie (known as a wook or wookie because of their resemblance to Chewbacca) acquaintance and his wookette girlfriend to crash on our hotel floor. I awoke in the middle of the night to the two of them loudly locked together (no, their dreadlocks hadn't tangled), forcing me to hold my full bladder *and* listen to their grunting and moaning until either I fell back asleep (impossible with my discomfort), or they climaxed and passed out, granting me access to the bathroom. Lucky me, the latter occurred.

Here in Denver, we non-wooks introduce ourselves and cross the pedestrian walkway to the lane devoted to hotel shuttles and taxis. The pickings are slimmer than the closing of a farmer's market, but a single taxi van idles at the end of the concrete curb. We hop in.

The conversation between two strangers with a Phish bond flows as if we're long acquainted. As we speak of Phish shows past, present, and future, I rifle through my recycled rice sack backpack in confirmation I haven't lost anything. Everything in its right place, I concentrate on my phone. I received a small deluge of texts during my race through DIA. They're all from Faris.

Hurry up!

Text us as soon as you get here.

Icculus!

You're missing a great set.

Hurry up! You need to get here!

I text him back. *En route now. Be there soonish?* I don't know the exact distance from the airport to the venue, but it can't be long now.

Another message—*set break*—confirms my arrival as I'd predicted, at the end of set one. Shortly after, our driver deposits us at the entrance. My buddy and I share the cost and voice our mutual appreciation of our Dick's sherpa. We give each other big hugs and depart.

And now I stand alone and ticketless. My chance to remedy both situations.

I text Faris, *I'm here!* and set off to find will call. People idle around the venue: folks who linger to hear the concert from outside, vendors from Shakedown who haven't bothered to venture inside, and various Dick's employees. I venture over to the closest fans, a young white couple with matching dreadlocks.

"Hey guys," I say. "Do you know where will call is? I need to get a ticket."

The dreadlocked dude laughs. "I do, but I also know a spot in the gate where I can push you through. Follow me."

I am gullible and intrigued, and don't need any coaxing to trail behind the couple. They saunter past an entrance marked with a large "E," leading me beneath a sign that reads "Eighteen76." Here, a vertical barred gate blocks the entrance, but, as I've been told, two bars provide ample space between so that a smaller human can fit through.

"Here you go," he says to me.

I give him a big thank you and he gives me a big push. There's slight resistance from my hips around the metal bars, but with some force, I emerge through.

It's like I have stepped through a wooden wardrobe. On one side, the surroundings stand quiet, and the breeze flows fresh and crisp. On the other, the buzz of conversation fills my ears, and the air becomes a musky wall depleted of all freshness. I'm here! And, I haven't even paid for a ticket.

My mouth opens into an involuntary Cheshire-Cat grin and I make my way out of the bar. For faster results, I call Faris instead of texting him. He answers immediately.

"I'm here! I'm inside!" I yell.

"Okay, I'm at a lemonade stand. Walk around toward Page side."

Turning and walking left to reach the pianist's side of the stage, I stay on the phone and follow his directions, dodging a plethora of fans who are taking care of bathroom demands and the need for more alcohol during the forty-five minutes between the two sets. My heart begins to beat faster, making its presence physically known. How is Phish Dick's going to go down? Will it play out like my fantasies?

"Where are you?" Faris demands through the phone.

I spot a bright yellow sign advertising both virgin and booze-filled lemonade. "I see it! I'm coming! I'm almost there!"

And there he is, standing in front of me as suddenly as I must have appeared to the patrons of the Eighteen76 bar. I'm sure my appearance hadn't caused anyone's stomach to leap as mine does at the sight of Faris. He swoops me in his arms, picks me up, and swings me around while I give a spontaneous scream.

It's no fantasy. My drunken friend surely must have just revealed his feelings for me with his wordless action.

Chapter 19

Faris sets me on the ground, and I throw my arms around him for a big, grounded hug. It feels so goddamn good to be reunited with and touched by a friend. I'd been craving such simple yet genuine human connections since the move and I'm starving for it. Our lingering embrace hits me like a gigantic dish of my grandmother's spaghetti after three nights of dancing to Phish. It contains everything I need.

I can't stop grinning. If a sloppy drunk were to walk by and step on my foot or spill a beer on me, I'd continue to radiate. We stand bullseye center of the walkway and act like Moses, forcing the Red Sea of people to diverge as they accomplish their various set break missions. The lights are turned on for the music's intermission and the venue shines as brightly as a helicopter searchlight. I squint up into Faris's face.

"How was the first set?" I ask.

"They played 'Icculus,'" he says, mentioning a rarely played song. Years can go by without it being played.

"Dammit. Don't tell me that."

"You should have been here! You know, Rachael, a real fan would have taken work off. What if they played, 'I Want to Know What Love Is?'" He grins and shakes his head at me.

"You know, Faris," I pinch his waist. "A real fan wouldn't have waited over four years to start seeing them again."

"Well, I'm here now and I didn't miss that set. I was here for 'Icculus,'" he says with a fake air of superiority in his voice.

"Motherfucker." I direct the curse at myself, my inability to arrive earlier, not at him. "Where is everyone else?"

"On the floor. Let's grab some booze and we'll meet them."

Faris buys each of us a double vodka lemonade. He hands me the drink and starts guiding the way to our small group. I haven't bothered to notify the others that I'm inside. Though it's Anna's bachelorette weekend, I'm more stoked to spend time with Faris than with some of my oldest friends, three women whom I love dearly. Out of the four of them, I may have seen Faris the most recently, but my heart feels the urgency to see his face more than anyone else.

I'm starving, absolutely famished, for all forms of human love, but it's the disconnect in my marriage that has me feeling the most despondent, leaving me grasping for ways to fill that void in my heart. Dependable Faris, through our rediscovered friendship and his availability to me every day via text messages, is doing exactly that.

We need his reliability to get me to the rest of our friends. Dick's splits its general admission into two sections, floor and seats, and floor tickets require a wristband for admittance. I may have been birthed into the venue free of charge, but that left me without a ticket and wristband. How am I to join our group on the floor?

Faris schemes an immediate solution. "I'll act really drunk and create a diversion to distract the workers from looking at your wrist."

"But how will I get to the floor?"

"Trust me, we got this," he reassures me. "Give me your drink."

I hand it over and watch as he descends the tier of stairs leading from the bleachers to the floor. At each floor entrance, two employees look for the coveted wristband, ensuring all who enter are permitted to do so. I follow him, my heart now pattering for different reasons.

As we close in on the bottom, Faris wiggles his hips from side-to-side dancing in an exaggerated fashion. He thrusts both his vodka lemonade laden arms high in the air. The giant man seems to double his appearance with this maneuver and would make a formidable sight to any black bear.

"Woooo hooooooooooooooooo! Phish! Fuck yeah, Phish!" he hollers.

I would have cackled over this, but my apprehension rules in my sobriety. What if I get caught? I needn't worry. The pair of Dick's employees train their eyes on Faris as he boldly arrives, and he engages them in conversation. While he asks them what they thought of the first set, I stroll onto the floor, not even looking behind to see if I'll be questioned for a wristband.

And exactly like I was through the gate, I am on the floor!

Dick's primarily entertains as an outside soccer stadium, with bleacher seats built around the entire playing field. The grass is transformed into a concert floor for the shows, disguised and protected under removable flooring. Faris turns up at my side and shepherds me through the crowd to stand in front of the soundboard, stage right, or, as fans call it, Page side.

I imagine if every fan was surveyed regarding their favorite member, Trey would come out on top, and excessively so. A true guitar hero, many regard Trey as a Jedi, able to bend space and time through his rapid-fire staccato bursts of instrumental expertise. Once touted as "Machine Gun Trey," his fingers may not move so swiftly anymore, but his genius has grown stronger with age.

Trey writes most of the band's music and incepts nearly all their creative projects, but people's affection for him goes deeper than his musical abilities. His redemption from drug addict to sober rock god symbolizes the chance for rebirth every one of us is capable of. He is proof that we aren't trapped in defeat and is mentor to many trying for their version of a second chance. There's video evidence of fans speaking with Trey, owing their sobriety, their very existence, to the man.

I love Trey. How could I not? The man is adorable, always taking the time to listen, to say hello, and introduce himself to fans with "Hi, I'm Trey," as if they didn't know. He gives me hope that my personal reset will be a success, even with its rocky start. But he's not my favorite. He's too popular. Rooter of underdogs, my preferences run from the obvious choice.

And though I love Fishman for his goofiness and Mike with his quirks, it's Page, master of all things piano related, who is my most beloved member of the band. My ears focus on his twinkling of the keys in all its forms, whether he's playing more classical notes while sitting behind the grand, standing upright at his clavinet and forcing us to get down to his funky grooves, or taking us through space with his synthesizers.

My admiration for Page extends beyond his piano prowess. He's the opposite of me. Soft spoken and quiet, what little he says holds meaning. I appreciate this quality in other people. Like my desire to be witty, I wish I could sometimes stop and think things through before speaking them out loud, or worse, immediately acting on my whims.

I've not met Page, or anyone in Phish, but I imagine if I did, I would burst into tears and immediately ask for a hug. I wonder if the band would find that creepy.

"Rae!" I'm enveloped in the most familiar of arms in an anything-but-creepy hug. It's not Page, Mike, Trey, or Fishman, but my cousin, Anna. Content to be so close to someone I know this intimately, I rest my head on her chest

Demaris and Selena offer similar welcomes. Mutual affection radiates between our bodies, an invisible bonded band linking us together. It had been thirst quenching to hug Faris minutes ago, and these three hugs are the ice in water on a sweltering day. A month of drought in the Vegas desert is relieved over these thirty seconds.

"You made it!" Anna throws her hands in the air. Her bright blue eyes shine with excitement and intoxication. She reaches into her cross-body mud cloth bag and emerges with a plastic flask adorned with Phish stickers. She takes a swig and offers it my way. "Glibbys?"

I accept and slug deeply of the Glibbys, eager to catch up to my friends' levels of inebriation. The Anna standard, a simple mixture of Crystal Light pink lemonade and Smirnoff vodka, works as another soothing signpost that I've arrived home. I get another sip in as the house lights dim.

The crowd roars.

My height barely permits me to see the stage, but the sound is a priority, and Trey's unmistakable muted guitar can only signal one song...

"Oh my god, *yes*," my cousin yells. "Punch!"

I'm with her on that. "Punch You in the Eye," with its palpable intensity, is my favorite way to open a show. And since I've just arrived, it acts as that.

The song starts with a pounding drive, building in tempo to a crescendo that works me, rockets the entire crowd, into a hands-in-the-air frenzy. The camaraderie fostered during those opening three minutes, twenty-five thousand people simultaneously shouting "hey," with the band, intensifies my love for them. For this community. For my favorite people I'm standing beside.

"Punch You in the Eye's" momentum almost always fires into ensuing songs and the energy escalates when "Sand" follows. A persuasive bass line lays the foundation for the rock meets disco groove, daring you to stand still. Even Faris, a concert boulder who rarely deviates from a simple bobbing of his head, bounces on his toes (though the vodka lemonade may have lubricated his limbs).

I, too, break out of character and turn my preferred solo dance into a duet, spinning circles and shimmying hips alongside Anna in an unsynchronized choreography. We may be replicating moves we busted during Phish's 2009 New Year's run in Miami.

2009 was the year I moved back to the States after a two-year absence, the same year Phish got back together post-breakup. They deviated from their usual New Year's shows in New York City to play in South Florida. I'd never rang in the New Year with Phish, and with Anna so close in Fort Lauderdale, how could I deny myself the pleasure? But the second of four concerts took place on December 29th, my one-year wedding anniversary.

Hmm ...

"Hey, Jay, I have the perfect way to celebrate our first anniversary," I'd said to my husband, bringing up the plan I'd conspired. "In warm and sunny Florida. Phish is playing in Miami for New Year!"

He scrunched his lips. "Oh, I don't want to do that. I'll have to use too much PTO at work. But you go. We can go out for dinner or something when you get back."

I didn't argue. I listened to Jason and attended the shows and had no regrets.

"Sand" opened set two on December 30th. Though not a remarkable version, it was my first time hearing the song live, and the funk wonder rocked my ears. Mike's syncopated bass backing Trey's persuasive call-to-action guitar combined to create my strongest memory from that trip. Anna and I swiveled together, knocking hips and twirling our arms within the small space surrounding our seats.

Dick's floor provides a more expansive dance room than our arena seats in Miami did, and Anna and I make full use of it throughout "Sand." When it ends, I resume my position in front of Faris and spend the next eighty minutes enmeshed in the show, occasionally breaking my musical trance to accept Glibbys swigs from Anna and to high-five Demaris with a "yay" when her beloved tune "Silent in the Morning" sounds.

Phish encores with a cover of the Velvet Underground song, "Oh Sweet Nuthin." I hide my forming tears behind sunglasses and dance in a gentle sway, quietly mouthing the words along with Page. Who are you to say I ain't got nothing? I'm reunited with my people, listening to the greatest band in one of my favorite cities. For the rest of the weekend, I have everything.

Chapter 20

Show over, I walk out in between Selena and Demaris. Though almost two years have passed since I last saw them, we pick up as if we hung out yesterday.

"Ladies! Friends! How was your day?" I ask them both.

"It's been lovely," Selena says, her large blue eyes glowing. "But you missed 'Icculus.'"

Selena is to blame for my Phish obsession. We befriended one another during my freshmen year of college. Though I was slowly getting into The Grateful Dead and the rest of the jam scene, then I was very much into (and I say this in a whisper) the Dave Matthews Band. A good sport, she jammed along to DMB CDs with me until several months of her inquiring "why Dave over Phish?" inspired me to borrow the Phish album *Hoist*.

I popped it into my car's CD player and listened without skipping a track. Heavily influenced by the classic rock my parents constantly played in our house growing up, my tastes skewed rock 'n' roll. Phish, the eleven tracks on *Hoist*, delivered this, and so much more. Funk. Bluegrass. Beautiful ballads with gorgeous vocals (provided by guest singer Alison Krauss for a track). A hint of big band. I never ejected it for another option. It stayed inside, playing repeatedly until I saw Selena.

"I need to borrow every one of your Phish albums," I begged her.

"Oh sweet, you liked *Hoist* then?"

"I fucking loved it. 'Axilla!' What a headbanger."

"If you liked 'Axilla,' wait until you hear 'Run Like an Antelope.'"

She was right. Out of the fifty plus songs on the four Phish albums I obsessively listened to, "Antelope," the raucous ten-minute mostly instrumental, was my favorite.

Over ten years later, she's my most knowledgeable Phish friend regarding all the things. Rumored tour dates and locations. Hotels closest to the venue. What that unfamiliar song playing is. She continues about "Icculus." "That was only the third time they've played it post-breakup."

"I was there for one of them!" Got to earn my street cred wherever I can.

"Oh, you were. That's sweet. Which show?"

"Hartford, 2009. But it still sucks to miss it. That's almost the first thing Faris said to me. You know you missed 'Icculus,' Rachael." I do a poor imitation of the sole male within our crew.

"Faris is a great guy! I recognized him as soon as I saw him," Selena says.

"Yeah, I vaguely remember him too," Demaris drawls. Her Tennessee accent strengthens when drunk. "He's cute."

I look up at her in alarm, feeling possessive. "Hands off, he's mine." The words fly out of my mouth, and I'm not joking.

Selena elbows me. "What are you talking about, Rae? You're married."

"Yeah, well …" I don't know how to follow that up. How can I? I am married, and even if I wasn't, I can't lay claim to any person. Still, the idea of Faris romantically connecting with anyone dismays me. I don't think I could stomach it.

We head to Demaris's place in the Capital Hill neighborhood of Denver, in a basement apartment she calls her hobbit hole. A little alcove off the front door holds her sewing machine. A plethora of brightly patterned material, used for making long flowing skirts, is draped over her sewing seat. Her open kitchen houses space to store her many homemade canned goods.

The hospitality flows in Demaris's southern blood; she opens her tiny apartment for us four out-of-towners to crash in. The air mattress is already blown up, with pillows and blankets, on the floor space between the living room and kitchen. Anna and I will rest our bodies there. Selena will crash with Demaris in her bed. Faris plans to sleep inside a sleeping bag resting on a camping pad.

"Is my box here?" I ask Demaris almost as soon as we walk in.

I can't wait to rip my contacts out. My backpack contains my makeup, deodorant, and glasses, but everything else I need is contained in the box I shipped out the week prior.

"What box?" she asks as she hands me a beer.

"I shipped a box here last week. You know that. I texted you the day I sent it." I sip the IPA. The strong ale is going to push me over the limits.

"You did? I never got one."

I stare at her in disbelief. My box never arrived! I'll be forced to wear the same clothes all weekend, and my contacts are useless without solution to overnight them in. I think fast. Good thing I have my glasses with me. I can borrow Anna's makeup. Demaris can take me to buy a pack of cheap underwear in the morning. Maybe I'll purchase some clothes too.

Demaris bursts out laughing. "I'm kidding! Your box is here." She points to a chair in her sewing alcove. Atop it sits the small cardboard cube.

I tear open the box, looking for my jammies and contact solution. I practically rip the silicon vision from my eyeballs. My lenses had been in for far too long and stick to my eyes as my stubby fingers pinch them out. They're replaced with my oversized plastic spectacles, and I change clothes.

Beer in hand, I plop into a Papasan chair pushed against a wall in the living room. The spherical cushion rests on top of a rattan base. A large bookshelf exploding with paperbacks and hardcovers faces me. I'm curious to peruse the shelves, but am rooted to the chair.

I'm alone until Faris settles on the couch adjoining me in the chair. He holds out his hand in a silent request for my beer and I pass it over. Our fingers graze and a zap shoots down my arm. His eyebrows and mouth raise in his goofy, teasing way and he tilts the bottle toward his open mouth. He slugs from the bottle and when I reach for it, his other arm shoots out, grabbing my hand, keeping me from the beer.

Holding onto me.

Several low-wattage lamps cast a warm glow. The subtle darkness surrounds us in a cozy envelope, increasing the sexual tension bouncing from the couch to the chair. He continues to grip my right hand. I could easily reach across the space between us and rest my left palm on his leg, inch it up, then bring it up some more.

I don't do that. Instead, I aim to make the connection with my mouth. I lean over in the Papasan chair, stretching my face toward him instead of my hand, beginning to pucker up as I decrease our physical distance.

And as I'm about to make contact, I'm knocked off my feet.

My body hits the floor. The pillowy orb that cushioned my bottom lands on top of me.

"Oof," I giggle.

I hear feet rush into the room. "What happened?" It's Demaris.

Faris laughs too. "She fell out of the chair."

"Are you okay?" she asks.

I sit, dazed but chortling. I'm clumsy while sober, exceptionally so when drinking. "Did I break the chair?"

Demaris picks up the cushion and plops it back onto the base. "No, asshole," she kids. "It rests on top."

I could never own a Papasan chair; I'd end up breaking bones. Even so, once Demaris has "fixed" the broken chair, I gingerly arrange myself on the cushion, waiting for everyone to join me and Faris in the living room. I'm ready to rage, rage, rage. Unfortunately, my fall acts as Friday's unofficial end.

"Time for bed, y'all. We've another big day tomorrow," Demaris announces. She helps me out of the chair. "Come on, Rae, I'll tuck you in."

I oblige, following her over to the air mattress. Anna joins me, and Demaris pulls the blanket up to our chests, even in the stifling heat of the un-air-conditioned apartment. The boogeyman may steal us without the fortress-like protection of quilted cotton, keeping all dark and evil entities away, and I cozy myself around it.

"Night, kittens," Demaris whispers as she turns the lights off.

Fading fast, I call into the darkness, "Faris, come cuddle with me."

Chapter 21

I awake in the morning to a roomy air mattress, my arms splayed across a vacant right side.

"Anna, where are you?" I whisper. My mouth feels like one of Demaris's cats shit in it while I slept. So dry. So gross.

"Hmm," I hear her murmur.

I spot my cousin. She's lying on the floor on her side of the air mattress, cocooned within a pillow and blanket.

"Why aren't you on the air mattress?"

"Faris," she mumbles.

I feel the weight keeping me buoyant and turn my head. Short brown hair, heat radiating from a large body, Faris passed out and snoring beside me.

"You called Faris to come to bed," Anna says. She sits up and blows her nose with a tissue. "Fucking cats."

Best friends practically from birth, my cousin—older by a year—and I have been sidekicks for our entire existence. All that said, she unintentionally contributed to my high school angst. With a slew of cute boyfriends and "cool" friends, Anna was the kind of popular that '90s teen movies depict. I tried to emulate my cheerleading, beauty queen almost-sister by borrowing her clothes and picking up similar hobbies. Alas, I attracted none of the things that came Anna's way.

We morphed into hippies simultaneously (not a surprise since we attended that fateful Phil and Friends show together), and I, with my action-packed weekends and a bevy of dates, finally felt her equal. My newfound confidence may have even given me an edge. Whereas she settled into a few long-term committed relationships, I dated and slept around in between my own shorter, "serious" relationships.

Yet I was the one to marry first.

Anna blows her nose again. "It wasn't very comfortable with three of us in the bed. I couldn't sleep anyway with my allergies."

"I'm sorry," I tell her.

I've vague memories of what happened before succumbing to sleep. I *had* requested Faris to come cuddle with me in bed, and he answered my request. He kept his back to me but allowed my tiny body to dominate over his as the larger spoon. We fell asleep with my arms wrapped around his soft waist.

Jason and I used to fall asleep intertwined in one another's arms. That bedtime habit disappeared with our sex life.

I possess zero guilt over the sleeping arrangements. Neither body fluids nor highly charged emotional words had been exchanged. Entirely innocent, just two people falling asleep to the comforting touch of another human. I had platonically cuddled with male friends, on couches and in beds, dozens of times. This was one of those moments.

But it's different now. I'm married.

And I can't say my feelings are platonic.

"It's fine," she says. "But no more. You're married. You shouldn't be doing that."

The newlywed holds strong opinions. She's been married three months, and I wonder if her and Edgar's love has been tested yet with real world married living. Like cat allergies, the power and struggle of marriage compromise can be hard to contend with, but perhaps they won't deal with the challenges that Jason and I faced.

Edgar grew up in our hometown. He graduated from the same high school as us and was raised in a similar culture. He enjoyed many of the same things as Anna. An integral part of our Phish crew, he would have been here, dancing beside his wife and as enraptured with the music as we were, if it wasn't Anna's bachelorette party.

A women's get-together that I invited Faris to crash.

"It's fine," I echo her words back. She's not wrong, but I'm not going to admit it.

And I do want it to happen again.

What do I mean by *It's fine?* Did I say it in agreement? *Yeah, Anna, you are right. What I did was wrong, and it won't happen anymore.* Did I say it to brush off what I had done? *It's fine, Anna. I just had my arm around him. No big deal.*

It was neither of these things. I said them in pacification and to change the subject as quickly as possible. I'd hate for Faris to wake up and overhear us. Around him, I prefer to pretend that my marriage doesn't exist. Nor am I keen on acknowledging my deteriorating relationship with anyone, not when our big Las Vegas reset is a whopping thirty days old. Too soon to admit failure.

This situation is becoming more convoluted than I ever intended and I don't want to talk about it. I don't know how to explain my feelings. Each of my emotions contradicts the other. I'm married, yet I have deep feelings for another man, and the guilt chokes me like a tightening wedding knot. Contrarily, I want this man to return my feelings, though I don't know what would happen should he have them.

But Anna is right. I shouldn't be doing any of these things. I won't cuddle up with, kiss, or screw around with Faris, and yet I want to find comfort from these thoughts by burying myself in his sleeping form. He saves me from possible scandal by waking up. So do Selena and Demaris. One person comes to consciousness, and the rest subconsciously copy.

Anna presents us women with gifts. We discussed wearing matching shirts during our Dick's planning, and the bride delivered on that promise. The form-fitting yellow shirt features a unisex silhouette falling in mid-air, hands thrown back with ten fingers spread out as if to catch the air like a parachute and ease the landing. The word "Caution" is emblazoned in bold letters above the figure, and "Jazz hands" below.

The T-shirt pays tribute to Anna, known for her vigorous gestures when busting a move. I hold it in front of me. "Are we going with these today?"

Selena's eyes widen in complete approval. "I can't wait to put mine on!"

Demaris claps her hands together. "Why don't you do that now? Let's rally, people. Time to eat."

"Are we meeting up with anyone?" I ask her.

She scrunches her face. "Who would we be meeting?"

"Your friends?"

Demaris, holding a newly earned master's degree in public health, moved to Denver in January. The Mile High City attracts a wide range of folk for the same reasons it appeals to me, and people are moving here in droves, including many Phish heads and other jam band aficionados. Surely Demaris has local friends who will accompany us to the show?

She gives a sarcastic laugh. "All my friends are here!"

The mountain air treats a gal good, and she looks radiant, but maybe she's hiding something. I've been doing the same. No one knows of my loneliness or unhappiness in Vegas.

"What about your local friends?"

"I don't have any."

It's hard to believe someone so thoughtful and charming hasn't made any friends in the nine months since moving here. Then again, I've had minimal contact with her since I returned from Korea. Our sparse communications focused on this weekend, and I flaked on inquiring about her new chapter here in Denver. An egregious maneuver, I silently promise to be a better friend.

"Ah man, really?"

"Yeah. It's fucking hard making friends as an adult." Her sentence rings true to my own recent experiences.

"Yeah, I hear that. I'm struggling to do the same in fucking Vegas."

Demaris envelopes me in a hug. "But I've got you guys and Phish!"

I squeeze her back tightly. "I wish it didn't have to end."

I wish to have magical powers to make it last forever, or at least transform my day-to-day so it will forever resemble this weekend. I don't possess these superhuman abilities. And because this weekend only offers an escape from what my life has become, it passes all the much quicker. Alas, I'm unable to assuage my sorrows with bedtime Faris cuddles.

I'm not allowed to do that anymore.

Chapter 22

"Geez, talk about too many choices." I gaze down one long row of vendors. There are still several more to peruse. "I've no idea what I want to eat."

It's Sunday. We've arrived on Lot early to make the most of our final day and have hours to carouse until showtime. My growling stomach reminds me to eat a solid base before diving into the bag of beer we brought. We head straight to the heart of Dionysus's quarters to grab food. An eclectic mix of Lot "chefs" abound in the rows of Shakedown, offering standards such as grilled cheese and burritos mixed with elevated plates of Thai noodles and Mexican street tacos.

"How about we split up and meet on the grassy knoll over there?" Selena suggests, pointing to a downslope hill surrounding one of the many soccer fields surrounding the grounds.

"Sounds good," Demaris says. "I'm gonna grab some pad thai and I'll meet you there. Anyone else want some?"

Demaris's lunch idea wins me over. We receive gigantic bowls of steaming noodles and move to the knoll. Hordes of concert revelers gather in the lush grass slanting down to the soccer fields.

We hung here last night for a post-show beer and watched a raucous soccer match between two impromptu teams of fans, of which, in the middle, one player stripped down, exposing the kind of dick this Dick's needed. Loud cheers and wolf whistles encouraged him to play the rest of the game naked.

There's no nudity yet. It's too early in the day. Demaris and I are the first of our friends to arrive at the designated meeting area. I luxuriate in the grass like a lizard warming itself on a heated stone, plate of food in my lap, an IPA encased in a koozie by my side.

The other three join us shortly, bearing cheesesteaks. No need to go hungry at a Phish show.

"This is great, guys," Selena says.

"Your cheesesteak?" Anna asks. "Mine's hitting the spot. It's so good!"

"Well, yeah, it's delicious, but I mean all of this. What a great Lot! The only thing that could make this better is if we had more matching shirts. That was fucking awesome last night!"

A contributing component to the magical world of Phish lies in song telepathy, the utter belief of message transmission via song—the band is playing this song just for you! This happens. A lot. Stories of this song wizardry abound. A father took his young daughter, Suzy, to her first show and Phish played "Suzy Greenberg." My non-fan friend Heather, obsessed with both David Bowie and her dog, Bowie, heard a "David Bowie" when her curiosity prompted her to check the band out.

Our turn came during yesterday's second set. Wearing our Jazz Hands shirt, we projected silent requests for a cover of "Also Sprach Zarathrusta (2001)," the song that originally inspired Anna's frantic hand movements.

Phish received our message. When Fish's drum rolled into the spacey ambient intro, we ladies lost our minds. Posted at the back of the floor for its abundance of dance space, we jazz hands-ed a plenty throughout the five-minute (too short a version) instrumental, showing our approval in spinning circles and weaves around a head bobbing Faris.

"You guys got your song," Faris says. "So, use your power of positive thinking and manifest a Reba for me."

"Ooh, that's so sweet. Are you missing your pup?" I ask.

"I am, but who doesn't want to hear 'Reba?'"

"Who's watching her?"

"She's at doggie daycare."

"How about Porter, Selena?"

Selena's beagle mix, "the handsomest boy" is her most treasured companion. I can't imagine her boarding him.

"My roommate is watching him. He doesn't mind, but it was a lot easier when I was with my ex. I knew Porter was in the best hands," she says.

"Speaking of your ex, have you dated anyone since you two broke up?" I turn to her.

In June 2011, we (Selena, Demaris, Anna, and many others) embarked on a mini Phish tour. Selena moved to Oregon as soon as she'd graduated college; it'd been six years since we'd seen one another. She hopped in my car for the trip from Philadelphia to Baltimore and we talked for the entire two-hour drive.

After discussing (my) Asian living and (her) emergency hysterectomy, the conversation pivoted to our love lives: my marriage and her recent breakup. Like Jason and I, she met and started dating her girlfriend during Phish's five-year breakup, when we thought our band existed no more. An integral part of our identities we couldn't share with our uninterested partners, would either of us have reconsidered the relationship if we knew the band would get back together?

"Why did you break up?" I'd asked her.

"We realized we weren't our best with one another. We had nothing to talk about and stopped having fun together. Fighting over nothing." She shook her head. "We had entirely different tastes in music. She could never get into this scene. But I did like knowing I could leave Porter with her when I was on tour."

"Was it a bad breakup?"

"No, not at all. We mutually parted ways. It was the most mature break up I ever had."

Even in 2011, this sounded familiar. Nothing to talk about, fighting over nothing, having dissimilar tastes in music. The resemblance between Selena's former relationship and my current one was striking. I nodded my head but didn't indulge my own relationship stories.

Selena now updates me on her dating status. "No, I've not really dated anyone since, but I met someone recently."

I elbow her. "Oh yeah? Tell me more!"

"We met in July. She's a fan. She's here actually. We hung out a bit on Friday."

"Do I get to meet her?"

"I'm hoping to hang with her some more, but I don't think anything's going to happen. She's always dated men. I like her, but it may be an impossible feat."

It seems our love lives continue to parallel in some way.

Chapter 23

Hours later, the show over, we walk away from the parties on Shake-down and the naked soccer games and traipse across the fields to meet our taxi driver on the other end of the venue. The land threatens our ankles and knees. It's covered in loose dirt, scratchy plants that cling to exposed skin, and prairie dog burrows. The darkness camouflages the latter. We're forced to keep our eyes on the ground to avoid tripping over one.

My wide-spaced steps are careful. I trail behind everyone else, but I don't mind, dancing to the music from the show playing in my head. Though the band didn't play "Reba" for Faris, dance opportunities abounded. As I dodge another rodent-created hole, I replicate the slow bluesy body swirl I used for "Meat." Once planted on the firm safety of a sidewalk, I burst into a run to catch up with my friends, my arms swinging frantically to mimic the quasi-Charleston I employed during "Weekapaug Groove."

Impulsively, I start turning cartwheels, my loose skirt billowing out as I spin topsy-turvy. Without a care that I'm baring my beer concealing granny panties to any who happen to be passing by, I spin until my arms fail to support me.

I land on my ass. Giggling, I climb to my feet, still intent on acrobatics. Channeling my inner Baby, I command Faris to stand twenty feet from me. My Johnny, he's going to lift me.

Despite my conversation with Anna, I've put little distance between me and Faris. Sure, he slept on the other side of the living room last night, body tucked inside the sleeping bag, but I sat next to him whenever possible. Eating breakfast at a diner. Lounging at the grassy knoll on Lot. Happy hour drinks at the dive bar near Demaris's.

We lunched at a Thai restaurant yesterday, splitting various curry and noodle dishes between the five of us. I passed all the unsavory parts of the meat—fat, bones, and questionable bits—from my plate to Faris's. It was an oddly intimate gesture between two people; I hadn't asked his permission, and he didn't voice any objection. Mid-conversation, he chopsticked my abandoned meats into his mouth as if they were an original part of his meal.

But there's been little physical contact, nothing more than hands brushing while passing a drink. High fives and playful shoulder punches when certain songs are played. Innocuous touches between friends.

To accomplish our *Dirty Dancing*, he'll need to grasp my hips. My pelvic bones.

I launch myself at Faris in a sprint. His giant hands grip me right where I want them to and I leap up, picturing myself rising gracefully like a heron taking flight. I lack the titanium abs and he the upper body strength. My feet gain less than three inches of air.

His hands stay around my waist. Electric pulses rush down my hips and travel inward. I look up at him. We're both laughing. His hands are so warm ...

"Rae. Faris. Let's go!" Anna calls. Our cab is here.

We're deposited at Demaris's thirty minutes later. Wired, high on the music, excitement, and alcohol, and not wanting our festivities to end, Demaris grabs two scratchy Mexican blankets and Selena fills a cloth bag with beers. Cheesman Park lies two blocks from the hobbit hole.

The green space occupies several blocks close to downtown. It's one of Denver's few coveted pondless parks, thus devoid of goose shit. The lawn is a favorite for joggers and dog walkers, weekend picnickers and readers, and leisurely games of volleyball. At 1:00 a.m., we're the only park dwellers.

Demaris spreads the two blankets on top of the dry, late summer grass, and we plop down. Anna and I sit back-to-back, pressed against one another, using the strength of one another's backs to stay upright. Selena sits in front of us, taking up the rest of the blanket's domain. Demaris and Faris stretch out on their sides, facing one another on the second one. The blankets partition us as if we're in two separate rooms.

The three former Pennsylvanians banter while the Southerner and Kuwaiti hold a distinctly different conversation. I'm half listening to my two dearest friends as I eavesdrop on Demaris and Faris.

I'm paranoid. Demaris expressed her attraction toward Faris on Friday. *"I vaguely remember him. He's cute."* My longing heart doesn't need much to arouse suspicion, and I've stalked their every interaction since. A simple offer to navigate to our destination, a seat close to one another, a sip from a water bottle, all things humans do for the good of one another, I take as a burgeoning sign of affection. I don't think either pays the other more attention than the rest of us, but each encounter feeds my paranoia. Their conversation held in the park is, to me, the flower handed out during the "Rose Ceremony" on The Bachelor.

"I almost moved here," I hear Faris say to Demaris.

"What?" she says, her voice rising in excitement. "Why didn't you?"

"My last transfer, it was either Denver or Fort Worth. I didn't get to choose. If I did, I would be here now."

"Hmph. That's too bad. I could use some friends. It would be fucking awesome if you did live here."

"Well, I get moved around a lot. Maybe I can bring it up to my bosses. Now that I know you, it makes the thought of moving to Denver even more appealing."

My eyes widen in shock. Even more appealing? The euphoria from the beer and music has faded by now, and my brain is awash with all the potential outcomes this seemingly inconsequential conversation carries. And by potential outcomes, I meant one. Faris is going to move here, and he and Demaris are going to become a couple.

In my mind, it's already happened. Ludicrous thoughts, yes, but these are the ideas that spring from my brain. These are the images I close out Dick's weekend with.

Chapter 24

"Are you sure you can't do any of Fall Tour, especially now that all the fun had this weekend is over?" Faris asks. He places the menu down and looks at me. "You know, Kylie and I both really want you there."

"Yes, I would love to, but it's impossible. I don't have the PTO or the money to do any of it." I reconsider. "Or maybe ..."

It's Monday afternoon. Faris and I sit alone, or as alone as two people can be at an airport on a holiday, inside the Denver Chop House in Concourse A. We're seated side-by-side at an empty communal table lining a large window that looks out into the busy corridor. I've angled my chair and pivoted my body to directly face him. Such a position blocks out the crowds shuffling by and offers a semblance of privacy.

His flight boards in an hour. I'm dreading it. Oh, these farewells. Why are we prolonging the inevitable? I'm devoting as much time to thinking about having to say goodbye as I am enjoying these final minutes together. Would it be best to get it over with as quickly as possible? Then I could start counting down the moments until I see him again.

Except we don't have one of those planned.

Never mind. I better stretch out these sixty minutes.

"Maybe what?" Faris demands.

I slap my menu down. I'd rather consider when I'll see Phish and Faris than debate lunch options. Our parting won't be so awful if we have a "next time" lined up.

"Okay, there's a slight possibility I can meet you for the two Worcester shows. I have that Friday off from work. But it all depends on the flight. If I can get a cheap one, I'll make it happen."

Fat chance any fares will be cheap enough for me to afford, but I need something to keep me hanging on. The post-Phish, post-reunion blues smacked me this morning. I feel my doldrums everywhere. Chest and shoulders heavy, third eye throbbing, my mouth involuntarily drooping, I've nothing in the coming months to look forward to. The possibility of a quick jaunt to Massachusetts in late October brightens my dark mood a bit.

He strokes his chin scruff and nods, a slow smile spreading on his face. "That's better. Don't tell me you can't go when you can! I'll keep an eye on flights. This will work out perfectly. Those are the last shows of the tour I'm doing."

In late July, Phish announced a short East Coast tour consisting of twelve shows commencing in Virginia in mid-October and ending a few days after Halloween in Atlantic City. Faris, euphoric about his return to Phish, sought tour buddies to join him for the first half of the shows. I couldn't commit to any, but Kylie accepted his offer and raised the stakes by promising to do the full run.

"You'll miss Selena then. She's doing the Halloween shows in Atlantic City."

"Is your cousin doing any? Or Demaris? I forget what they said."

My stomach twists, capturing my tumbling heart as it turns. I'm briefly frozen over my worries born from last night's conversation. My mind travels back to forty-five minutes ago, to our airport drop off. Demaris, accompanied by Anna and Selena (who aren't leaving until tomorrow), drove us. We all exchanged hugs, and I meant to spy on Faris's goodbye with Demaris, but I was wrapped up in Anna's arms. Did their embrace linger? Did they exchange numbers? Make plans to meet up another time?

Why is he asking if she's doing any of Fall Tour?

"So, are they?" Faris asks me again.

I shake my head and blink. "Oh, no. No. I know Anna isn't planning to, and I don't think Demaris is either. Why? Would you do the other half of tour if they were?"

Yeah, Faris. Will you rearrange your plans so you and Demaris can do Phish tour together?

"No, I have to go back to work. I was curious."

We order our food, and though it comes quickly, Faris requests a box as soon as our dishes are dropped off. Uh oh, the moment for goodbyes has come. My bite of chopped salad feels like it's lodged in my throat. He places his sandwich in the box and stands. I do too, on knees that threaten to collapse, and not from three solid shows of dancing.

He hands me a twenty for his lunch and gives me the quickest of hugs, nothing like the ones exchanged with our friends earlier. I want to lock my arms around his back, sink my head into the cruck of his neck, inhale the woodsy scent of deodorant, secure this memory of us, how he feels, how he smells, and steal away with it, tucking it into my annals to conjure later. Two seconds isn't enough to do that.

"Uh, this was fun. Thanks for including me," he says, not even looking at me. He bends over to retrieve his backpack from the floor.

"Of course, dude. Let's do more if it and soon. Worcester!"

"Make it happen," he says as he leaves the restaurant and disappears from my sight.

I'm dejected. The logical part of me knows Worcester isn't happening, making this departure resemble our last goodbye in college when tentative plans for future meetups were made but contained plenty of doubt that they'd happen. Faris had stopped by my apartment in mid-August 2004, days preceding his permanent move from State College. I had something to give him. He had something to show me.

"Yo, Rachael!"

Though I'd been expecting him, I jumped. Distracted and buried deep in my dresser drawers, I hadn't heard footsteps on the stairs leading to my attic bedroom.

"Jesus Christ." I put a hand to my chest. "You startled me. And since I'm already scared, let's get this over with. Let me see it."

He obliged, removing his baseball cap as he drew closer. There it was. Or wasn't. Ponytail gone, Faris's light brown hair was shorn close to his scalp in an unremarkable haircut that required zero styling. He twirled for full effect, and his naked neck, the pale skin where his ponytail used to hang, shone like a warning signal.

"Oh my god, I knew this was coming, but what happened? Why did you have to do this?" I mock wailed. He'd warned of this hippie-to-young-professional morphing for months, but still, I wasn't prepared for this, for how it would affect me.

"I need a job. The short hair will help. What, you don't like?" He runs his hands along the sides of his head and purses his lips in a *Blue Steel* gaze.

"This shirt I got you won't look nearly as cool." I handed him the lime green Phish shirt I'd been digging in my dresser for. I'd returned from Coventry, Phish's final "we're breaking up" music festival, a few days earlier. I'd skipped my graduation ceremony to attend it. Though I'd begged Faris to come ("Our band is breaking up, and you're not going! What's wrong with you?"), he refused, claiming he had too much to do in preparation for his relocation. He'd already moved on, ready to begin adult life.

He held the shirt by the shoulders to examine the screen print of the four men floating through the sky on a giant hot dog. "Thanks for getting this for me. How was it?"

"As bad as expected. Trey looked fucking awful. I kept thinking he was going to die in front of us. And Page, I want to cry thinking about it."

"What happened?"

"He started crying right in the beginning of 'Velvet Sea.' Absolutely heartbreaking. And you had to hear the crowd, how they were cheering. Why? It was nothing to cheer about. It was miserable."

"See. I'm glad I didn't go. Sounds like a shitshow."

"But I'd feel awful if I didn't go. I still can't believe you didn't."

He shrugged in response. I slapped his shoulder playfully. "Whatever dude. But make sure you wear your shirt in Delaware to help you make friends." I sat on my bed. "Now, I'm depressed. College is over. Phish is done. Your ponytail is gone. What's happening?"

Though I kept my voice light and exaggerated, none of what I said was hyperbole. So much of what I treasured, of what had helped shape me to become this version of Rachael, was ending. College acted as an incubator; Phish and the friends I made during this period provided the hefty nutrition. How would I continue to evolve without this life-style?

"It's called adult life, Rachael. We all have to grow up," he said with a straight face.

There he was, displaying the mature side found in his classic Faris dichotomy of "I'm ready to party and throw down" versus "it's time to put my big boy pants on and buckle down." I saw an opening and teased his responsibility. "Can you still have fun, Wilson? Loosen up. We just graduated college."

"Well, I also think my parents would disown me if I didn't get out of here. It did take me an extra year to graduate."

"Okay, okay. I'm fine staying here and delaying all the grown-up things, but my parents haven't given me any shit yet." In my stubborn-ness to hold on to this era, I'd made zero plans for my future. I would end up seeking an alternate version of college by sticking around State College, partying hard, and working minimum wage jobs for another two years.

We hugged when he left. It lasted mere seconds. His arms hung around my back as loosely as the extra-large shirt I had bought him would have fit me.

"Will you visit?" I asked, pleading more than I intended.

"I'll try! Maybe next summer."

He kept his promise.

It would be the last we saw one another before our SPAC set break run-in.

I hope I can keep my tentative Worcester promise to make up for this pallid goodbye. After all my daycreaming and daydreaming, we said our farewells atop a chicken sandwich. We didn't talk about my attempt at a make out or our cuddled-up slumber. Our relationship status is exactly as it had been entering the weekend.

Deeply in the friend zone.

But what did I want? Had my attempted seduction been successful, where would that leave me and Faris now? My fantasies never went beyond the instant gratification of a whirlwind Dick's romance. Would that have been it, three days and then back to being friends? Or maybe sex would completely fuck up the friendship.

Or maybe it would have been the start of an affair. I'd jet off for weekend rendezvouses in Fort Worth. A horrible liar, I'd never be able to keep such deception from Jason. I don't think my moral compass would acquiesce to such a thing anyway.

But maybe a successful Friday night kiss would have been the first step in ending my marriage.

Only my messy mind of contradictions still believes it's best for Jason and me to continue searching for an oasis together to flood out the lengthy drought in our relationship.

Then why does my heart ache as I look at the vacant seat beside me, imagining how things could be if we'd kissed?

I finish my salad, head to my gate, and check my phone. Missed call from Mom and nothing from my husband. Figures. I call Mom. She's eager to hear about the weekend, how her newlywed niece is doing, and how the music was. She entertains me in conversation for a while, and when we hang up, my flight information reads on the electronic placard.

Las Vegas. 5:35 p.m. On time.

Here I am, waiting for an airplane to bring me to a final destination I want no part of.

In 2010, Jason and I were delayed over four hours in the Newark airport on a layover coming back from Fort Lauderdale visiting Anna and Edgar. The return flight to Pennsylvania was only forty-five minutes; renting a car and driving would have been quicker. But we waited. While we waited, I checked out the destinations of other flights. An aircraft bound for Lisbon caught my eye. I closed my eyes and wished I could board the plane to Portugal. Why did I have to head back to Pennsylvania?

It's the same now, but oh, how I wish to board a plane to Pennsylvania to see my parents, eat my mother's cooking, and sleep in my childhood bedroom. I look at that Las Vegas sign and wish to head anywhere but there. Such a highly sought vacation spot for so many people holds no magic for me. Instead, it contains a husband I don't miss, a stressful job that requires too much of my free time, and zero friends to decompress from either of these with.

I made this bed, I must sleep in it. The cruel saying goads me. I'm stuck. I chose to marry Jason and I must make it work with him. We decided to settle in Vegas, and I must make a home of it. I wanted to work in a Title One public school, and I must be present in my classroom tomorrow morning. I can't diverge. My path trodden from the choices I made; I'm so deeply embedded that I've no other option but to continue with it.

To Vegas I will go.

Chapter 25

"You look exhausted, Molly," I say as soon as my friend opens the door.

It's been over a month since I've seen her, and I'm alarmed by how sunken her eyes appear. And though her emerald dress complements the auburn in her hair, the green washes out her fair skin.

"I am exhausted. School and work are kicking my ass," she says, forcing a smile.

"We could have rain checked. It would've been no problem."

Was that the truth? Though the couch beckons on such a chilly October Saturday, I never have plans. Molly had texted this morning inviting me and Jason over to her boyfriend's, and I'd looked forward to it all day. Even once darkness settled in and the wind picked up, conditions perfect for sweatpants and a book, I impatiently paced my apartment, waiting for Jason to get home so we could head out.

He's newly employed, dealing blackjack at the Stratosphere on the sketchier north end of The Strip. Securing a job proved more competitive than either of us had anticipated, and though disappointed Jason couldn't find work at a chicer casino, we're pleased he's working, manning a blackjack table from early afternoon through the evening on weekends. He arrives home reeking of cigarettes and drained after most of his shifts, but it's easy to cajole him out for a late dinner, especially if Korean meats are involved.

Rare plans with friends enticed him even more than barbeque. He freshened up and we were out the door much quicker than we would have been if only a restaurant awaited. Yay plans!

But then I saw Molly and her appearance indicated we wouldn't be getting into much this evening.

"It's fine. I wanted to see you!" Molly argues my idea of rescheduling.

"I know. I wanted to see you too. We don't see each other enough and I have no friends."

While I try to make this statement sound like a joke, my desperation leaks through. It's no hyperbole. I don't have any family here, and, other than Molly, no friends. Socializing ranks number one on my long self-care list, and Vegas living isn't providing any. This is my first night out with someone other than Jason since I returned from Denver six weeks ago.

"I don't have friends either. I go to school, and I work," Molly says.

She doesn't sound sad, or light, just tired and matter of fact. Things currently suck for her, but she's making sacrifices for the future. Her situation is temporary; she's living in Vegas for nursing school. She'll eventually graduate and move on, but this right here, this is my new start.

Is this it?

My life in Nevada reminds me of the one I was trying to escape in Pennsylvania. I still dislike the town I live in, and my shitty marriage remains unchanged, only now I'm without my family and friends. It sounds worse off.

I am worse off.

Wait, is this it?

At least I'm currently out and among friends.

"And we're both liars. We're not totally friendless. We both have one and we're with them now," I tell Molly. "Oh man, I sound like such a fucking dork. This is what having no friends will do to you."

Molly guffaws in appreciation and leads me over to the fridge and hands me a beer. "My goal is to have at least two beers with you before I pass out. This is what having no life will do to you."

We join our significant others in the living room. The two men are cushioned on opposing sofas, conversing airplane mechanics. Molly sits beside her boyfriend on the larger of the two couches. She turns to him, staring at the side of his face, at his baby-faced profile, as he explains the art of maintaining an Airbus motor. My vantage point shows his blue eyes wide, his smirks of exasperation, his round cheeks rising and falling while regaling Jason with stories of flying to various parts of the country to repair aircraft. He's into the conversation. So is Jason. When I sat on the carpeted floor near his feet, he acknowledged me with a pat on my shoulder without breaking contact from the younger man's face.

It's hard to join in mid-discussion, but we've arrived at an entertaining point, with a blizzard and an airport stranding in North Dakota. I sip my beer and listen in. My gaze momentarily settles on Molly. She's no longer looking at her boyfriend, but fidgeting with a string on the hem of her dress. The attention she allots him tracks what she's divulged to me concerning her feelings toward him.

She met him immediately upon her move to Vegas in the spring, and they labeled themselves an official couple following date number one. It's clear (and it would be even without hearing it from Molly) that he likes her more than she likes him. A sometimes-needed situation, my friend's self-esteem benefits from a doting partner, and he worships her.

With an older sister gifted the winning combination of popularity and supposed beauty, Molly's confidence had been on a poor trajectory since birth. Alas, she never discovered a musical community and culture to enable her esteem to soar.

I think she's an amazing human and I far prefer her to her sister (who is lovely in her own right but not to Molly's level). Intelligent and kind, she possesses that quick wit I envy in others and can crack a joke or deploy sarcasm within nanoseconds. She's also self-deprecating. Her height (she's almost six feet tall while her sister is tiny) is a typical victim of her humor.

Our year together in Korea, in a country full of petite women, amplified her insecurities over her body. She struggles with shopping in the US; it was impossible to do so in Seoul. Her legs were too long, her bust too big, and her feet too large for anything to fit. This wreaked havoc on her already low confidence, and so, once back in the States and living in Nevada, insecure and lonely for friends, Molly settled for the first funny, kind-faced man to come along.

Her problems with such a quick coupling developed soon after they declared themselves girlfriend and boyfriend. Since I moved here, Molly has been asking me if she should break up with him. He's crazy about her and she's just okay about him. His sense of humor didn't live up to her expectations (oh, how those online dating profile pictures can fool), and though sweet, he is dull. With zero intentions of getting more serious with him, Molly wonders if she should continue dating him to abate the loneliness of being single or end things before he becomes too attached, if he isn't already there.

As her elder with six more years of dating experience, I'm full of advice and suggestions. *If you're settling for him, why waste your time? You're so young. Why be unhappy?* I tell her this whenever she complains about the boring airplane mechanic. Her loneliness always wins. I admit my misery without confessing. *Molly, trust me, nothing is lonelier than being in a miserable relationship.* But he's her first boyfriend in many years, and she's waiting for her feelings to change.

I'm too familiar with this frustrating patience.

Once the Fargo marooning story finishes, Molly seizes the opportunity to change the subject. "Ji Soo, how is working at the Stratosphere? Are people winning big money?"

The topic sticks to work for a while. When it pivots, it dives no deeper than routine trivialities. School, my hatred of mornings, a newly discovered Korean restaurant that makes the best *jjajangmyeon* (black bean noodles). I forced myself out to have a good time, but the good time isn't presenting itself.

Molly passes out first. She joins in on the conversation less and less until going completely silent. I leave the room to use the bathroom and when I return, her boyfriend has joined her in peaceful slumber. Even Jason's eyes are half closed. I wedge into the open cushion on the loveseat and gently place my stockinged feet in his lap. He grips the balls of my feet firmly for a moment and lets them go, surrendering to the sleep hanging thick in the tiny living room.

Amazed that all three of my companions have fallen asleep on me, I reach for my purse placed on the floor near the loveseat. My hands need little digging to find my phone.

Faris and I were texting earlier. Not unusual behavior, we text daily. I'm learning more about him from five months of messaging than from dozens of college weekends. How he and his siblings always meet to celebrate major birthdays. The time he whisked his brother away to San Francisco following a difficult breakup. That his parents permanently moved to Florida from Kuwait following Maryam's high school graduation, and that he hasn't been back to his home country since he visited the year following his own commencement ceremony.

Our communications offer a brief respite, giving me escape when I need it, provided he's available to volley messages back and forth. He recently entertained me on a five-hour return bus trip from visiting my brother in LA. Jason hadn't responded to my pleas for a distraction from the long and depressing drive through the desert. Faris came to my rescue. He told me, through a myriad of texts, a long story of a recent work-related hunting trip for geese. A little lab ran into the bushes to scare the geese into the sky, doing most of the work and aiding the eager hunters in bagging over ninety geese. Faris stood back from his peers. He didn't possess an accurate shot, nor did he care.

Recently, Faris learned his job was transferring him, of all places, to Denver. I worry what this move means for his future with Demaris, or the future I imagine they'll have. I dig for information. *Have you told Demaris yet?* His response caused my blood to run cold.

Not yet. I need to send her a message.

I want to know more but don't think I can handle it, and so have asked no more about her.

Our more recent texts focus on the logistics. *When are you going to look at places?* or *You can host everyone for Dick's next year!* and *What day are you moving?*

My feet rest in my sleeping husband's lap as I stare at my phone, hoping to read a response from my crush, but my blank phone provides more disappointment. I shouldn't be. My last message was sent past his bedtime in Texas. He's an early sleeper, and I'm two hours behind his central time zone. I hadn't expected him to reply this late, but I sent it hoping he stayed up later than usual, being it's Saturday.

Where's an escape now? I dragged my ass out on a dark and chilly night to flee the day-to-day of depressing desert living. I wanted to reconnect with friends and use our laughter to temporarily forget about the realities of my new start. Instead, my companions all passed out on me. Faris, snoozing thousands of miles and two time zones away, can't offer me a reprieve either.

I hadn't paid much attention to the radio earlier, but it's now my only entertainment. My ears focus on the modest folk song beginning on the airwaves. It's not immediately recognizable. The tune is missing the lengthy instrumental introduction from the original version. Without the syncopating synthesizer masquerading as a flute, the song isn't as obvious.

Ten seconds of simple guitar strumming leads to the lyrics and the song reveals itself to me. The singer yearns to be at home. The DJ at the college station must be a sadist who senses my isolation. I don't know who is covering The Talking Heads masterpiece among love songs, but the words mean the same to me. Home is not a place. Home is being with the one(s) you love.

I moved to Vegas in hopes of building a home with Jason. I'd wanted so much out of it. I wanted us to laugh together over inside jokes. Drink late into the evening as we shared stories we'd not yet heard. Hike into the desert. Enjoy music and concerts. Fuck regularly. The problem is we didn't share many of these things from our beginnings. I don't know why I assumed we'd start to once we moved here.

Four months into this "new life" and I feel more alone and isolated than I've ever felt in my thirty-one years, but I'm stuck, so stubborn on the idea that my feelings will change. Through so many conversations, I've reiterated to Molly *nothing is lonelier than being in a miserable relationship*, but I'm in complete denial of my own relationship. Time to wake up. Take off my eye mask and remove the earplugs. Time to face my reality. My truth.

I don't love Jason.

I say those words to myself, not out loud, but in my head. Still, it's a moon-sized step. An inaugural moment. It's the first time I admit my true feelings in speaking that sentence.

I do not love Jason.

The song serves as a catalyst to wash away my months, perhaps even years, of denial. This marriage reset is an absolute marriage disaster. All our bad behaviors as a couple are exacerbated here with no one around to occupy us or to distract us from our issues. We designed disparate goals for ourselves, forming five-year plans without consulting the other and living separate lives like two roommates who tolerated one another. I stopped accompanying Jason to his soccer games. He preferred hanging on the Wee House's living room floor while I entertained friends in the kitchen. He spent his vacations visiting gigantic out-of-state casinos with friends, and I absconded to Phish shows since learning it was best not to invite Jason on my respites from married life. Years of anger, avoidance, unilateral decision-making, and disconnecting coalesced in the southwest, amplifying our marriage crisis to the point of no return.

This move was supposed to be our second chance, but we aren't restarting. We won't be falling back in "love." And I don't want to. I endured this shitty relationship for too long.

I'm done.

From such a profound awakening comes a different crisis.

I don't know how or even if I will be able to end it. There are too many things keeping me tied to him. We've nine months left on the leash for our freshly furnished apartment. Who gets to stay? Where would the other go? What about furniture? Do we divide it and repurchase what we each lost? Neither of us can afford that, nor can we support a single living lifestyle.

Our hooks in each other dig deeper than apartment logistics and the dismal finances we earn individually. I can't push for a split with Jason. His citizenship so recently acquired, leaving him seems tantamount to abandonment. He doesn't know anyone in Las Vegas. He hardly knows anyone in America. I can't leave him to fend on his own. It's too cruel.

Even if I was ruthless enough to abandon Jason, I don't know where I would go. I can't leap backward to Pennsylvania or leave the teaching job I'd just begun, and I can't afford to start again elsewhere.

By allowing this marriage to continue past its expiration date, in choosing to remain with Jason despite years of discontent, our detached lives are still somehow intricately entangled. I've no other option than to stay in Nevada.

Married to Jason.

The tears come instantaneously with this realization. They pour down my cheek silently. My shoulders heave up and down and I cover my face in a decorative pillow. I don't want to wake anyone up. How will I explain my crying? *Sorry, Jason, I don't love you.* I want to be able to say those words but I'm unable to open my mouth. I won't let them pour out. Even with my newfound awareness, I've conceded to this cruel stage of love, the dying and dead phase.

What I lack in sound I make up for with product. My weeping could provide southern Nevada's lengthy dry season with adequate moisture, if only flora thrived under such salty nourishment. My tears fall as the product of a confused encyclopedia of emotions. Regret over my rushed marriage to Jason, the disappointment in this ostensible reset, the grief in my inability to be truthful to my husband, my needs, and my own happiness, frustration over all these choices I've made. I'm unable to get out of this *Choose Your Own Adventure* because I'm out of pages. There are no more possibilities. This is my life because I'm unwilling to write a different chapter.

The song ends.

I compose myself.

Jason wakes up.

With my tears wiped away by the sleeve of my sweater and deep breaths, many of them taken, nothing seems amiss. Molly and her boyfriend continue to snooze on the couch, and me and my husband sneak out.

Chapter 26

Kylie texts. *We need to talk!!! Call me now!*

I can't. I'm still working. I message back.

It's a Tuesday in early November, and I'm alone in my classroom. My students at specials, I'm allotted these forty-five minutes to complete my non-teaching responsibilities. Any grading, lesson planning, collaborating, email writing, and parent communication I don't finish in these three-quarters of an hour must be attended to at the end of the school day. Rare are workdays that end at dismissal. Judging by the amount of exclamation marks following Kylie's words, I'll try my best to make today one of those occasions.

Kylie has recently returned from Phish's Fall Tour, having attended all twelve shows. I had stalked airline websites since Dick's for a cheap flight, but, as I anticipated, prices turned in the wrong direction. Faris joined in on the daily flight search, bombarding me with links to flights whenever a relatively reasonably priced (to him) flight surfaced.

Rachael, here's a flight for $400!

Faris, my budget is $200 or less.

Check this one out! $375!

I can't afford it. Besides, it has 2 layovers, and I don't get to Boston until 8 p.m.

But Rachael, you need to be here!

Alas, an affordable flight to Massachusetts never materialized, and I was unable to join my friends in Worcester as I'd so hoped to.

I spent that first weekend of tour sulking on my couch watching reruns of *Modern Family*. Phish had kicked off the first three shows of tour in Virginia, at the Hampton Coliseum, the site of my first Phish concert in 2003. I zoned out from Phil Dunphy's televised face and pictured myself back at "The Mothership," prancing around the fountain outside the beloved venue's spaceship-like exterior as I did ten years ago.

Faris and Kylie were there, raging with a group of Kylie's friends from Pennsylvania, several of whom happened to be single, good-looking, and female. Paranoia that Faris would fall in love, or at least hookup, with one of them, struck. If only I were there, bopping around to the drum circle pounding near the fountain's epicenter. (Though drum circles have since faded out of the Phish scene, there was a huge orbit of djembe and bongo bangers when I was there in the early aughts so in my imagination they stayed). Playfully tapping Faris's hip with my own, the suggestion in my hips wouldn't lie, forgoing my need to rely on Kylie's promise to cock block for me. She'd known of my crush for a while now; I'd confessed my feelings to her while sitting at my darling flower table during one of my frantic Saturday morning marathon phone sessions.

But I wasn't there, and I had to depend on her. Kylie has never let me down before, but the power of hormones and booze may have trumped her possible interventions.

She reached out the Saturday morning following night one to let me know Faris went to bed alone in his hotel room like a good boy. I laughed and thanked her for the babysitting, but then jokingly scolded her for calling me instead of enjoying the start of Phish tour.

The next day, I was couch-locked in front of the TV (where else), sinking into the dark abyss of my cerebrum, shoving my face with carbs, grease, and dairy. If I couldn't be rollicking in Hampton, Virginia, I should have at least planned to be out and social, but there was no one for me to be out and social with. With Jason working and Molly studying, my two options were exhausted. However, in reflecting on our outing from two weeks ago, perhaps the couch and *Modern Family* made a better choice.

Though normal to be in my jammies and on the couch early on a Sunday, my feast was not. I was working through an entire pint of Ben and Jerry's in this single sitting, eating the emotions of my loser life away with the power of a caramel core and chunks of peanut butter covered pretzels. The paranoia of Faris hooking up with someone returned. As I scooped up baby spoonfuls of ice cream, I willed myself to remove the pictures of Faris fucking one of Kylie's friends out of my head, but they stayed, my stubborn brain overpowering the pleading in my heart.

But then came a text message.

I wish you were here.

The simple message arrived attached with a picture from the show. The entire room was dark, save for soft blue lights beaming in on each of the four band members. It looked as if The Coliseum had indeed transformed into an alien spacecraft, hovering above the stage ready to teleport the musicians into the wonders of space. The audience held their lighters high into the air so the dark bowl surrounding the stage glowed with the complementary yellow hues from the hundreds and hundreds of low-lit flames.

I wish you were here.

I froze. Gasped. Could not look away from the message.

I wish you were here.

It strengthened my belief that my feelings weren't so unrequited this time around.

I wish you were here.

Then Jason came home from work. I put my phone down and joined my husband to see how his workday had gone.

Kylie had not only promised to cock block Faris. She had also threatened to talk to him. About me.

I protested. I didn't want him to know about my silly crush. My feelings would eventually fade and disappear, like every other crush I've had before him. But then Faris had sent me that text message and I hoped such a conversation occurred during their nine-day adventure.

I hadn't heard from Kylie since she and Faris parted ways after Worcester. And now she texts, over a week later and at the most inopportune moment in the middle of a school day, and, according to her message, *we needed to talk!!!*

I hurry out of work as soon as my last student is picked up. Tomorrow, I'll have to go in extra early to make up for lost time, but this phone call is too important to postpone. As I rush out of the classroom, I glance at the apple placard displaying my name hanging outside my door.

Mrs. Wesley.

It's a name I don't identify with. My administration knows I'm married but they hadn't consulted me prior to sticking the letters in place. Had they, I would have requested Ms.

I reach out to Kylie as I walk to my car. She doesn't pick up. At a red light on my way to the gym, I try again. No answer. I text her. *This suspense is killing me.* She calls me while I'm working out, and her phone goes straight to voicemail when I dial her back. Sleep won't come without talking to her.

We connect after dinner. Kylie is a night owl; it's eight o'clock on the West Coast when she gets back to me. Jason stretches out on the living room floor, watching sports. He's relaxed, digesting food, zoned out, and paying little attention to me. I pick up my phone from the island separating the galley kitchen from the living room.

"Kylie, it's you!" I cry.

"Rae!" she shouts back. "I've missed your voice!"

I don't want to be rude and demand that she tell me everything Faris said right away. Instead, I ask her about the tour. She tells me about the Halloween show and catching up with Selena, who flew in from Oregon for the last of the concerts in Atlantic City.

While we talk, I nervously pace the entire length of my apartment, from the front door to my bedroom, back and forth, impatient and nervous to get to the nectar of "we need to talk!!!!"

"So Faris and I had quite the conversation during our drive from Virginia to New York," she finally says.

I nod. Silly. She can't see me. "Okay."

"You're going to have to break up with Jason, confess your feelings to Faris, and move to Denver," she busts out.

I laugh. "Imagine that!"

"No, I'm serious. You have to break up with Jason, confess your feelings to Faris, and move to Colorado. Denver is where you want to be, anyway. This all works out."

I walk by Jason as she says this. His gaze absorbs the cheering crowd on the television screen. No matter how captivated he seems by the sporting event, I can't have this discussion here. Not with my husband in the same room. The bathroom makes for the best place, behind a locked door with the sound of the fan concealing my words.

"What are you talking about?" I ask her once I flick the fan on. The annoying whir relaxes and assures me. It's a first for the white noise.

"Faris has feelings for you," she says.

"Wait, wait, how did this conversation even get started?" I demand. I feel like a middle school student. *Faris, Rachael likes you. Do you like her?*

"I said to him that you two seemed to have quite a connection. I could see it in our group texts and from things you would say. He agreed. He likes you. A lot!" Kylie's voice rises with her next words. "You have to tell Jason."

My body wants to levitate toward the whirring fan, this body buoyancy signaling how close the seemingly impossible inches closer into a potential reality. But the most unfeasible part of this scenario is not Faris's confession. That's not the true burden; I've suspected he returned my feelings since Dick's and Kylie merely confirmed that. Me telling Jason my true feelings, uprooting whatever I'm trying to establish in Las Vegas, and moving to be with Faris in Denver is. It's such an outrageous, out-of-reach scenario I would have laughed if it didn't make me want to cry first.

"I can't," I tell Kylie.

"Faris said it was pointless having feelings for you. You're married and he can't do anything about it."

"That's true," I murmur. I keep my sentences short, still fearful that Jason will overhear.

"Rachael," Kylie pleads. "You need to get out. You're not happy."

"I know."

"You can leave!"

"No, I can't."

Three simple words for a situation anything but straightforward. It's convoluted. I don't love Jason. I don't want to be married to him. And my emotions touch upon every feeling south of happiness. I'm scared, sad, overcome with guilt. Petrified to talk with him. How will I file for divorce if I can't even talk to my husband about it? I'm miserable and lonely, utterly dissatisfied with my path, but acting on nothing to alter it.

Yet nothing will change unless I make it happen.

"Faris is moving to Denver in a month. Demaris lives in Denver. They are both single and amazing." Kylie paints a picture in my head. "What if they get together?"

The butterflies flipping through my stomach in elation earlier move to my esophagus. I feel nauseous. I hear Demaris's words from the first night of Dick's. *I vaguely remember him. He's cute.* What Kylie says seems more likely than Faris and I getting together. They are both attractive, fabulous, and single, and they will be living in the same city.

"Don't say that," I plead.

"It won't happen when you leave Jason and move to Denver to be with Faris."

"I can't," I say. "We just moved here. I just started teaching. I can't move on already."

"I know," Kylie admits. "And I'm sorry. I want you to be happy."

"I want to be happy too," I smile sadly at my reflection in the large bathroom mirror.

"What are you going to do?"

"Nothing."

This statement is carried out to fruition, and I don't do a thing. I continue to attend hiking meetups and occasionally hang out with my colleagues, but no friendships emerge from either endeavor. Korean dinners on Fridays with Jason and the dead air space between us continue as our weekly ritual. Hanging on opposite ends of the couch, not speaking and engaged in activities removed from one another, remains routine. I go to bed alone.

And I still allow the relationship to continue.

Faris and I don't stop exchanging daily text messages. My crush refuses to go anywhere. It's gained strength since my conversation with Kylie. Every subsequent text from Faris is like protein powder. Each message causes my diaphragm to ache and groan. My marriage may be sexless, but my libido has returned, and I will satisfy it. I masturbate like I did in college, with images of his head between my legs.

I look forward to going to bed alone.

Chapter 27

This Saturday in late November is like most of the fifteen other Saturdays I've experienced since moving to Las Vegas. Wake up, make myself a cup of coffee with a push of a button, stir a teaspoon of coconut oil into my instant dark roast, and sit outside on the yellow petals of my flower table. The fall morning sun keeps me company for hours. Vegas gets major points for permitting me to sit outside this late into the season, needing nothing more than a hoodie to keep me comfortable.

While caffeinating, I smoke my weekend-approved menthol cigarettes and dial the numbers of family, friends, anyone really who might be available to speak with me. I make call after call until someone picks up and I persuade them to spend thirty minutes of their day catching up with me.

This is how I socialize on Saturdays and Sundays. Jason works, and I spend my days alone. The sole reason for the weekend's existence is the brief two-day respite they offer from the stressors of my job; I barely look forward to them anymore. They intensify my despairing loneliness.

Though I frequently tell Molly there is nothing lonelier than an unhappy relationship, my weekends sometimes cause me to question the truth in my statement. Here in the desert, I experience several varieties of isolating solitude. There is the loneliness that comes from the disconnect in my relationship. And then there is the actual seclusion from the multitude of hours I spend alone.

The first few hours are relaxing. I crank music and clean. Later, I settle on the couch with a book.

Then the sun goes down.

The nervousness emerges, a product of an extrovert physically by herself longer than necessary. I make sure a light is turned on in each room, but the low glow they produce highlights the gloom of night. Small pockets of muted light meet darkened spaces, making my world seem smaller, intensifying my feelings of isolation.

I wish I had plans. I wonder what's happening on The Strip.

There's probably a decent band in town. Wish I had someone to go out with.

It's 5:30 on a Saturday evening, and I'm in my pajamas.

This is loneliness.

I suffered from it when I first moved to Korea. It was an ache of homesickness, the pain of wanting to see and be with my people back in America. Standing on the tiny balcony off my bedroom, I'd smoke cigarettes and wish I owned a pair of ruby red slippers to transport me to Pennsylvania. I felt like I was the only person alive; the wind whipping my hair and causing embers of cigarette ash to fly around me.

I'd stare across the parking lot, looking at the Korean letters spelling out the names of the gigantic apartment buildings across the street from my own building. My gaze would then turn down to the parking lot filled with white cars fifteen stories below while I nervously chain-smoked cigarettes and took in the newness of this country, wondering what the fuck I had done.

I frequently mused about my decision to teach in Korea in those early days. Had I made a mistake in moving across the world? Regardless of that, I was stuck, committed to a yearlong contract. These fears, aggressive and real, permeated my head, but it didn't take long for me to acclimate to Korean living or meet people whom I hung out with regularly.

Still, these friendships I'd formed were fresh and possibly, (most likely?) fleeting. Could I count on them to include me in their plans? Would they be there for me should I critically need them? Could I put my complete trust in them? There was no foreseeing where these relationships would go, and such unpredictability caused a pale shadow of loneliness to linger.

And then Jason came along.

These evenings spent alone in my apartment bring me back to those thoughts I had on my fifteenth-floor balcony in South Korea. Once again, I feel like the last person left in the world, the lone survivor of a plague or atomic blast. And if I struggle with weekends here in Vegas alone, what will happen if Jason and I split and I'm constantly by myself?

I'd thought maybe my loyalty to Jason, my guilt at abandoning him in a strange country, made me stay with him, but it's more than that. There's selfishness in my sacrifice. Kylie had questioned the state of my marriage on the drive to SPAC, had asked if it was one of convenience. It's become that for me.

My loneliness played a large role in why I clung to him in the beginning, why we became so serious so quickly, and it's a huge reason I stay with him now. I know I won't last on my own, either. I don't know if my mental health can acclimatize to being completely alone.

This evening, television noise keeps me company. It's turned to the movie *Thirteen Going on Thirty* and I alternate between watching it, reading *Maddaddam*, and perusing Facebook. Of the three, social media is winning most of my attention. I'm not an active Facebook poster, but I lurk regularly. Faris recently made his move to Denver and I've been stalking his profile daily, investigating to see if he is settling in, making friends.

Hanging out with Demaris.

His profile shows his social media style has altered little over the years. As of yesterday, he hadn't posted anything in months. I don't see any recent status updates, photos, or check-ins. His profile picture has never changed. It bears an image of a hairless and chubby-cheeked young man, the Faris I remember from college.

Maybe he stalks as stealthily as I do. Is as disappointed in my boring page as I am in his. Perhaps I will brighten his up with a post, something I've never done, something to put me on the forefront of his mind, not Demaris. I can tell him how I look forward to spending the next Dick's at his place. Generic, yet effective.

His space is almost bare. I notice the most minute change. Someone posted on his timeline.

You moved to Denver and didn't tell me. Shame on you! Let's hang out!

It's from Demaris.

She knows! How the fuck did she find out? I look at Faris's information beneath his dated profile picture. He's been uncharacteristically active and has listed his current city as Denver.

My stomach flips as if I've crested the top of a coaster and am on my way down. I think back to what Kylie said to me. *"Faris is moving to Denver in a month. Demaris lives in Denver. They are both single and amazing. What if they get together?"*

Faris is going to reply to her message, and they'll meet for a beer. One beer will turn into several, ending with them going home together. This is exactly what will happen; I can think of no other alternative. I imagine the two of them as a couple, kissing passionately as they undressed one another.

I've never made myself nauseous through the power of thought, but my stomach turns even more aggressively, and a wave of bile rises in my throat. Running to the bathroom to dispose of the acidic liquid burning my esophagus and mouth, I spit out the teaspoonful of sadness in the sink and keep my head hovered over the smaller porcelain god in the chance more arrives. None does, but when I glance at myself in the mirror, I see a pathetic woman who looks as if she spent the morning with her head hanging in the toilet.

Though it's early evening, I wear no bra and am still in the old T-shirt and leggings I slept in. Both hair and teeth remain unbrushed, and my oily face has flaky patches of dry skin around my mouth and chin. My mouth tastes even more decrepit than my appearance, the grossness of unbrushed teeth combined with coffee drunk hours earlier mixed with a raunchy layer of bile.

I am disgusting.

I tear off my clothes, throw them to the ground, and reach into the tub to turn on the shower. The water pours down at my preferred temperature: hot enough to tinge my skin pink. I step into the wet heat, ready for the water to clean my rankness and relax me. Enough of this day! Enough of this foulness of my body and breath! Enough of this … this … new life that I created for myself.

I want to become a whole new me, an entirely different entity.

David Byrne has asked himself time and time again and I ask the same of myself. How did I get here?

My relationship with Jason progressed quickly after our great Bungalow make out of 2007. When my parents visited for Christmas and New Year's eight weeks later, he and I were already spending all our free time together, including during my parents' trip. He tagged along on our city adventures for the two days he was off work, enriching our sightseeing by acting as an unofficial tour guide with his curated list of must-see places.

He charmed my parents. How could he not? He grabbed Mom and me hot coffees while we waited in line to buy tickets (that he purchased) for Seoul Tower, and he tried his best to distract Mom from her fear of heights during the cable car ride to the top. He insisted that Dad pose with the rat at the statues of the Chinese zodiac circled outside the National Folk Museum of Korea. He led us to a near-secret restaurant down an alleyway in crowded, antique-filled *Insadong* to dine upon the tastiest *mandu* I'd ever tasted. The doughy, gigantic dumplings enveloped the meat and veggie filling in a chewy yet firm consistency. I'd have never discovered this simple perfection if it wasn't for Jason's knowledge.

His understanding of the city—of subway lines, neighborhoods, and places to eat—and how quickly he recalled this information highlighted the advantages of dating a local, along with his ability to translate from Korean to English and English to Korean. Throw in his good looks and sense of humor. Wow! I was dating the local heartthrob! Evidence of this was apparent when I hung out with my fellow foreign teachers and overheard the "more beautiful and popular" women talking about my relationship with the cute and funny Korean.

So, on top of curing my residual loneliness and fueling my always-in-need-of-a-boost self-confidence in his affection and compliments,

Jason was somewhat of a status symbol. People wanted him around, to play on soccer teams, to travel with, to go on bike rides, and dating him gave me a sense of importance.

All of this intensified my feelings for him. I thought I'd been in love twice before and assumed the fierce emotions causing my stomach to whirl in a pleasant loop and wanting to spend every spare moment with him was love. We exchanged those three most powerful words in any language in January.

In February, we took advantage of the Chinese New Year and took off to the mountains with a mixed group of friends for the long holiday. When we arrived at our shared accommodations, we immediately busted out all the Korean alcohols. We pounded the winter chill away with *soju*, *makkoli*, and Cass beer. Jason sipped on a small glass of beer while the rest of us got wasted.

Hammered, I pulled him away for a mid-party liaison in the privacy of our room. Post coitus, overcome with booze and love, I stared into his sleepy brown eyes, thinking I'd never feel this strongly for another man, and a wave of sadness washed through me. This relationship was doomed. It'd never last the thousands of miles of distance placed between us when my contract ended in June. Unless ...

"We should get married," I impulsively whispered my future to Jason.

His face came to life. Eyes sparkling and lips outstretched, he said, "Okay."

It was a *Sex and the City*, Trey McDougal, alrighty-then moment. I cavalierly suggested we bind together forever, and he so casually accepted.

At twenty-five years old, my frontal cortex, the part of the brain responsible for rational thinking, had just recently fully developed. Plus, my Korean existence made me feel like I was a Disney princess in an animated movie. You know, the one where the poor, white princess moves to a foreign country and almost immediately meets a handsome local who treks ninety minutes on a bus each way twice a week to see her. They fall passionately in love and live happily ever after.

At least, that's what my heart told my brain.

We got engaged three months into dating. We married in December, ten months later. Unfortunately, our happily ever after came with an expiration date, once the lust that I mistook for love faded without real love to take its place.

Meanwhile, Faris and Demaris are going to fall for one another.

I linger in the heat of the shower, the water cleansing my body and easing my mind. The hot water soothes my breakdown. It pours over me, lifting both my physical and emotional funk and carrying the grime and anger away to disappear down the drain. I give myself a thorough cleansing: lathering, scrubbing, and exfoliating dead skin to reveal a fresher Rachael beneath, like a reptile. I renew my legs, shaving my prickly extremities with my little pink razor. I'll slather my smooth skin in an uplifting grapefruit-scented lotion.

As I am carefully running the razor up the fleshy part of my calf, an image of Demaris and Faris passionately intertwined involuntarily fills my internal vision, and I burst into tears. My sobs explode like a storm surge breaking through a weak levee. My stoic exterior is no longer a formidable opponent against my repressed emotions; I comply and allow my heart, beat up by years of this exhausting marriage, to break down. I love Faris, but I don't know how to proceed.

The only thing I can think to do is stay the course. To keep on keeping on. I'm threading in the rip current of life on a familiar routine that tethers me on a stagnant course.

I realize I am not to have real love in this lifetime.

Maybe I'll get to have it in my next one. But, at thirty-one years old, I've resigned myself to living a loveless existence. It's not new, nor is it the different one I expected to begin in the southwest. It's the same exact one. It sucks that I've just learned this, as it's far too late to change anything.

Chapter 28

I stare across a tiny two-top table at Jason a few hours later. He texted me earlier to make plans for a ramen dinner. Though I don't feel like a "better me" post-breakdown, the cry worked some cathartic magic, and I was able to shake off the most draining and volatile of my emotions to pull myself together.

I'm tired of being sorry for myself and have dressed for how I want to feel rather than how I actually do. My favorite pair of slim-fit stretch jeans compliment an orange sweater, and I stuck my contacts in and finished my look with a pair of oversized wooden earrings. A light dusting of pressed powder, a sweep of blush, and a stroke of mascara brighten my face. While my insides may burn with secrets and regret, I do look like myself, and for this, I am pleased. And hungry. I'm ready to pig out on a big bowl of noodles.

"Rae," Jason says to me as a spicy tuna appetizer is placed at our table.

"Yes?" I ask him. I aim my wooden chopsticks toward a tasty rectangle of sushi basic-ness. My appetite screams in full force, ready to chow down.

"I've been thinking about something …" He trails off, hesitating as his words come out.

"Yes?" I wrestle with my mouth full of food and am half paying attention to him. I want to eat my food and avoid our half-assed attempts at conversation.

"I think I want to join the army," he says quite casually for his reticence seconds earlier.

I, meanwhile, nearly choke on my tuna. I don't know what I expected him to say, but it certainly wasn't this. The army? Where the fuck had that idea come from? He gets my full attention now. "The United States Army?"

"Yes. The United States Army."

"Why?"

Yes, husband, why? Up until this very moment, he never mentioned, never hinted, he was brewing such an idea. Jason highly regarded his two mandatory years in the Korean Army. He enjoyed the camaraderie fostered among the other young men in his unit and appreciated the routine and known expectations. He was even fond of the rigorous physical challenges he was given. I just never expected him to be rehashing these adventures now, over a decade since they ended.

He sticks a piece of crunchy tuna in his mouth and chews, thinking about his answer. "I'm almost thirty-five, so this would be my last chance."

"Last chance for what?"

"To join the military. The army has the highest age maximum, and the cutoff is thirty-five."

When Jason and I first met, he was finishing up his undergrad and planned to attend law school. At twenty-eight, he graduated with his bachelor's degree much later than many of his peers. This was one of the things that had attracted me to Jason. He didn't abide by many of the norms expected of adults his age in Korean society. He was in no hurry to enter the soul-sucking force of Korean work culture, where eighty-hour work weeks and zero hours spent enjoying an annual vacation was standard. It appeared to me that Koreans, even more so than Americans, judge success based on career, and Jason hadn't started his yet.

After we met and married, Jason figured he would attend law school in the States. He changed his mind when he settled at the Wee House and decided to pursue a more easy-going yet potentially lucrative job as a table games dealer at the casino. He didn't mention law school much more in the proceeding months. A few years of tossing cards segued into an interest in accounting. He took some prerequisites last year when we were back in Seoul, and he was looking into attending the local community college once we established residency in Nevada.

No wonder Jason's announcement baffles me. He's constantly changing his mind. Perhaps his constant shifting is a rebellion from his upbringing in that career-obsessed "live to work" culture. My own life philosophies revolve around love and enjoyment, not work, but I do want us to reach our own terms of success. I don't care about living in a big house, driving a fancy car, or wearing designer clothes, but I desire regular simple travel and the security of not living paycheck to paycheck. I even picture retirement someday, now that I contribute to an employee-matched 401K. By eschewing all ideas of having a set career, Jason moves us further away from that goal.

"What about going back to school to be an accountant? I thought that's what you wanted to do," I say.

"The military will pay for school if that's what I want to do."

"But we just moved here!" I protest. "We've been here less than half a year and you want to uproot us so soon?"

"We made this move for you," he says. "So that you can become a teacher. You decided that. Now I'm making the next decision on what we'll do."

"But Jason, you knew this wasn't temporary. You knew we were moving here for good."

"I've changed my mind. This is a good opportunity for me, and I want to do it."

"What about my opportunity? What would I do?" His unilateral choice to join the army would essentially force me, as his spouse, to come on board as well, to assume the role of a military wife, to base my very existence around my husband's orders. No, thank you. Even if our marriage was strong, even if I still loved him, I'd balk.

"You can teach wherever I get stationed," Jason says nonchalantly.

Our ramen had appeared in the middle of this conversation, and I look down at my bowl of pork *tonkatsu*. I swirl the noodles around and mix the greens, dispersing carbs and vegetables throughout the bowl.

Weren't we growing past this bad habit? But here's Jason trying to make a life-changing decision based on opportunities for him with no regard for me. For us as a couple. He reinforces our lack of cohesion, how we aren't a team.

I wish I'd not taken his thoughts and feelings regarding our move into consideration and laid down my law. *We're moving to Denver!*

Inspiration suddenly springs from Jason's blind-siding revelation. If he is serious, if this is truly his next step forward, his own second chance, I'll encourage him to do so while also explicitly communicating that he made the decision without me, it's something I want no part of, and that I'm out.

Perhaps this is the necessary step to get me that new life.

This may be my way out of the marriage.

Chapter 29

Sunday, December 29, 2013. It's our wedding anniversary, and thousands of miles separate me and my husband. I migrated east for the holidays, but Jason, unwilling to take a break from the casino (surprise, surprise), stayed behind in Nevada. It's not the first anniversary we won't be spending together. Four years ago, on our paper anniversary, I elected to celebrate one full year of marriage with paper ticket stubs and chose Phish and their New Year's run of shows in Miami. Jason shockingly chose work.

I was never one to make a big deal out of holidays and birthdays, so I didn't look too deeply into it. An anniversary is just a day, like Tuesday (the most worthless of them all). Do we need to spend the day wrapped up in one another's arms to prove our love? But, if we are in love, wouldn't we want to spend the occasion wrapped in one another's arms?

Once again, for our fifth wedding anniversary, neither of us selected the other. In defense of my choice, I also opted for family and another much-needed escape from Vegas. It's my winter break from school, and there was no convincing me to spend my sixteen days of holiday in the southwest desert. In what's become my typical fashion, I didn't question why Jason had to work, nor did I push him to join me.

Communications with him for the past nine days consists of daily, albeit brief, two to five-minute conversations. It's been over a month since Jason revealed his intentions to join the United States Army. He's visited the recruiting office but hasn't signed anything to make it official yet. I've been encouraging while also expressing my truth. *I'm not on board with this path, Jay.* Okay, part of my truth. I've failed to blatantly explain how splitting up would make the most sense if he does. I use the passively neutral—"*do it if it's what you really want to do*"— to close these discussions, chickening out from delving deeper into the full repercussions of his aspirations.

I don't bring up the military or divorce during our long-distance conversations. Best to save those for a future in-person exchange. I promise myself it's going to happen once I'm "home" (yuck). I'm wishful, trusting that my uterus (not my nonexistent balls) will return, leaving me able to participate in such real and necessary discourse. While I'm at my parents', we speak of mundane events, listing the day's happening. It's more of an obligation, a checking off a box in marital expectations, than a desire to talk with him.

"How was work?"

"It was kinda busy."

"Did you talk with anyone interesting?"

"No, not really."

"Not at all? Did you see any drug deals or men with paid dates?"

"No."

I earnestly try to stretch our conversations, but I don't know what to talk about with my reticent husband. It's so much easier with Faris, who provides complete sentences in his written and spoken communications. I've connected with him eighty percent more than with Jason since I've been in Pennsylvania.

Faris and I texted late Christmas Eve, and I sent him a photo of Mom and I both decked out for the birth of the baby Jesus. I wore a fitted red dress that showed off my curves, long dangly earrings, and the fire engine red lipstick I normally reserved for the weekends when I had plans.

You look amazing. Read his immediate text.

I can't wait to see you! I replied.

Me too.

Our exchange left my vagina in a vibrating tickle of cravings.

And in a few short hours I'll be hopping on a bus headed to Manhattan to meet him.

Though I've cherished every moment with my dearly missed loved ones, my brain, in the great paradox created through merely existing, has been preoccupied the entire trip, focusing the bulk of my time on this exact day.

Our rendezvous is innocent enough. It revolves around seeing Phish. The quartet is sticking to their usual late December plans, ushering in 2014 at Madison Square Garden over four nights of music. Though we missed yesterday's show, Faris and I have tickets for the next three. The original plan, conceived at Fall Tour's end and advocated by me and my butthurt over missing it all, included Kylie, but she canceled on us sometime between Thanksgiving and Hanukkah. It'll now be Faris and I exploring New York City by day, raging Phish at night. Sleeping in a shared hotel room.

Kylie and her master plan, I wonder if it was a ruse, concocted to get me and Faris alone.

Because I am the married woman, I've zero intentions to pursue anything. I have morals. And integrity. And I want to stick to them. So, if we're going to hook up, Faris must make the first move. I certainly won't reject him if he does, but I refuse to be the initiator. The nuance of my justifications nonexistent, the anticipated cuckoldry seems less intense, less cold, if I allow Faris to make the move. My premeditated affair becomes less intentional.

I've not seen him since we parted ways in Denver, and he's plagued my thoughts every day since. Nighttime brings about many do-it-yourself pornos, but it's more than physical. There's plenty of "lets' go get a soda at the counter" reveries. What life could be like if he and I were together? What my life could be if I weren't married to Jason? I'd have a dependable show buddy, hiking partner, conversationalist, and a comedian all in one. Someone to grab a beer and to eat the gross parts of the meat. A lover who wanted to fuck me.

Essentially, the exact opposite of everything now.

I dress casually for my big day, opting for comfort in leggings and a sweater that I jazz up by dangling multicolored peacocks from my ears. I ponder necklaces and fidget with the plain silver band around my left finger, spinning it round and round as I debate. It's worn out of habit, not out of the bonded union it represents. I don't want that implied representation pervading my escapades with Faris.

Off it comes, as easily as it did in Saratoga Springs. Then my simple objectives were for the innocent fun of flirting. Now, my intentions aren't nearly as innocuous.

I place my discarded ring on the lacey doily covering the dresser top. It blends in among the rest of the jewelry I'm leaving behind.

"Rae, you ready to go? Your bus leaves in half an hour."

I look into the mirror and see my mother at the door's threshold. Did she see me take off my wedding band? No, she couldn't have. She's only just appeared.

I talk to her via our reflections. "Yeah. Let me pee and we can go."

The mom taxi from my pre-license days resurrects when needed, though our relationship is much evolved from when I was a miserable teenager. We chat easily, openly, during the drive to the bus station. I do, however, shield my left hand from her vision as much as possible as we converse. I clasp my right one around it, dig in my purse for nothing, conceal my naked finger under my phone. My actions totally unnecessary; with Mom's eyes glued to the road, she's not paying any attention to a single finger.

"Did you ever find out why Kylie had to cancel?" She asks me.

A few days earlier, I had asked my parents if either of them could give me a ride to the bus station because Kylie was no longer attending the shows. I didn't divulge that I'd learned this tidbit weeks prior and (terrible liar that I am), feigned surprise as if she'd let me down with the news minutes ago. There's little I don't share with my parents. I can use one hand to list the three things I keep secret.

1. My abortion
2. My misery
3. My crush on Faris

Even if Mom doesn't know about my current crush, she remembers my former one to Faris (my fault for reminding her of it after our random reunion in Saratoga Springs), and I don't want her using those mom superpowers (the ability to magically know things) to sniff out the possibilities that await me. If I made it seem like I just found out Kylie canceled, sharing a room with Faris looks less suspicious. Less premeditated. *Do you know how expensive it'll be to book a hotel last minute this time of year in New York?*

But neither of them had hesitated at the information. Mom immediately replied, "I can drive you," and Dad asked, "What happened that Kylie can't go?" to which I shrugged and said, "Who knows?"

Liar!

But I don't have to lie to Mom now. I give her the reason Kylie supplied, which may have been a fib on her end. "She's having problems with her car and didn't want to spend the money at Phish if she has to spend a lot on her car."

"That's too bad."

"I know. But such a grown-up decision. Look at us acting like adults."

"So now it's you and Faris."

"Yeah. I don't know anyone else going."

"You two will still have lots of fun. Your favorite band in New York City. I wish I could see the Stones like that."

No "does Jason know you're spending three days with another man?" or "make sure you behave." It's almost as if she's granting me permission to surrender to whatever will happen. I'm sure she senses my unhappiness, whether I reveal the truth or not.

At the bus station, Mom promises to pick me up when I return on New Year's Day. I board the 10:20 a.m. Martz bound for Port Authority in Midtown. My stomach twists in a torrent of nervous anticipation for the entire two hours of transport. Faris is flying into LaGuardia from visiting his parents in Florida and will meet me at the Port Authority subway station.

I've taken the bus from Scranton into Manhattan on dozens of trips, but always with at least one other companion and never with such exhilaration coursing through me. I exit the bus and enter the gigantic station, as anxious as navigating an unknown subway station in Seoul.

Port Authority is cavernous, and its many corridors all look the same. I would hate to be running late to catch a bus there. The fluorescent illumination shines muted and faded from its dirt-eclipsed lightbulbs; it's a movie from 1985 still waiting to be digitally remastered.

I follow the overhead signs, crossing passages, going down short flights of stairs, and through a subway gate to exit the lifeless void of the bus station and into the unorganized chaos of the train station. People stand around as plentiful as ants on a tossed popsicle stick, waiting for transportation, using the bathrooms, looking for their correct gate of departure. Faris texted me during my bus station traversal. I've forty minutes to kill.

Dunkin shall keep me company. Coffee will always be the most wise and delicious way to pass time. There is no better beverage for a woman with a tiny bladder and an anxiety disorder.

Rather than sit tight with my large coffee and wait for my Prince Charming to arrive, I walk laps, pulling my red suitcase behind me, burning off nervous energy. I think about what I'll do once I'm face to face with Faris. Will I play it cool and hide my excitement? Pretend that the texts exchanged on Christmas Eve had never been written? Trouble is, rarely am I nonchalant about anything and it'll be near impossible to keep a smile from stretching across my face.

I can own my feelings and act sexy and flirtatious? I picture myself strolling toward Faris with an extra wiggle in my hips and a duck-like purse to my lips. Nope, that's not going to happen. My natural awkwardness intensifies, especially so when in such a heightened state of nerves, and my default move during uncomfortable situations is to laugh at everything.

When we were kids, Anna and I had been playing on top of the gigantic tires at my grandfather's trucking garage when one toppled over and landed on her leg, pinning her to the asphalt. Instead of going in search of help, I froze and looked at her while giggling in shock. Will the same happen this weekend? I imagine Faris in the middle of a subway track with a train barreling down on him while I stand on the platform, stuck in fear but chuckling as the lights draw closer.

I hear a ding. The cartoonish tragedy disappears from my head.

I'm here.

Faris is here.

Faris is here!

Chapter 30

My heart pounds like a tom tom drum, bouncing off my chest wall in a deep and steady rhythm. Twenty ounces of newly consumed caffeine aids the tachycardia. Faris texts me his gate number and I head off in that direction. My pace competes against the finest of speed walking athletes, even with a rolling suitcase. As nimble as a cat, I dart left, then right, dodging upcoming human traffic and moving around slow-moving families ambling in front of me. I've never had such finesse. Maybe I am going to play it cool and confident.

"Hey, Rachael, where are you going?"

I hear my name but continue to confidently moonwalk. A few seconds of processing elapses and then I stop and turn around. There he is, standing taller than most neighboring him, dressed warmly in a black coat, the usual goofy grin spread across his face. The drum in my chest is replaced by a tambourine shaking my entire abdomen from my belly to the top of my sternum.

"I was looking for you."

I walk toward him, and we hug. It's not as dramatic as our reunion at Dicks, when he took me into his arms and spun me around, but somehow more meaningful. He wraps his long arms around my lower back and pulls me close. I drape my shorter arms behind his neck and touch the right side of his face with my left cheek. I inhale, a subtle move of intimacy he won't detect. He doesn't wear cologne but smells so distinctly of Faris, slightly spicy and herbaceous with a hint of sweat. The masculine smell turns me on. I want to kiss him but don't, standing firm in my resolve to not make the first move. The condom is in his court.

He pulls away first. "Shall we go to our room?"

I thought you would never ask.

We walk side-by-side pulling our suitcases while reading the overhead signs in search of the correct train that will take us to our midtown Manhattan hotel. Faris reserved a room for us at the most ironic sleeping establishment two liberals could ever bed down in, and we'll be bunking at The Women's National Republican's Club.

The "Club" provides conservative women a space to dine, meet, and hold events that, I imagine, espouse the evils of sex before marriage and the importance of being a submissive wife. It also serves as a hotel. And because Faris prioritized walking distance to the venue above anything else, it'll act as our home base for the next three days.

Once we're on the train, I try my best to not play it cool, but to show I'm cool, i.e. a hip person who's traveled to New York City enough to be familiar with the subway system. I study the map and emphatically tell Faris we need to ride it three stops to our destination.

"Are you sure?" He asks.

"Yes!" I insist. I analyze the map for confirmation. "Herald Square is right near Koreatown. Our hotel is close to that. We'll only have to walk a few blocks."

We exit the train at my suggested three stops. When we emerge from beneath the earth's surface, into the hailed shopping district of the world's busiest city, we discover that it's raining, and that I had been wrong. We should have traveled one more stop. Instead, we roll our luggage through a dichotic barrage of harried city folk completely attired in black and gaggling, gawking tourists an additional five city blocks in the rain to arrive at the hotel.

In striving to play a trendy version of myself, Awkward Rachael prevailed. Faris acts a good sport. "I did need a stretch after sitting on a plane for hours."

Our room is on the fourth floor. It looks like a hotel room should. A desk stands against the farthest wall and a window makes up half the wall to the left of it. The bathroom is located on the other side of the room, with a heavy door I hope will block out all bathroom sounds. Thick, wooden bedside tables flank the bed.

Not the beds, but the bed.

One queen-sized bed for two humans.

I am fucked. We are fucked. How can something not go down in the sharing of seven feet of such a soft and sensual space? A soft and sensual space that serves two main purposes.

Sleeping and fucking.

Faris focuses on the bed too. "I could have sworn I requested a room with two beds."

I somehow manage to say in a steady voice, "It's big. We can share," and change subjects faster than a standardly played "Bouncing Around the Room" (d'oh, perhaps not the best song reference to use if I want to maintain my composure). "I brought us something."

I poke around my suitcase and when I find the bottle, I brandish it in his face.

He frowns. "Eww. What is that?"

"It's some sort of vodka, sparkling wine combo. I got it at my family's White Elephant exchange. I had my heart set on a pair of sock monkey pajamas and ended up with this instead."

He takes the bottle from me. "Sparkling wine and vodka?"

"It's called a Marilyn Monroe Martini, and I drank them on camping trips in State College, but I never had a pre-made version. I wonder if it's as gross as a bottled Long Island Iced Tea."

"I guess we'll find out." Faris opens the warm bottle of Christmas won spirits and pours us each a glass. We clink our glasses.

He takes a sip and wrinkles his mouth. I scrunch my own face. "Oof, it's bad."

Faris excuses himself to use the bathroom. Once he's out of sight (please don't let me hear any noises coming from inside), I whip out my phone, take a fuzzy, pixelated shot of the queen bed, and send the picture off to Kylie sans message. She won't need anything more to understand.

With Faris in the bathroom, I change my clothes and apply a fresh layer of deodorant. Dressing for shows in the winter isn't nearly as comfortable or as fun as warmer weathered concerts. It's too cold to go bare legged with a flowing sundress kissing the bottoms of your legs, and putting leggings beneath, while providing more warmth, doesn't deliver the same freeing effect. I clad myself in jeans and layer a black sports bra and white tank top beneath a restrained gray and white tie-dyed hoodie. I am guaranteed to sweat inside even with the twenty-degree temperatures outdoors and will strip away some layers indoors once I start dancing.

Despite our distaste in the cocktail, we loiter in the room to finish the bottle. I sit in the left corner at the bottom of the bed, my tiny legs tucked in, and the glass of too-sweet bubbles held loosely in my left hand. Using both pillows, Faris cushions his back against the middle of the headboard. His long legs stretch out to practically touch my right hand.

He sticks his tongue out whenever he takes a sip from his glass. "I didn't expect my first taste of booze this holiday season to be so bad."

"You haven't had anything to drink? It's the holiday season!" I'm stunned, especially given Faris's penchant for partying.

"My dad's Muslim. We don't drink in front of him."

"But you're over thirty years old." Again, his statement shocks. It's not like he's sixteen and has to hide his vices from his parents.

"I know, but he's very religious. He doesn't drink, smoke, eat pork, curse, nothing. And we all pretend we don't either, so when the family gets together, there's no booze. Or pork. It's a respect thing."

"Oh, wow! Okay. I get it. How admirable. Cheers to that!" I hold out my glass to him.

"Cheers!" He obliges and clinks back. "And now I need to catch up on my lack of holiday cheer." He quickly swallows the contents of his glass and refills it.

"What about your mom?" I ask.

"She'll occasionally have a glass of wine. She'll have more if he's not around. She cooks pork then too. Ironically, I think pork is our favorite meat as a family." He laughs as he says that and rests his hands on his outstretched legs with his glass of wine nestled in the middle of his upturned palms.

"Is she Muslim too?"

"She converted to Islam when they got married. They wanted to raise their kids within the same religion and since we lived in Kuwait, Muslim was it. And then none of us grew up to be religious anyway. My mom switched back to Catholicism when they moved to the States."

"Did they move directly to Florida?" I'm so curious and will continue posing questions until Faris stops me. He nods and so I ask another one. "Why there? Is it the heat?"

"No, it wasn't the weather. They're not snowbirds from New York. My mom has a bunch of family in Florida. She lived there when she was a teenager. That's where my parents met."

"Oh, I was wondering how that happened."

"My dad came here for school. Met my mom while waiting for the bus. Next thing you know, they're married and she's moving to Kuwait."

"Hmm. I wonder if it was as big a culture shock for her as if was for me?"

"What, getting married?"

I freeze at Faris's mention of the taboo. Six months ago, on Phish Lot in Saratoga Springs, less than twenty-four hours since we randomly crossed paths, I told him I was married. A universally prioritized topic (I would think) to mention when catching up with an old friend, I stated it as a fact "I'm not sure if you know, but I got married" not a gushing "I'm married to the most fabulous man," but I would never have foreseen we'd end up here, with my feelings as they were. Even so, almost an unspoken agreement, Faris and I overlooked my marriage in every conversation since, covering every subject from camel testicles to the corn bulging from my baby toe, but I avoided mentioning Jason, and anything related, since. Oh, of all the times and places to reintroduce it.

I squeak out, "No, moving to Kuwait."

"I'm sure it was, but enough about my family," Faris says. He reaches for the bottle of wine on the bedside table and tops off both of our glasses. "I've been with them for the past week."

"Alright, let's talk about Colorado then. How is that treating you?" I ask.

Though I've been able to glean an idea of his life in Denver through our daily texts, I figure now makes the most opportune moment to learn if anything is going on between him and Demaris.

His reply is generic. "It's good."

"Come on, that doesn't tell me anything."

"I'm a few blocks from a dog park. Reba likes that." He smiles. Perhaps he's thinking about his pup.

"Have you gone out much? Met anyone?"

"Nope. Not yet." He shakes his head.

"Man, meeting people was a top priority for me when I moved to Vegas." I grab his socked foot and pinch his big toe. "What's wrong with you?" I tease him.

"What's wrong with me? What's wrong with you? Who has the energy to go out and meet people after moving and trying to settle in at work?" He leans over and places his hand on mine, the one that's grasping his foot, and squeezes.

His fingers send a zap down the sides of my body. The charge causes me to leap in surprise. My wine dances within the confines of the glass and threatens to spill, but its contents shockingly stay inside.

"Woah, cat-like reflexes! What happened there?" Faris asks with a chuckle.

I compose myself, sitting cross-legged at the bed's edge, and shrug, so cool and casual. *Your touch had zero effect on me.* "I startle easily."

"Jeez, I guess you do."

The body jolt derailed our conversation, but its crux remains unknown, and I need to find out before we leave this room. Dancing around the issue didn't reveal the necessary information, so I just come out and ask. "Anyway, I guess you haven't seen Demaris yet?"

While I can anticipate what his response will be, my heart quickens with the intensity that accompanies anything high stakes, and my palms instantly slicken with a sheen of perspiration. I inhale deeply and slowly, disguising my breathing patterns by holding my glass against my mouth.

He shakes his head. "Not yet."

Though it's the answer I'm expecting, my hand still spasms. The wine I succeeded in not spilling a minute ago splashes on my face. "Ah shit, I'm such a klutz." I wipe my face with my free hand, but skin on skin is no way to mop up a liquid. I use my sleeve to dry my chin.

"I guess you do startle easily," Faris says. "Was it the wind? Did you hear a door slam down the hall? A dog bark outside?"

How could I explain this? "A ghost pushed me," I say.

"Hope it doesn't come back," he says, chuckling at me. "You want me to grab a tissue?"

"No, it's only a little bit. I'm already dry. But back to Demaris." I'm not dropping this subject yet and don't want tissue retrieval to interfere with it. "How come you haven't met up yet?"

"I moved a month ago."

"Do you think you will soon?"

"Rachael, I don't know," he says breezily. "Why the interrogation about Demaris?"

"Well, you're my friends and I want you two to be friends." And I do, as long as it's platonic. "You're in a new city, and she sounds lonely. Perfect recipe for a friendship." I take a breath and spit out the thought that's haunted too many of my waking moments. Might as well get to the point. "Or maybe even a relationship?"

"Are you trying to play matchmaker?" He laughs as if it's the funniest thing he heard all day. "No, Demaris is great. I'd love to be her friend, but that's it."

"Why not? You're in the same city. I think you both happen to be fucking rad. And you're Phish fans." I'm a masochist, but I must ensure there's no possibility of romance between them.

"Don't try to make a love connection, Rachael. It's not going to happen," He wags his finger playfully at me. "But we'll hang out, I'm sure. I want to get settled before I start socializing."

I relax and allow a sigh of relief to escape my mouth. Demaris, my friend, my friend, my dear friend, poses no threat. My anxiety stuck to her typical MO in creating a convincing narrative through over-thinking, over-analyzing, and overreacting. So positive of Faris's and Demaris's imminent coupledom, I'd been more worried about contending with their burgeoning relationship than I was with the repercussions of my own failing one.

I drain the last of my wine to cover up my auditory relief and Faris finishes his too. He makes one last lemon-puckered face as he touches my shoulder, rounding his long fingers around it and giving me a squeeze. "Come on, let's get out of here. I need a decent drink."

His contact lingers. While it elicits another instant physical response, I don't twitch, jerk, or shudder, only revel in this subtle, yet stronger sensation. A tingle travels in two distinct routes from my shoulder: one path to the tips of my fingers and the other to my crotch. My head and body simultaneously turn to ether, floating pleasantly light above the bed.

I've no handle on either my reactions to his touch or my emotions. If I did possess the power to sway them, I would have saved myself from the heartache brought on by a lifetime of unrequited crushes. I could make myself fall back in love with my husband and force my more-than-crush feelings for Faris to disappear. Mere mortal I am, I do not control the yearnings of the heart. I can, however, control how I act on my emotions.

But I'm not going to do that. The good angel perched on my right shoulder flew away the moment Faris and I bumped into each other on July 5th. Should he at some point make a move, I'm all in, guilt free in my desires.

The smell and intangible heaviness of potential sex diffuses throughout the room, but neither of us acts on it. My marriage reigns miserable. It is, essentially, over for me. It may not be legally finished, yet, but I'm checked out emotionally.

It's been over for ages. If I'd spoken this truth to Jason when I first felt it, the marriage would be a tangible "no more" rather than this abstract. I want to kiss Faris, wrap my arms around his body, tackle him to the bed.

But, and a big "but" at that, the marriage is not "no more." My legal husband still considers us to be a happily married woman and man.

And the truth hovers over me and Faris.

Instead of kissing him, I bounce off the bed and grab my coat. "Let's go."

Chapter 31

Nicknamed "The World's Most Famous Arena," Madison Square Garden takes over two city blocks in the heart of New York City. Electrical placards illuminate the front façade and display the night's entertainment. Prior to these four shows, Phish has played The Garden twenty-seven times and has celebrated the New Year here a lucky number seven December 31sts. Seeing the band's name emblazoned on the flashing lights fills me with childlike glee. Simple pleasures for a happy life.

I'm also pleased with our spot, located in the lowest level of seats in section 116. Not only are we close to the aisle—a quick escape to the bathrooms and concessions—but we're Page side, sure to offer clear and unobstructed sights of my favorite pianist.

These are my first indoor Phish shows since I was at this very venue (almost) exactly two years ago, on December 31, 2011. Inside Phish presents differently than outdoor Phish, offering superior sounds and stronger visions of their incomparable light show. We're positioned to have perfect views of the latter.

The band's lighting director, Chris Kuroda, has been at the helm of their visuals for over two decades and is able to anticipate their every note, cuing the beams to shine and change with perfect timing to the music, even the improvised jams. The lights can morph in an instant as if breathing along with the band, going from hundreds of individual spears of purple shining on stage to lasers of green beaming into the crowd, channeling the Mardi Gras spirit with purple, green and gold parades of color, transforming to speak directly to me in my favorite shades of green and orange, then shifting to an eerie yet illuminating wave of red. The spectacle pierces eyes as deeply as the music penetrates ears. Sometimes I close my eyes to hear the music deeper, but tonight I'll keep them fixed on stage to behold CK5's wizardry.

I've commenced my pre-show rituals of bathroom and beer run and I whip out my iPod (still no iPhone) to capture some sharper-than-my-dumb-phone, yet still heavily pixelated, selfies of me and Faris, a ruse to get close to him.

"Smile Faris," I command, and he obliges, tipping his head so that it touches mine.

He seems looser than he was an hour ago, no longer stiffening at our contact. We'd stopped at a bar en route to the venue to clear our palates of the sickening sweetness of my White Elephant wine. Through two pints of pale ale, Faris had regaled me with stories of growing up in Kuwait.

"The first time I ate bacon, I was at a sleepover at my friend's house," he started his first story. "She offered me the devil's meat at breakfast, and I couldn't pass up on it. Temptation, right? Well, as soon as I got back home, I got sick with the stomach flu. It would be years before I touched pork again."

"Talk about instant karma," I had laughed.

His next story was even funnier.

"I was in Model United Nations in high school and every year we went to Amsterdam for a Model United Nations conference."

"Man, the best my shitty high school offered was a springtime trip to DC."

"The first time I ate mushrooms was on that trip. I ate an eighth myself at the hotel and lost my mind. I communed with a shaman inside the bathroom for hours and went through like six pairs of socks."

"Were you throwing them at people?"

"No, my feet kept getting hot, so I'd take my socks off. But then they'd get cold, and I'd put on a fresh pair."

I cracked up. Fueled with the liquid courage of beer, I leaned over him as I cackled. The laughter poured out of me with my forehead propped on his shoulder. I anticipated a return touch with an arm around my shoulder or on my knee. Instead, the foundation beneath my head moved and Faris stood up.

"We should head over to the venue," he said.

He'd walked half a step ahead of me the entire way to The Garden. Had I fucked things up for us? Did I make him feel uncomfortable? Maybe I had misread the signs. Goddammit. I should have stuck to my original plan and waited for him to make the move, if there was even a move meant to be made.

But, with our heads pressed together, looking at the blurry photos on my tiny iPod screen, things between us seem back to normal. I relax, as calm a person vibrating with the tingling energy of desire can be. Even with my trembling, I feel euphoric, as though I'm mere feet away from the stage, not hundreds.

The first set passes in a booze and pheromone influenced blur. Though I'm focused on the music, I'm unable to get completely lost in it, too aware of Faris's presence, the inches that separate us, that it's only he and I together, no Kylie, or his sister, or any of my friends to buffer and distract. Because we're squeezed into seats and not spread on a lawn or dance floor, my shoulder grazes his arms continuously, my hips bump back and forth into his leg, my right hand continues to brush his back and belly. With such limited room to move, it's all by accident. Every thirty seconds, I tap his body and a charge runs through me, igniting my insides whenever we make contact.

I'm convinced Faris senses his effect on me. How can he not? I feel so electrified that I could help power Phish's light show. He's a static fan today, bouncing his head to the music without moving any of his limbs but doesn't complain about my constant body bumping, and though we exchange words and smiles when stoked for a song ("It's Ice" followed by "Gumbo," yes!) he ignores my dancing, my touching, my body, for the entire set. There's no hand on my back or shoulder, no hip bumping back into me. He's treating me like a platonic friend, exactly as our relationship has always been. What happened to the man that an hour ago had pressed the side of his head against mine?

"No dancing from you, huh, Faris?" I say to him at the end of the set, trying to discern his stiffness.

"There's no room," he says, pointing to the inches of concrete our feet are allotted to move in. "Besides, you're doing enough for both of us."

"Come on, give a girl a little action. A little twirl or a shoulder tap. Let me know you're feeling the music." I stand up in the space he's pointing to and bop around, modeling the actions I recite.

Touch me, please, touch me!

"I'll show you action. If you keep bumping into me, I'm gonna toss you on stage," he teases and grabs my upper arm around the bicep. It's the most contact we've had all show, but he releases me too quickly.

"Oh please! Throw me right by Page!" I say. *Or throw me down on this beer and grime covered concrete floor and make out with me.*

Set break ends and I've made no ground with Faris. Trying not to let his abrupt indifference fuck with my headspace, I turn my attention to the stage. The band picks up their instruments and plays a short, ambient jam that unfolds into a classic "Down with Disease," a song frequently extended to eclectic and dark improvised jams. I, of zero musical talent, frequently wonder how four men can create such intricate, layered sounds with a guitar, bass, drums, and piano.

This version of the song transports us to space. I soar. Though my body remains tethered to the floor, I feel as if I am floating around and above it. My eyes stare, transfixed to the stage, beholden to the mesmerizing lights flashing on, in front of, and behind the band members and glowing out into the audience. The beams, shards, and angled rays of blue and purple further propel us into the outer atmospheres above.

This is the start to a set that demands reverence: ninety-minutes of music consisting of a mere six songs, with the end of one song seamlessly segueing into the next one. There's no clear ending or beginning to the music in such a harmonious stream of consciousness, sure to cause confusion for the uninitiated and roars and hollers of approval from the zealots.

We're offered zero breathers once an almost twenty-minute "Down with Disease" ends, for after it comes the dark, familiar guitar licks that begin "Carini." The song's lyrics about Lucy taking a walk and ending up dead match the evil and psychedelic tones of a song that climaxes in a crescendo of madness. I'll never grow sick of hearing it.

Too bad I miss it.

I turn to Faris as soon as I hear those oozy, murky riffs that open the song and lock eyes with him. His mood seems to have worsened. At least during the first set he wore his usual Phish inspired ear-to-ear grin. Now his straight mouth expression speaks with a silent seriousness.

Uh oh, what the fuck happened now? He's debating to tell me how we're friends and that we will only be friends. That I touch him way too much and it makes him uncomfortable. That I'm disrespecting my husband and now he's unsure if he even wants to continue our friendship because of it.

Instead of expressing my pleasure in the song choice, I pivot to ask him what's wrong, otherwise I'll obsess over what he could possibly be thinking about. Maybe he's capable of reading my mind because, as I open my mouth to speak, he's bending down to hear me better. But no, he's not listening to me. He's turning to me, and his lips press on mine. His mouth opens, turning the kiss from a friendly and gentle peck on the lips to a fervent exploration.

I've been burning for this man, absolutely yearning for his touch—this very touch—but right here, right now? If this were Jason, so clueless to the unspoken Phish rules, I'd have admonished him to leave me alone. *Pay attention to the music!*

But this is Faris. He knows them, as do I. When the band is playing you don't talk, you try not to leave for the bathroom or to get a drink. You certainly don't make out. Yet, I eagerly kiss him back. I wrap my hands around the back of his neck to pull him down, closer to me. I can't remember if I'd ever been kissed with such passion. Nor can I recall when anything has made me feel as rapturous as I do now.

I will forgo all Phish rules for this.

But what do any of us know about the rules of marriage? I've conducted five years of personal experimentation and I'm still not aware of the dos and don'ts that make-or-break wedded bliss. Nor do I know how to escape an unhappy one. This kiss, something I've been waiting for and wanting to happen for months, years even, must break every single one of the rules. But all my fantasies and daydreams, evolving from my first vision of a simple kiss in Saratoga Springs, have boosted me through my disappointing life and marriage reset, while my friendship with Faris offered me a greater reprieve from my new existence. To think a random set break encounter launched what could actually be my second chance.

And so, I don't withdraw from Faris and scold him to listen to the fucking music and to keep his fucking hands off me, a married woman. Instead, I wrap my arms around him and kiss him back as ardently as he kisses me. His mouth tastes familiar and offers me warm comfort. If there's anything I value more in this moment than Phish's music, it's this relationship finally—*finally*—evolving to the physical.

My mind explodes with the surrealness of this moment. *How can this be happening? Wait, is this happening, or am I making it up?* My brain rambles on a litany of stream of consciousness *holy shits* until I tame it enough to enjoy the present. Faris's normally clean-shaven face has grown several days past due, and the stubble pricks roughly on my face. I welcome the abrasiveness. The subtle pain heightens my senses and adds to my pleasure. It also allows me to register reality.

I briefly wonder what the fans sitting next to and behind us think.

I refuse to break our connection and I don't pull away from Faris's embrace. He doesn't back away either. The music becomes the background soundtrack to our innocent yet insistent make-out session. We remain intertwined through all of it, from "Carini" and into "Waves" and "Twist" and "Golgi Apparatus." We don't part our lips until we hear the band play the abrupt ending to "David Bowie."

We miss the entire set.

I have no regrets.

Chapter 32

"Let's continue this back at the hotel," Faris wiggles his eyebrows at me suggestibly.

Show over, he and I stand outside The Garden. The chill of the air doesn't seem to sting as harshly as it did hours ago.

He likes me. He really, really likes me.

At least that's what all the signs are pointing to. Six months of daily texting, occasional phone calls, and not enough Phish meetups have finally culminated with that satisfying ninety-minute smooching session. Now to take things to my ultimate NC-17 bedroom fantasy.

My synapses and clitoris send the identical message to my brain. "Fuck yes," I respond immediately.

Back in the hotel room, I switch a single lamp on. It throws off a warm glow and provides enough light for our eyes to absorb one another. Faris takes off his coat. I remove mine as well, tossing it in the corner of the room. With the first move made by him at the show, I don't feel the need to hold back anymore. Like a tiger stalking its prey, I push him down on the bed and attempt to look my sexiest as I crawl up the length of his body until I'm straddling him. My mouth covers his, kissing him with an unbridled urgency to make up for the months of denying ourselves this physical step in our undeniable connection.

I unbutton his flannel, clumsily removing the T-shirt below, both of us laughing when it sticks around his neck. The shirt is tossed to the floor. My lips brush the left side of his collarbone and I start to trail my kisses down his chest. His flesh presses against the thin cotton of my hoodie, but I need to feel him with my own body, for his warmth to radiate onto my bare skin. I draw myself away for a moment to remove my outer layer and he helps me with the rest, taking off my tank top and bra beneath with a bit more grace than I had with his clothes. The satisfaction of our naked abdomens pressed up against one another is immediate, and I want the rest of him right now.

"Do you have a condom?" I ask him.

"No, I don't. Do you?"

"Why would I have a condom?"

"Why would I have a condom?" He echoes.

"What do we do?"

I'd been lectured about AIDS and all its STD cousins since I was a young teenager. Throw on my deep disdain for possible motherhood (and my accidental pregnancy) to almost always ensure sex with a partner was protected. Yet, here we are, condomless and I desire this man more than any other intimate moment of my lifetime. Am I going to turn down sex with him because of our lack of protection?

Fuck no.

"If you're okay not using a condom, I am too. I haven't had sex in a while, and I've been tested recently," he says.

He'd never given me any reason to doubt him before. I believe him. "Well, I've been with the same person for over six years and have also been tested. I know I'm STD free." We both ignore the allusion to my husband.

"Are you on birth control?"

"Nope." I stopped years ago. Fucking stupid hormones. It was easy to use condoms with Jason for how infrequently we had sex.

"I can pull out."

Faris's level headedness and dependability have shone through in all other situations. I trust him not to fail on this promise. I kiss him deeply in response. It rightens our headspace, sets our attention on one another and our bodies. I unbuckle his belt, unbutton and remove his jeans with our mouths still pressed against each other. Like his shirt, they get stuck, this time around his knees. He takes care to remove them properly, while I lose the rest of my clothes.

Faris watches me rip off my socks. "Okay, I guess I'll take mine off too." He tosses the discarded pair at my naked chest with a chuckle, but the socks miss their target.

"Eww, keep your stink off of me," I say and lightly slap his hip.

His naked hip.

We're completely exposed to one another. While Faris's eyes take me in, I look back at him. My eyes immediately focus on the body part that will bring me the most pleasure.

I climb back on top and grab him. The first joining of my body with another person's is one of my favorite parts of sex. I love the physical aspect, that initial fullness of being entered, but there's an emotional side as well; I feel closest to my partner in that instant. I slowly place Faris where I want him, and he finishes our merging with a force I feel throughout my entire being.

With that singular, fluid move, our relationship is changed forever.

♫

I wake up far earlier than I would have liked to. Early Monday morning sunlight, bright enough to blaze through my closed eyes, peeks through the sheer curtain hung over the single window. We must have passed out without shutting the blackout layers. Hey, at least the sun came out, though it will do little to heat the day.

I snuggle under the covers, Faris passed out and snoring on my right side. Curling my left arm over his waist, I spoon him as I had on the air mattress in Demaris's living room. I kiss his broad back, intending to take advantage of both my early wake-up and our birthday suit slumber. He stirs, but doesn't open his eyes. I apply more pressure with my next round of kisses but fail again at getting a response.

I move to his neck. My lips brush the stubble prickling beneath his jaw. This provokes a more positive reaction. Faris rolls over onto his back. Yes, go time!

Instead, he opens his eyes a crack and mumbles, "Rachael, please let me sleep. I'm so tired."

How can he be so sleepy? I'm naked. He's naked. Let's be naked together. I'm riding high from our encounter—and possibly still beer buzzed—and I need to be with him again as soon as possible. Right now! And yet he sleeps, denying me in a similar manner to how Jason last rejected me. How is Faris refusing me, especially now? We have months of sexual tension to release.

I'm wide awake but attempt to steal more shut eye to cushion me for the long day ahead. When sleep doesn't return, I acquiesce and rise to the day, thinking a warm bath may soothe me back to bed.

The Club's bathroom is cold and cavernous, the tiles frigid beneath my bare feet. I turn the knobs of the tub, differentiating the hot faucet from the cold one. Once discovered, I let it flow. The sound of the water pouring into the wide porcelain rectangle reverberates off the bathroom walls and tiled floor. I wonder if, and hope, the sound will rouse Faris. I expect him to burst in through the door I've intentionally left unlocked, swoop me up, newlywed-style over the threshold, and have his way with me.

He doesn't. I clumsily climb into the tub. The hot water envelopes me as warmly as I want Faris to. I slide down so my entire body is submerged with my face poking above the surface and my hair floating buoyantly around me. As a kid, I would float down to this particular position and imagine myself a mermaid, loving the way my hair felt as it drifted above my head, soft and swollen with water. Eight-year-old me envisioned I looked as majestic as Ariel perched on a rock with the waves crashing behind her. Now, I want to look as sexy as a mermaid, floating around in my adult-fantasy-turned-real world, waiting for my lover to awaken and come find me.

And still, he doesn't. I continue to soak in the tub, intermittently turning the hot water on as the water cools. This solo time gives me the opportunity to reflect on the events from the night. The disbelief causes me to feel out of body. I float above the tub, watching myself relax in the hot water. Here is my moment; something I had long wished and waited for. With all the odds against us, without any guarantee of coming to fruition, it had happened. I can barely believe it!

This amazing reality brings me back inside my physical self. I gaze over at my naked body and run my hands down the length of my abdomen and I think of how Faris touched me. I can't wait for him to stroke me again.

My thoughts drift briefly to Jason, and what this means for our marriage. I try to keep them from invading my bliss and disbelief, to stop the guilt from consuming me. Like a bad psychedelic trip, they loop in my head anyway. *You're the worst human in the world, Rachael. How could you cheat on your husband? Who does that? What are you going to do now?*

What am I going to do now?

Such a weighty question could, should, invade my head space. Long ago, a good friend gave me solid advice about LSD and mushrooms: Once the slightest smidge of darkness creeps in, you need to think about something else. Channel the positive, you'll have a good time. I picture my friend and her advice now and turn my thoughts to Faris and the next two days we have together, vowing to stay present in each moment, to not think of the implications our actions have, or of what lies ahead for either of us until they're through.

I emerge from the tub and wrap myself in a cheap and threadbare towel. Sleep is no closer than it had been forty-five minutes earlier, but I'm going to crawl in bed and snuggle up to Faris anyway.

I open the heavy bathroom door and find his eyes open and on me. He smiles sleepily and opens his arms. He's awake now and doesn't disappoint in showing his excitement for our newfound connection.

Chapter 33

Faris and I wander back to The Club in the first hours of New Year's Day. Close to two o'clock, it's later than our returns of the previous two nights. Phish's holiday shows offer three sets of music instead of the standard two and involve a "gag," or a pre-planned theatrical event. Tonight's gag, an homage to their thirty years as a band, may have been the simplest and most low key of their history, but, like a perfectly executed rib eye dinner, it was absolutely unforgettable.

In between sets one and two, an old white box truck with a simple label of JEMP (Jon, Ernest (Trey) Mike, and Page) written across the box was carefully driven into the middle of the floor at Madison Square Garden. The four musicians ascended to the top of the truck and took their places behind basic rigs and microphones held in place by hockey sticks, a throwback to their original stage set in the early '80s.

Clocking in at over an hour and composed of vintage Phish songs written no later than the early '90s, the classic set included favorites such as "Reba," the song Faris's dog is named for, the dark and oozing "Split Open and Melt," and the ultra-rare (but played twice this year) "Icculus." "Reba" contains the most melodic and exquisite composed instrumentation in all of music's history. I'm unable to hear the middle jam segment of the song without producing an eye full of liquid emotion. And to think in my beginning days of fandom, I considered it a bathroom break song.

Midnight struck shortly after set three began and Faris and I kissed tenderly as hundreds (thousands?) of rainbow-colored balloons fell from the ceiling and gently rained upon every person in attendance. *How many more kisses do we get to share?* I wondered, my thoughts stealing me away from such a sweet turning of the year for a moment too long.

A clock set on stage had displayed and counted down 2013's final moments. It was a tangible device keeping track of our fairy tale, the inevitable ending approaching much too fast for my liking. From the moment Faris and I met at the train station on Sunday, my internal timer began ticking, keeping track of the days, hours, minutes, seconds to Wednesday morning, when our New Year's "weekend" ends. I attempted to live in the moment, enjoy every meal eaten together, our many hand-in-hand strolls through the West Village and midtown, our trysts in the hotel, but I could not stop my brain from its constant awareness of this finite time. I was much more cognizant of the hours passing than Cinderella had been at the ball. Three more sleeps together, two more sleeps together. Now we are down to one final sleep and this last stroll to The Club.

Bittersweet, I want nothing more than to get back as quickly as we can and close ourselves off from the rest of the city. I can't wait to press my body against his, feel the heat radiating off his skin, the weight of him on top of me. But the sooner we get back and make love, the faster sleep, and the morning, will come.

By staying present, or trying to, these past three days, I hadn't given any thought to our, to my, next steps, and with my fantasies becoming reality, I hadn't wanted to awaken the light-sleeping bitch that my anxiety is by thinking of a plan. Old habits die hard. Anytime my brain wanted to think about my future, mine and Faris's future, mine and Jason's future, I repressed it for later thinking and discussion.

During our drunken stumble back to the hotel, we trade banal lines concerning the show without mentioning anything that truly matters.

"Dude, 'Fuck Your Face!' That was my first one," I say when I should have said *I don't love my husband and I want to be with you. We can do this. Give me some time.*

And while I want him to say, *Rachael, I like you. What do you need to do so we can be together?* He answers, "That was my first time too. And what did you think of 'Fuego'? That's my favorite of their new songs."

Maybe he's thought about our future as little as I had, but I'm doubtful. Logical Faris must be thinking of what happens next. Perhaps he, too, is avoiding a difficult conversation. But if he isn't bringing anything up, neither am I.

In the hotel and on the elevator, we kiss for the thirty seconds it takes to get to our floor. I follow him to our room, my arms wrapped around him from behind and linking at his chest, but into the bathroom he goes. Our connection breaks as he takes care of business, still in his thick Patagonia jacket.

I take my winter coat and hat off and throw them to the floor. Beneath my layers, I wear a red dress. It's the same red dress I wore on Christmas Eve, the dress that received a text of approval from Faris. I knew, once I received the *You look amazing* message from him, I would be wearing it tonight. A woman complimented me on it earlier at the show, while standing in line for beer.

"That dress is beautiful," she told me. "I hope you have a special kiss lined up for the New Year."

I felt the warm liquid of knowing comfort wash through me as I nodded and told her I did.

Alone in the hotel room, I run my arms down the sides of my hips and remove the sexy fitted sheath. There's no beer bottle-holding granny panties or joint-concealing sports bra beneath. I've planned my lingerie for the evening: a rarely worn black push-up and a black lace thong. Saving the best for last.

I light the candles we found yesterday. We had ventured out of our room later than anticipated on account of some lengthy post-bath fun. Before heading out for the day, curiosity got the best of us and we set about exploring The Club, wandering into a large open room on the lowest floor. Positioned dead center was a gigantic showpiece fireplace. Large windows, from which thick, cascading curtains were hung, lined the perimeter of walls. Mirrors almost as large as the windows interspersed between each one. It surely had to be one of the spaces where the Manhattanite women of the Republican party held their exclusive meetings and events.

"Are you two getting married?" I heard a male voice ask.

I looked around the massive room and spotted a hotel employee with a kind, grandfatherly face standing in the doorway from where we had entered. I must have looked confused at his question, for he explained more in the next inquiry.

"You two checking out wedding venues? You must be getting married, huh?"

I smiled and nodded at him, wanting to kiss him instead. Oh, wishful thinking. If only. "Yeah," was the only answer I could give him, afraid I was turning beet red at his mistaking us for a future bride and groom.

Grandpa smiled at us. "Good luck with everything." He turned and left.

Faris and I looked at each other and chuckled, though we didn't say anything. I didn't know how to react to such an encounter, but, like a mating bird, there was something bright and shiny to distract me.

"Oh, look." I pointed at a handful of discarded candleholders piled in the hallway between the banquet room and stairs that would lead us back to the main reception area. The cylinders were made of shiny mosaic tiles, and each held a white, six-inch candle. Impulsively, I grabbed two and stashed them back in our room before leaving the hotel. When we returned later, I lit both and placed one on the desk and another on the bed stand closest to the bathroom. They set the darkened room in a romantic yet sexy glow as we undressed one another. The sex that followed was the best I had had in both far and recent memory.

I'm wet thinking about putting the candles to the same use.

I debate how to position myself best for maximum sex appeal and not look contrived or cheesy. On the bed, hands arranged above my head with a minimal bend to my elbows? On my hands and knees? Bent over the bed so that my practically bare ass beckons to him when he emerges from the bathroom? Oh, how I would hate for him to call me out for my pre-planned centerfold, but we never take one another too seriously. There's a small chance he will.

I debate what to do for too long; Faris walks out of the bathroom and lies on the bed, still fully zipped in his winter coat.

It's an odd maneuver. *Why are you getting in bed fully, fully clothed?* But I don't give it any thought. I approach him from the bottom of the bed. I crawl up his body in a similar move used on our first night together. I kiss his neck once, twice, on one side then move my mouth to the other, kiss him there, and settle on his lips. Innocent closed mouth pecks at first. His lips barely move. I open my mouth, expecting him to copy, but his lips remain an unresponsive dead fish.

Frustrated, I sit up and take both his arms. I place them on my breasts, which bulge, unnaturally perky, from the tight band of black lace pushing them up and together. I know I look good. Why is he resisting me?

He withdraws his arms almost immediately from my chest. The ultimate rejection. I stare at him, stung. My alcohol stunted brain processes things at the rate of a toddler wading through waist high water.

"What's going on?" I ask.

He doesn't look at me, nor does he answer. I press him again. "Faris, what the fuck is wrong with you?"

He looks at me and finally answers. "We can't do this, Rachael."

I look down at him, still zipped up to his neck. His coat closes him off like a fortress I'm besieged to, keeping me from not just his body, but to his heart as well. He won't, or can't, reveal any emotions to me.

"What does that mean?"

He gestures to me as I still straddle his hips, my body upright, then back to himself. "This. Us. We can't do this."

With that, I understand what he means. He is indeed refusing me, denying us a final chance of pleasure in being together. We've spent days together as a couple, reveling in not only physical intimacies, but all aspects of a romantic relationship. The past three days found us immersed in dozens of personal conversations—though none about us—and we cozily shared meals and drinks, explored New York City by foot and subway, and took part in our Phish obsession as giddily as a partnered duo would. Why would he allow such a façade just to do this?

I feel more than unwanted at this realization. My heart skips a beat and seems to freeze. It waits for its removal from my chest, knowing it will be on full display for the two of us to see before being discarded to the floor. It's a painful taunting, something a cruel owner would do to his dog with a bone. *Why show me what we could be like, Faris, if you were going to break my heart?*

Tears quietly run down my face and fall on my open neck as my legs remain locked around him. I feel exposed. Vulnerable. It's not because I'm perched practically naked on top of him, but because I hate revealing how much his words affect me. My intent is to appear strong, that I agree with him and no, we can't do this, but my tears disprove any of it.

Rolling off and away from him and the bed, I stand upright beside it. I should cover my body with a T-shirt or blanket. Instead, I compose myself and look him in the eye. Anger bubbles inside of me. "So, we're going to spend this entire time together as a couple and now you're rejecting me?"

He looks back at me. "You're married, Rachael."

"That didn't stop you before."

He sits up and unzips his coat to remove, finally, that hard, outer layer. "Because I do want this, Rachael. I want us to be together, but I've been thinking about it since Sunday. You're married. We can't be together."

Ah, his dependability, one of the things I love most about him, presents as integrity now, and it's breaking my heart. "But I don't want him. I want you."

There, I've said it aloud to someone else other than myself or Kylie. I say it to the person it matters to the most. Out into the open world, the confession of my feelings soars loose. Will it now take flight and encourage me to do something, to act for the sake of these feelings?

It's his turn to challenge me. "What happens when I go back to Denver and you go back to Vegas, back to your husband? What happens next?"

And here's his logic. It's come out to talk sense, and I want no part of it. I don't respond. Will we continue with our affair? Will I leave my miserable marriage and try to make it work with Faris? Will I continue dredging on with my status quo?

My tears return as I confess to Faris. "I don't know."

He sighs and opens his arms to me. I return to them, burrow into the escape they've provided. I kiss his cheek. Close my eyes. We fall asleep wrapped up in one another, he in his clothes and I still in my bra and panties. Our tiredness from the day's events and exhaustion of our emotions push pause on continuing this conversation.

His phone wakes us a few hours later. Leave it to Faris to remember to set his alarm. Without doing so, he would have risked missing his flight.

I'm feeling out of body again, only now it's due to pain and not pleasure. Still drunk, I watch my motions from above, the harried woman with mascara caked to the dry skin under her puffy eyes, hurriedly brushing her teeth and changing clothes, not exchanging any words with Faris, robotically shoving dirty garments and toiletries into a suitcase without bothering to organize anything.

I barely give a thought to what transpired hours earlier. I'm numb. It's the one singular positive from the amount of booze I consumed the previous day. My brain isn't ready to focus and I'm not going to force it.

We check out of The Club and hail a taxi. It'll drop me off at the Port Authority and then deposit Faris at LaGuardia. We're silent until the taxi pulls to a stop in front of the bus station. Time for this magical ball experience to be over. The pumpkin doesn't just materialize. It's rotting.

"So now what?" I turn to him at the same moment I open the taxi door.

"I don't know. Like Phish says, 'if life were easy...' But it's not. I don't know what's going to happen."

"I don't know either," I reply, resigned. Fucking fool.

I leave the car. Faris exits his side and meets me for the briefest of hugs, weak of all feelings, and is back in the taxi, gone from my sight and touch. Is he feeling as dejected and heartbroken as I am, or does he want to get far, far away from me? There's no way for me to tell; his face betrays not a single emotion.

The car drives off, and I watch until it's out of my vision. He's gone. It, whatever it may be, is officially over.

Chapter 34

Between the hard plastic chair I'm slumped in and the overhead fluo-rescent lighting boring into my eyes, it's as if I'm in an interrogation room. The Port Authority bus station buzzes with the traffic of holiday revelers heading home, causing my already pounding head to throb more. Slowly starting to process the last eight hours, I register one single emotion: abject misery.

Phish had played "Icculus" last night, Trey yelling at us to "read the fucking book," referencing his made-up (and integral to Phish lore) *Helping Friendly Book.* Its pages contain all the universe's mysteries, most importantly, the secret to eternal joy and never-ending splendor. Trey's lyrics could have been aimed at me; I absorbed an in-between-the-lines meaning as he screamed the words.

"Read it." (*I've had my second chance.*)

"Read it." (*Phish has had a second chance.*)

"Read it." (*This is your second chance.*)

"Read the fucking book." (*Take it! Do what you need to get that second chance.*)

Read the fucking book, Rachael. Since July, the universe has been presenting me with the ingredients for a happy life, and still, I don't know how I'm going to proceed. Now that I'm shifting back to reality, what am I going to do in Vegas? What will I say to Jason? Am I ready, and brave enough, to end our marriage? And is that really how Faris and I are parting ways? Am I going to see him again? Are we still friends?

I chew on a greasy ham, egg, and cheese bagel and wash it down with a bitter slug of coffee, all the while internally asking myself these things in an unsettling spiral during the hours of waiting for my bus and the travel back to Scranton. If I'd been present for the "Icculus" at Dick's and had heard Trey demand I "read the book" then, would I have started 2014 with my problems resolved and already behind me?

Mom picks me up, all smiles at the bus station and obliges my request for Chinese takeout, even though she cooked the traditional New Year's Day meal of pork and cabbage. We eat two big meals that afternoon.

Tomorrow is my final day in Pennsylvania; I head back to Vegas on Friday evening, and I'm determined to know what the fuck I'll be doing with my life by then. My computer stays on my lap while I watch movies with my parents and inhale *lo mein* noodles—later when I'm hungry again, it's pork ribs and sauerkraut—clandestinely googling away. *I'm having an affair. What can I do? I left my husband for my lover. Success stories of women who left their husbands.* Each nuance to this search yields the same websites and articles, but I read them all again and again and again.

I'm not just looking for advice, but for a crystal ball to predict my future based on which adventure I opt for. Will I choose silence and wait, hoping for Jason to join the army? End things and be alone? End things and try to pursue something with Faris? This decision won't come from the mouths of internet strangers or from my parents, who sit three feet away from me and are unaware of my inner turmoil or my secret research, but from me. I need to trust in my heart to give me the right answer and for my brain to establish the way to get there. But while my heart may be screaming its wants at me, my brain isn't listening.

Chapter 35

It's Friday and I'm not sitting down with Jason having the most difficult conversation of my life, nor am I unpacking my suitcase and settling back into my routines and rhythms. Nope, instead, I'm stranded overnight in Chicago.

My flight out of the Wilkes-Barre Scranton Airport was delayed and I had a tight connection at O'Hare. I almost made it. When my plane touched down in Chicago, I immediately turned on my phone and received the alert minutes later that my flight to Vegas had already taken to the skies.

So here I am, trapped in the Windy City.

Serves me right. I left earlier that afternoon an emotional wreck, no tears shed but weeping internally, needing a force as strong as the jaws of life to rip me from my parent's embraces, yet I broke my promise to myself and am no closer to a decision.

One would think my choice shone crystal clear after Faris stated, "I want to be with you, Rachael, but you're married. We cannot have a relationship," but it's not that easy. The move to Vegas, Jason's citizenship, my teaching career. What was supposed to be my progress has stunted everything for me. How can I acquiesce, at thirty-one years young, to continue leading such an unfulfilling and lonely existence? Yet, how do I go about deconstructing something that's so new? Something I so meticulously planned for. Something I thought would change everything.

Either choice, to stay and wait it out with Jason or to cut the torn and badly frayed wedding knot, will be the emotional equivalent of having my heart ripped from my chest. If I stay, and Jason waffles—like so many other of his considerations—on the army, my misery continues. And leaving opens a door to the great unknown. Everything undetermined, I'm terrified, exacerbated by my always-present anxiety, of not knowing what will come. What will happen to Jason? And me? I have no influence over whatever follows once I set the course.

Goddammit. What the fuck am I going to do now?

I haven't deplaned and am sitting in the back of the aircraft. With no one in the seat beside me, I unclip the tray table, prop my elbows on it, and support my head in my hands, taking deep breaths and refusing to cry. Silver lining this happenstance, it seems the universe granted me more contemplation time. And I'll have a free hotel room to do it in. I discover this when I step into the terminal, where a woman in a navy suit stands at the jetway's threshold.

"Who are you?" she asks.

"Rachael. Rachael Wesley."

"Here you are." She hands me an envelope. "Your plane ticket for a flight tomorrow and vouchers for food and your hotel room tonight."

"Oh, wow, thank you!" I accept the packet and step aside to inspect its contents. Talk about an anomaly of customer service, my name is written in black ink cursive on the front and inside are two meal tickets, twenty-five bucks apiece, a voucher for the Holiday Inn Express, and a ticket to McCarren Airport leaving at 8:30 tomorrow morning.

The woman tells me a shuttle will transport me to the hotel and I head in its pointed direction. I text Jason, who is expecting a call to pick me up, to notify him of my prolonged delay. He texts back instantly. How rare for him! *Oh, I'm sorry. Be careful and I'll see you tomorrow, my honey.*

Would Faris have been more curious about my stranded situation? Call instead of texting? Try to find a flight to get me home as soon as possible? I know the answer is yes.

Outside, the frigid cold is almost overwhelming and I'm most relieved when the shuttle pulls up. I sit in the back, absorbing the heat on full blast, and am dropped off at the hotel in minutes. The late hour proves a boon for me; check in is immediate, and I enter my room as quickly as I breezed through Scranton airport security screening.

Without hopping in the shower to cleanse myself from my evening travels, I wash my face, strip down to nakedness, and hop beneath the soft covers, too tired to search through my suitcase for something to sleep in. I did grab my book, though. I'm halfway through Meg Wolitzer's *The Interestings* and want to read it until my eyes close. The trouble is it causes me to wallow. The main character, Jules, is also stuck in a bad marriage and considering an affair with an old friend and I can't escape my reality in it; I picture that awkward goodbye with Faris, of the life in Vegas I'm heading back to.

Do I really need to decide my fate at this very moment? I can choose tomorrow, next week, a month from now. I've survived with my charade of feelings for over a year. What are another few days?

I search the television for something to soothe me to sleep and find an episode of Anthony Bourdain in Peru on CNN's *Parts Unknown*. The TV screen displays a crisp image of the man who introduced me to the wonders found through travel, and, in a butterfly effect of sorts, landed me in this hotel room. Dressed in a striped button-down shirt more suited for a city stroll than a hike, Tony stands alongside his best buddy and fellow chef, Eric Ripert, among two other men, preparing to go on a search for elusive Peruvian white cacao. How fitting, I purchased a bar of dark chocolate with one of my food vouchers on my way out of the airport. I unwrap the bar and pop the first square of chocolate in my mouth as Tony and Eric begin their trek through the Andes.

Like the book I was trying to read, the show offers little distraction. It places my huge real-world problems at the forefront in Rachael's land of make believe; watching a few minutes triggers my brain to churn out a fantasy. It's not a sexy one, well, aside from the handsome man I'm crouching next to, huffing and puffing halfway up a mountain in the foothills of the Andes. I've replaced Eric, so instead of Tony bitching over how fit his Frenchmen buddy is, he's chastising me.

"Rachael," he says once he catches his breath. "What the fuck are you doing?"

"Umm, I'm climbing a mountain." Why am I always so literal?

"No, with Jason. Why haven't you ended things? What the fuck are you waiting for?"

I shrug. "I don't know. I guess I'm waiting for him to sign with the army."

He sits on a rock, wipes the sweat off his forehead. His thick, graying, practically white, hair is glistening from his exertion. "It's not like you to wait on other people."

"I was stuck in Scranton for years because of him."

"But that changed, right?" Tony speaks forcefully. "You forced a different direction. You didn't want to live there any longer, so you made a plan to get you where you wanted to be. Why can't you do that now?"

I sit too, not on a rock but directly in the dirt across from him, and bend my knees to my chest as I explain. "But all these recent things, I don't know what I can do about them. I've been wanting to settle down and find a place to call home, but I hate living in Vegas. I've been waiting for my crush on Faris to disappear, but it only intensified. And my marriage? Talk about a disaster. I was insane to think the move would save us."

"At least you tried something. But why aren't you doing anything to change things now?" His voice rises even louder, and he holds his hands out to me, palms upturned.

"I told you, I'm hoping that Jason will join the army."

"Did you ever think he's waiting for you to tell him you support him? That you're on board with it. Maybe you're what's holding him back. You're screwing him over by not being truthful with him. That's not fair. Besides, why are you counting on him to make a change for you?"

I start to cry. It's my own fucking imagination, and I'm bawling my eyes out in front of my brash idol. Guess it makes it all the more life-like. If this conversation was taking place in real life, I'd be sobbing. I cry too much anymore. "I'm so scared. I don't know how to tell him. What am I going to say? That I don't love him anymore and that I'm in love with somebody else. I can't do that. It'll break his heart."

"You wouldn't necessarily have to say that. Things weren't good, even before Faris came into the picture." He eases up on me and uses a softer tone.

"But I don't want to be by myself either. I worry so much about being lonely and what that'll do to me."

"And you don't have to be. No one says you need to stay where you are. But think about this. Are you happy now?"

"No, I'm absolutely miserable, and I'm terrified I'll always be this miserable." I'm like a child, blubbering away without listening to the wisdom of someone who knows better.

"Listen to me. We only get this one life. You will only be Rachael Wesley once. Are you going to die disappointed in how you chose to live it and angry that you let that happen?" Tony smacks the dirt path beside him with his fist for emphasis.

"But it's too late. He just became a US citizen. We moved to Las Vegas five months ago. I had it all planned out. How do I change things now? I'm stuck." I close my eyes and shake my head, wishing things were anything but what they were.

"What? Is there a law that says you must stick to your plan? Will you get in trouble if you don't? You're not stuck, but you can't wait for others to do that for you. Stop being such a chicken. Remember, Rachael, you, and you alone, control the power to change things. Make life what you want it to be."

With that final bit of advice, Tony, the mountain, and its trees filled with cacao pods, Peru, everything fades away. I'm back in the Holiday Inn Express room. Present. Aware. Dare I say, empowered.

I visited with Kylie briefly yesterday. How could I leave without telling her what had happened in New York? She was thrilled, obviously, and though she encouraged me to act, "Rachael, it's now or never. Do it!" and despite my promise to have a plan in place before leaving Pennsylvania, I wasn't ready to discuss any possible scenario at length. She must have picked up on my reticence and didn't press me.

Kylie was the sole person I could confide in, and I missed the opportunity through my silent act of self-sabotage. Thank god for those second chances, for here, in the privacy of my brain, I had the chance and space to process, somewhat externally with a figmented Tony. I can make sense of things. Finally.

My husband and I don't connect over anything. We have nothing to talk about and don't engage in anything together. I turn(ed) to Faris for this. Phish shows? We've tried and he didn't enjoy them. Thankfully, I have a plethora of phamily to attend with. I use hiking groups since Jason doesn't want to trek anywhere with me. Key decisions, like figuring out a city to move to, were single-handedly left to me. I found us an apartment with the help of my father. I attended Anna's wedding, a top-tier family event, with my mother as my date. I read on the couch, and he watches sports. I connect with people through phone calls made from my flower table outside while he Skypes inside at the dining room table with friends back in Korea.

I don't have a husband. I have a roommate. A roommate I don't relate to. I'm terrified of being alone, but I'm ostensibly living single and surviving fine on my own.

The universe, in her wonderful wisdom and power, has been highlighting this alternative road for half a year. She offered me another course, sent me all the signs to take it, but it's up to me to make that choice. Sure, I've stumbled over the freshness of Jason's US citizenship, my job, my apartment lease, but each offers an opening elsewhere. Jason couldn't join the military without his citizenship. I can finish out the school year at Jesse Martin Elementary and use my experience there to land a teaching job in another city. My apartment lease runs for twelve months. No need to sign for one more year. Fuck this despairing loneliness. I'm going to a city filled with people I know, and I'm moving with my half of our newly purchased furniture.

All of this, it's all possible, but it's me, and me alone, who can set them into motion.

And though I don't know what the future holds for me and Faris, I don't care. No matter what happens next, whether Faris and I get together, or whether I am to be alone, I know I cannot continue my life with Jason.

Chapter 36

I would love to say I wake up feeling like a resolute woman, or that the old me, the fierce and independent woman who once moved across the world to realize a dream, is back. The truth is, when the morning arrives, I'm nothing but nervous.

Perhaps the shift to my former self occurred unnoticed because I'd never left. Through all of this, I've remained me, only my sure and confident side had been muted and in competition with her confused twin, this latter self juggling too many simultaneous life changes and a high school classroom's worth of emotions to realize what she needed to do to live happily and fulfilled. Wiser now (so I hope), I have the solution for this suffocating weight. I just need to carry it out.

After putting on the same clothes I wore the previous day, I make my way to the lobby minutes before the six o'clock shuttle picks me up. The opposite of last night, the lobby is packed with people headed to the airport aboard the van.

I rehearse what I plan on saying to Jason while on the crammed and boisterous ride, pausing while I check in and breeze through security. The speech resumes as I'm sitting at the gate. It's easier to organize my thoughts in the quiet corner than aboard the shuttle. I focus on my opening statement, paramount to how successful the worst conversation of my life will play out.

Should I come out and say it? "Jason, I think it's best if we split up."

Start with a bunch of positives and then break it to him. "I think you are one of the funniest and most intelligent people I know but we stopped working together a long time ago."

Encourage him. "Jason, go live your dream and join the army, but I'm not coming with you."

Be completely transparent and tell him the whole truth. "I am in love with someone else."

No, not that last one. No need to reveal an unnecessary detail. Tony, my subconscious, was right. Things were over long before Faris reentered the picture.

Though I practice my options (except for that final one), each one causes my stomach to turn and my heart to pound faster than a HIIT workout. I'm on the verge of a panic attack and I'm not even in Jason's presence yet. How am I going to initiate this conversation without having an anxiety induced heart attack?

Turbulence fills my flight to Vegas. It matches my inner chaos and deepens the pressure weighing on my brain and heart. Imagine the plane going down the instant I've made up my mind to move on with my life? I try to rehearse the various breakup scenarios in my head while the lead bird shakes, but my brain prefers to use its telekinetic powers to hold the plane in the sky instead. Fuck it. I'm optimistic that my mouth and brain will work in tandem to give Jason the news in the best way possible when I'm in his company.

We touch down safely and punctually at McCarran. It's only 10:30 a.m. and I don't text Jason to pick me up, I call him. I suspect he's still sleeping, and a brief beep of a message won't be enough to wake him. But the ringing fails to do the job. Another attempt is made while walking toward baggage claim and once more as I wait for my suitcase to come along the conveyor belt. No answer.

Anger bubbles through me. Boiling, I grab my suitcase and take some rage out on my luggage by slamming it on the ground. Jason promised to pick me up and he knew when I was arriving. Couldn't he have set an alarm? I'm stationed in the taxi line when he rings me back.

"Ah, Rae, I'm sorry," Jason says, yawning. "I just woke up."

"It's okay, Jason," I say. *No, it's not.* "I'm going to grab a cab."

"No, Rae, let me pick you up," he insists. "I'll be there in twenty minutes."

I accept and reverse my steps, baby striding a slow walk to the passenger pick up area, acknowledging and begrudgingly accepting that I'm back in Las Vegas. When I left two weeks ago, I'd pleaded with the universe to stop time, to please let my trip back East crawl by so that each day felt like a week (while simultaneously counting down the days to New York). (Humans. What's wrong with us and our mess of contradictions?) Those fourteen days had not especially flown by, but here I am anyway, back in the Vegas Valley. My anger subsides and I'm hit with a deep wave of sadness, both in knowing the conversation I'm about to start and for what my immediate, unknown future holds.

In my absence, the purple mountains bordering the valley appear larger, rising high above everything and forming an inescapable bowl. They, more than anything else, not the slew of tourists exiting the airport, or the multitude of billboards lining the interstates advertising casinos and restaurants and all the supposed fun to be had, aggravate my unhappiness, the suffocating loneliness this place stirs for me. Of all the things, how are my beloved mountains inspiring the most existential dread? Could it be that this foreboding they offer is a gift, a reminder to carry through?

Jason arrives thirty minutes later. He envelopes me.

"I missed you so much," he says, giving me a quick peck on the lips.

"I missed you, too," I say, obliging him with a peck back.

More lies. *No, I didn't miss you. And I dreaded coming back here.* If our relationship had been open and honest from the start, all this could have been avoided. We could have parted ways years earlier, when I first realized we didn't work as a couple. But I'd been lying to myself then as well.

No more of that. It's time to spill.

I open my mouth, but the action is as effective as shouting his name into the wind. Save for the radio turned to a low volume, the car is silent. We don't speak. We haven't seen each other in two weeks and yet we still don't have anything to say. It's another obvious indicator this needs to happen. I try again.

"Jason?"

He looks at me for a second. "Yes, my honey?"

"I … I'm hungry." *Fucking chicken.*

"I am too," he says. "You want Hawaiian barbecue?"

"Sure." I close my eyes to hide the tears welling beneath my lids. Now that I'm in his company, a wave of memories rushes through me. Happy ones, only the good. A random Tuesday at my apartment in Seoul. I'd gone out for dinner with my roommates. They stretched the evening with beers, but I called it after eating. Jason and I weren't married yet and he still lived with his grandmother, so I was home alone, relaxing in bed with a book.

Bang!

The unexpected slamming of the front door ripped me from the pages of *Free Food for Millionaires.* My first thought was that my room-mates had arrived home, but I didn't hear the two of them chattering. Rarely did any of us walk in so silently.

"Hello," I yelled, expecting one of them to reply. Nothing but the creak of the wood floors indicating footsteps.

Oh shit, who is here? What the fuck was that?

I clenched my body, preparing to leap from my bed and flee. My bedroom door flung open and my heart fell to the bottom of my stomach. Surely, this was my demise, murdered by an intruder who somehow knew the code to our apartment.

"My honey!" Jason's beaming face, framed by his thick mop of hair, poked into my room, a benign version of Jack Nicholson's *Here's Johnny.*

"Jason! What are you doing here?" Given the ninety-minute commute that separated us, we rarely saw one another during the week.

"I had to see you! I couldn't wait for Friday."

"Really? This is the best surprise!" My heart rose back to my chest and swelled. Oh my, what a way to show someone you loved them.

I recall the weekend we headed to the Eastern Korean coast and took an overnight train to get there. On it, I reclined my body on his for a comforting cushion to sleep on. We arrived in time to see the sunrise over the ocean and then fall asleep in the sand in one another's arms.

Other images fight for space. A sweaty and smiling Jason tuckered after a soccer game and advancing toward me for a giant victory hug. Him bringing me a bowl of steaming hot chicken soup when I was sick with a cold. The two of us bathing a tiny lost dog we discovered during a summer storm.

I'm flooded with memories. I open my eyes to no longer see them, but now I'm fully present with my husband, the one person I just decided I need out of the way. How am I going to do this?

But then I realize my bittersweet reminiscing has captured lost moments from what seemed a lifetime ago, on another continent, from a joyful but expired phase of our relationship. I try to conjure up a recent memory, something from the last year. I recollect road trips, dinners, Phish shows. There's Kylie, Anna, Mom and Dad, Faris, so many of Faris, but none involve Jason.

This does help me picture a parallel existence. In it, I no longer reside in Las Vegas. I made the move I always wanted, and call Denver home. And it feels like home, like a place I was meant to exist in. Here, I don't struggle to meet people. Demaris and I develop an even stronger friendship and I have a variety of friends both through and independent of her. Some I grab beers with on a Friday, others to meet for a stroll in the park or for a Sunday morning hike. There are dinners together, coffee dates, trips to the dog park, dancing at shows.

My life in Denver includes a support system I can rely on. My friends care for me, check in on my mental well-being when my anxiety flares. They guarantee I'm not alone. It's symbiotic. I have my "Anna," my "Selena," and my "Kylie" in Colorado, and I get to introduce them to one another.

I teach in Denver and eventually master my skills in the classroom. I'm respected and highly regarded for the environment I cultivate for my little ones, where students feel safe and comfortable and learn not only academic skills but social and emotional ones as well. Teaching doesn't get any easier, but I get better, and I'm rewarded by the magic churning in an elementary school, the *oohs* and *ahhs* of my students turning on to the wonders of reading fill my classroom and my heart.

And though I'm content with or without one, I visualize my alternate partner. He is tall and broad, with blue eyes and a face prickly with stubble. My blue-eyed, bearded partner and I, growing from the initial communication bumps our relationship (almost never) started from, actually have discussions in order to plan our lives together. We ensure the other is satisfied when making decisions. We can sit around in comfortable silence together. He watches TV while I read next to him, pausing our solo decompressions to check in on the other. To laugh at our dog. To smother one another in smooches.

We see as much live music together as possible: Phish, of course, and My Morning Jacket, Trombone Shorty, Railroad Earth, so much music because Denver is never short on bands passing through. Sure, I'm occasionally sad, and my anxiety will become uncontrollable at times, but that can happen to anyone. What's most important is that I've finally found my home and am living happily and satisfied.

The biggest obstruction blocking me from this alternate universe stands in front of me, literally and figuratively. We've arrived at Arabella Apartments and Jason rolls my suitcase ahead while I languish behind, taking deep breaths, willing myself to do it.

It's now or never, Rachael. Just do it. These thoughts need no more interior space. Release them! If I delay any longer, I'll never set them, or myself, free.

"Jason, sit down. We need to talk."

Chapter 37

Jason sits at our dining room table. I follow him, my litany of classic anxiety symptoms bursting simultaneously and cranked to ten. Tunnel vision causes me to stumble over my discarded suitcase standing in the path between the living room and kitchen.

"Rae, are you okay?" Jason asks me.

"Yeah, I'm a bit lightheaded. I've been up for hours and haven't eaten yet." My eyesight fades in and out, and I work my mouth to spill the words. *Jason, this is over.*

Proving they're more formidable than my lust for something more, my nerves defeat me in a pivot. "Let's hurry up and order that food."

"Is this what you wanted to talk about?"

"Yes! Hurry! Get me teriyaki chicken please."

We forge on. Jason picks up our Hawaiian BBQ and we eat it at the table. Silence prevails. Afterward, I unpack, and he naps on the living room floor. This is my life. I better get used to it. I'll adapt eventually.

While I hang my clean dresses and sweaters—freshly washed by my mother—I think of me and Faris, of our antics in New York. Me dancing, him bobbing his head, both of us consumed in the music. Sitting beside one another at a bar, my hand resting on his knee and our faces turned to each other in conversation. My naked chest pressing to his.

In real time, Jason wakes from his nap and hurriedly readies himself for work. He pecks my cheek and rushes out the door. I plop on the couch and turn on the Dunphys to distract the Sunday scaries though it's Saturday.

New year. Check. New me? No way.

This is no way to live.

I pass the evening on the couch. Jason returns from work and there's more takeout and silent eating. Jason controls the television remote, and I read, or pretend to. I think of Faris and New York again. I look at Jason and my heart pounds, Pavlovian style. My hands lose power and drop the book I'm holding.

"You okay?" he asks.

I want a divorce, Jason.

I can't say that. I stand up. "I'm tired. I'm going to bed."

I fantasize for hours, unable to sleep. Jason remains in the living room. Eventually, he comes to our room but I, thankfully, surrendered to sleep with the bed all to myself. When I wake in the morning, his prone figure lies beside me. I picture that first morning we spent together, long ago in a faraway place. In another life. I had left him dozing in my bed while I crept quietly away to work. Before closing my bedroom door, I snuck one last look at him. Eyes closed, his high cheekbones highlighting the handsomeness in his sleeping face. How I wanted him to always be in my bed.

He opens his eyes now. Smiles. "Good morning, my honey."

"Morning."

We linger under the sheets, not speaking, not touching. Jason used to prefer morning sex. Rarely a weekend morning would go by without him pressing up against me from behind, but we haven't been intimate since copulating on the living room floor, my pre-Trader Joe's seduction of desperation. That was, or it seemed, so long ago. Maybe I should touch him now ...

Except I don't want to. The only person I want to touch is Faris.

"What shall we do today?" he asks.

"I need to go to the grocery store. We have nothing here." Our cupboards and pantry bare, it looks as if Jason hadn't grocery shopped in the two weeks I was gone. He's left that chore as a return gift for me.

I don't want to do that.

I don't want to do any of it.

"I picked up things here and there when I needed them. I was going to stop on Friday, but I ended up going to the recruiting center."

I turn to him. "You did! Why? Did you sign up? Why didn't you tell me?"

He shakes his head. "No, I didn't sign anything. I had some questions."

What's he waiting for? Was my subconscious right? Is he not going to join unless I give the green light, tell him I'm on board with being an army wife?

He has stated countless times he intends to join the army, but if I don't initiate the split, will he ever do it?

The meanest thing Jason had ever done was not tell me about his American citizenship ceremony. When he initially confessed this to me, my blood turned cold, my limbs froze in shock. But the truth is, his cruelty had set me free. If I went to his citizenship ceremony, I wouldn't have gone to the Phish shows in Saratoga Springs. The universe wouldn't have been able to place me exactly where I needed to be.

A chance run-in with an old college crush, not a fresh start in the Nevada desert, offered me my true rebirth.

This divorce isn't just about me. Jason and I must go our separate ways. It's the one, single thing that will allow either of us to live. As harsh as it'll be, it's my turn to set Jason free. Even if he doesn't follow through on his military aspirations, he deserves the chance to build a life without the burden of someone who doesn't love him.

I pull myself into an upright position and glance once more at my husband. "Why haven't you signed the contract yet?"

"I don't know."

"Are you waiting for anything?" I stare down into my lap. There's no way I can look at him when I do this. I take a breath. And then one more. I let it out, and along with it, before my brain stunts or my heart pauses out of fright …

"Jason, I don't think we're right for each other."

Chapter 38

"What are you saying, Rae?"

I steal a glimpse at my husband. He's frozen, supine with his head cushioned on his pillow and facing me, eyes wide and mouth slackened There's no going back in time to take back what I said, and I can't chase my words with a net and capture them, tucking them out of sight and out of mind until he forgets. In my morning unleashing, I've started to expose what has haunted me for far too long and I need to reveal the rest.

With my gaze once again in my lap, I continue to purge in a shaky voice, dancing over the complete truth in a partial confession. I've already struck the blade in; there's no point in twisting deeper into the wound. "I think there are better people for us. We don't connect over anything anymore, do we? And you want to join the army and I want no part of that, but I don't want to hold you back. There's another woman out there who would support you, but I'm not her. I think we should get a divorce."

I look at him. His face has collapsed. It's an imploding building; his eyes close, perhaps in shock, and tears soak his lashes while his lips squeeze together in a thin, downturned line of agony. He covers his grief with his hands, and I turn to the calming green ferns that dot our bedspread, using my palms to gather the fabric in bunches. Silent, I stay in that position, my head and back upright and supported by the wall, neck craned down, and hands fidgeting with the cover, listening to my husband sob. For once, I'm not the one weeping.

After what seems like hours, but is probably minutes, Jason stops crying. The mattress moves with his body as he propels himself into a seated position and stands up. I sense him walk away, but I stay behind, numb, processing the momentousness of this morning's events.

This is it. This is so much of what I'd feared, and it's happening right in front of me. No, I'm living it. A contradiction of emotions washes through me. Self-Loathing. Elation. Dismay. Confusion. I just ended my marriage, yet I never felt so light, so unburdened. I've no idea what follows, but it's done, or at least I've begun the process of dissolving our marriage. I said it, finally, and there's no going back.

Only forward.

I force myself out of bed and walk into the living room. Jason lies on the couch scrunched on his side in a fetal position, hiding his head in the crook of his arms. I slump to the ground at the foot of the couch. The day passes, neither of us moving. Not speaking. Breathing. Existing. The shadows in the room alter with the shifting sun. As darkness approaches, the living room dimming so that we're practically silhouettes, Jason speaks, his voice low but steady.

"If you think the best thing for us to do is get a divorce, then we should get one."

"I'm sorry, Jason. I think we really aren't meant for each other. Moving here showed me how much we've drifted away from one another. I want the best for you, and I want you to be happy. But I'm not happy. I haven't been for a while."

"I guess I'm not all that happy either." He pauses for several moments. "And I do want to join the army. I think I'll sign the papers sometime this week."

♫

The sun has barely touched the bottom of the horizon, hints of yellow and pink in a rising day contrast with the blue-black sky, but I'm awake, eyes wide open without my alarm. I haven't slept. My heartache wouldn't grant me any rest. Instead, I watched Jason's slumbering form beside me and thought of our final months together, of the memories we created to close out our marriage.

Keeping true to his word, Jason did sign his enlistment contract in early January. His basic training would take place in Georgia, but it didn't begin until April. This meant he and I, not yet technically divorced, would continue to live together for over three months.

I expected awkwardness to prevail in our marriage purgatory, the one hundred days of cohabitation with my soon-to-be ex-husband filled with an aggrieved Jason devoting his days to making mine a living hell while I hid behind locked doors and the white noise of bathroom fans.

I was wrong. There was no animosity, little tension, zero fighting. Our final three months reflected a bastardized version of the reset I hoped for. While I was awash with internal disputes, looking forward to Jason starting boot camp so I could begin my next phase but trying not to take our remaining days for granted, it was the strongest he and I had been in years. We hiked through abandoned railroad tunnels on a trail to the Hoover Dam. Cosmic bowled in an alley filled with black lights, lasers, and fog. Road tripped to LA to visit my brother. Our dinners out, though never a verbose affair, became somewhat chatty.

He chose pho and boba tea as his final civilian meal. Sucking up tapioca balls through the oversized straw, he confessed what he was most looking forward to. "I can retire early. I only need to stay in the army for twenty years and then I can be done working forever."

I almost spit my taro tea out from the laughter that bubbled up from this so very Jason remark.

Finally, I have some recent, happy remembrances with Jason to accompany the older ones. They are bittersweet souvenirs, not just of what we became but of what we once were and how we treated and felt about one another when we knew our marriage was ending and our time together was finite.

And after this morning, we'll never share this bed or any bed again.

I wake him up. We brush our teeth and wash our faces, but while he chooses his clothes carefully, I stay in my pajamas. I won't be exiting the car. It's Jason who's leaving.

The sun is coming up in full force on our right as I drive the short distance to drop him off. I park the car and we turn to one another in the small space in the front seat. With downcast eyes and his right hand palming his rigid cheeks, Jason's face betrays little emotion. Mine probably bears all of mine.

"You may be the oldest recruit, but you're going to kick everyone's ass. Show those eighteen-year-olds how boot camp is done," I tell Jason as I slap his knee, attempting to force some levity into the sadness suffocating the car's interior.

He stifles his laughter with a weak smile but doesn't say anything.

"Make sure you call me as soon as you can," I say.

"I will," he promises. "I love you, Rae."

"I love you, too," I say, and I mean it.

We hug tightly and then he grabs his duffle bag, gets out of the car, and walks out of my life and into the recruitment center. An army bus that will shuttle Jason's cohort of newly enlisted to the airport idles at the curb outside. I don't stick around to watch the would-be soldiers board.

Once I'm back at the apartment, I immediately go to my closet, to the gigantic walk-in that helped sell me on this place. Jason's wardrobe used to claim the right side. He'd hung his jeans and khakis and his multitude of button-down shirts on plastic hangers that now swing empty. The shelves that held his T-shirts and his one hat (a Red Sox baseball cap with its sticker still clinging to the bill because Jason thought the trend looked cool) were cleaned bare and are waiting for my workout clothes and plethora of hats to spread out upon the blank racks. This space is all mine. The closet, the bed, the couch, the television. The entire apartment. My life.

All mine.

This is what I had wanted.

I lie down on the carpeted floor inside the closet and cry myself to sleep.

Chapter 39

I write the date in the middle of the board as I do every morning before the school day starts. My second graders learn the concept of time, of the days of the week, and the months of the year. Time, and the passing of it, is something teachers are constantly aware of, lying in wait for our closest three-day weekend, the winter holiday, summer vacation. It's like we're wishing our lives away.

I've been counting down the days since mid-January, using weeks instead of days to make it appear shorter. Twelve weeks seems less of an eternity than eighty-four days. Never in my life have I wished my life away with such fervor.

Friday, April 11, 2014

This day desperately needed to arrive, and finally, it's here. It marks the last day of school before my weeklong spring break. I'm hosting my first house guest (other than my parents, who visited last fall), and they arrive tonight.

I haven't had any physical contact with family or friends since I left Pennsylvania at the beginning of the year. For four months, I've been stuck in a limbo reality of existing in my former life while waiting for things to happen that will allow me to spring into the next one. This break commences this next phase.

Because I've looked forward to the break with the anticipation of a child with their sights on Christmas, the school day snails by. I experience a full twenty-four hours inside every sixty minutes; it feels like the equivalent of a week has passed when the final bell rings. I usher my students out the door and into the safety of their loved ones, run into my classroom to grab my purse, disregarding my computer to fully honor my week away from school, and I'm out the door, free.

Only to wait. Though my apartment looks spotless, I kill hours by cleaning, sprucing up my bathroom with a fresh layer of bleach and my kitchen with the crisp and clean aroma of lemons.

The text pings after nine. *I'm here.*

I bolt out the door to retrieve my visitor. They're standing outside the passenger pick up at the airport, wearing a look of contrived impatience that morphs into a smile once I pull up.

"Kylie, you're here!" I shout through my open passenger side window. I exit the car and we capture one another in a bear hug. "I thought this day would never arrive."

"Woman, I thought you would never arrive." She squeezes me. "Do you know how long I've been waiting here?"

"It's twenty minutes from my house. So, maybe two minutes?"

"I walked outside a minute ago."

Back at Arabella Apartments, I give Kylie a tour of my tiny abode, grab a twenty-four-ounce bottle of stout beer to share, and lead her outside to my favorite spot.

She takes a seat on a pink petal and looks at me. "How are you doing?" she asks. It's not a blasé question meant for small talk.

I grimace. "No, ignore that face," I tell her. "I'm great. Even better now that you're here." I lean over and touch her forearm.

"Do you feel like talking about it now that I'm here?"

"Yeah, I do." I nod, suddenly hit with a wave of melancholy. "Last weekend was rough. I didn't expect to be that sad, but Saturday, as we were packing up the last of his things for storage, I couldn't stop crying. And then I dropped him off on Sunday and came back here, and I sat in the closet and cried. I looked at all this space, all the shelves and racks to hang up my clothes, but Jason's things were all missing. The entire space was mine. Everything I wanted to happen was happening, yet here I was crying myself to sleep in my fucking closet. I don't know how someone can feel so devastated yet so happy at the same time. What the fuck is wrong with me?"

Kylie reaches across the table and gently grabs my wrist. "Rae, you're grieving. This is natural. Jason just left for the army, what, not even a week ago?"

"But I had been looking forward to him leaving for basic training since he signed up! I couldn't wait for him to officially join the army. Why am I so fucking sad?"

"You guys were together for over six years. You loved him! Of course you're going to be sad. And it's a huge change for you. You need to adjust to that as well! But look at it this way. How would you feel if you hadn't brought up the divorce?"

I consider this. Intuitive Kylie. Everything she says is correct. My last words to Jason were true. I want nothing but good things for him. And though I'd been eagerly awaiting his start date with the army, I now must adapt to life without the person I spent the last six years with. Change is tough, no matter how much it's wanted.

I laugh. "Oh god, that would be terrible. We would still be together. He probably wouldn't have joined the army."

"Feel your feelings. It would be fucked up if you weren't sad. And you didn't tell him about Faris, right?"

I shake my head vigorously. "No, no, oh no. I couldn't do that. What would be the point? I mean, I kind of told him when I said I thought there were better people out there for us. But what would I have gained by telling him?"

"Nothing. It would have made him angry."

"Yeah, exactly."

"Look at it this way. You guys weren't happy. You would have eventually divorced him, with or without Faris."

"We would have, right? At least I hope so."

"*Yes!* You may have hidden it for a while longer, but eventually, you would have got the fuck out." Kylie extends and enunciates those last words.

I sigh. It sounds exaggerated, but it's anything but. The solitary exhale wordlessly sums up my frustrations and disappointment in my actions. "I wish I hadn't let it drag on as long. That's my biggest regret.

We should have split up sooner. And then I had to go and fucking cheat on him. Who wants to admit to having an affair? I'm such an asshole. Such a bitch. If I'd ended things when I really should have, if I stopped lying to myself sooner, it would never have come to that. And then there'd be less drama for me and Faris to contend with."

"Stop being so hard on yourself. You were in a tough situation. Look at it this way: once you and Faris slept together, you knew you had to end things with Jason. You didn't stretch on this physical affair for months and months."

"Well, Faris kind of helped me end things with Jason. Who knows what would have happened if Faris didn't call off everything with me? Would I have gone on with the affair while still trying to make my ridiculous marriage work?"

"No, no. I don't think so at all. You're not that kind of person. And like I said, I think you would have reflected on what you wanted anyway, whether Faris ended things with you or not. You're not some bullshitter who creates wishes and goals and never acts on them."

"Who knows how long that would have taken?"

"That doesn't matter. You did it. And if you hadn't initiated the divorce now, Jason might have missed his opportunity to join the army. He would have aged out. So you actually helped him pursue what he wanted. Look at that!" Kylie is animated, stretching her open and upturned palms in my direction.

I digest this. "You're right."

"I know," she nods.

"Thank you. This is helping."

"And I'm here! Let's celebrate all of this." She leans in close to me and clinks her glass to mine. "And don't forget about Wednesday."

"I'd never be able to forget that!"

Wednesday. It's gone from eighty-four to five days away.

Chapter 40

It's Kylie's first trip to Vegas, but we do minimal Strip carousing. A single afternoon poking around the botanic displays at The Wynn and marveling at the cloud-filled skies decorating the ceiling throughout The Venetian satiates her Strip desires.

"Show me the real Vegas," she insists.

I do my best to meet these demands. We hike, taking part in an early morning Meetup in the Spring Mountains. Our charismatic guide is the one male in the group and the women pepper him with questions, a front, I believe, to flirt with him. His girlfriend trails behind the rest of us hikers; she may not be the trekking fan her boyfriend is. He checks in frequently, calling back to her, "How you doing, honey bunny? You hanging in there?"

I forget to reapply sunscreen and my amateur mistake rewards me with my first sunburn of the season. My arms, neck, and face wear a painful base of red. The burn forces me to rethink my wardrobe for our nighttime excursion. I can recycle my planned outfit for later in the week. Maybe for Wednesday. I mask my scarlet skin with makeup and layers.

We venture to Fremont Street, Old Vegas, to The Beauty Bar. One wall is lined with vintage seated hair dryers, and though they won't dry a potential rolled-up beehive, they do make a statement seat when guzzling down a cocktail. Kylie and I aren't there for the ambiance, however, but for the music. Outside is a backyard bandstand where we are introduced to the music of The Jon Spencer Blues Explosion. Kylie bought the tickets on a whim, and we didn't know what to expect. They're good. Real good. We dance the entire show.

We spend Kylie's last day sipping Bloody Marys poolside at the Green Valley Ranch casino. We leave my car there, grab a taxi to get us safely back to my place, and order a gigantic margherita pizza for dinner. Her flight doesn't leave until tomorrow evening, so we overdo it with beers at my flower table until close to 2:00 a.m.

She collapses on her belly in my bed, on Jason's former side. Since arriving, she's slept beside me, her presence in Jason's old space offering a warm comfort. It's been easier for me to sleep, knowing there's another person, a much-loved person, here with me. But tonight, with the sugar from the booze coursing through my bloodstream, I toss and turn, thinking about Wednesday. Wondering how the hell I got to this point. Physically, mentally, and metaphysically.

Was it all through calculated design, all my deliberate planning? One step led to another, steering the way to this city, this career, to Kylie snoring ten inches from my head. Was this all because of the choices I made? The places I opted to work, my decision to teach in Seoul, Kylie and I attending those Phish shows at SPAC when we could have gone the week later instead. Where would I be if I took an alternative at any point?

Or was something larger at play? The universe. Lifeforce synergy. Cosmic destiny. I couldn't deny the power in the bizarre coincidences that crossed my path. How working at The Order People with its plethora of young northeast Pennsylvania hippies coincided with my dive into the counterculture or that random set break encounter hours after I took my wedding ring off. These events all planted seeds, shifted energies, and set me into motions I couldn't deny seeking.

It's both, right? It has to be. Though intentional in choosing my path, the most unexpected and unplanned things appeared, either further enforcing what I already decided or helping to alter what I thought otherwise was meant to be. A melding of the spirit and human world to create my present existence.

Go to sleep, Rachael, you're drunk. I chuckle at myself, at my 2:00 a.m. Jack Handy deep thoughts. Kylie's light snores deepen. I blow a kiss her way, another toward the sky, and drift off to slumber.

♫

It's Wednesday.

I'm back at the airport again. It's my third trip in six days, but now I play the visitor role, stepping on an airplane to take me far, far away from this desert sand trap. With a mix of luck, effort, and time, I'm hoping that what's temporary for now will transform into a permanent vacation from this place.

Kylie left yesterday. I dropped her off at this very terminal I sit in. Though bummed to bid her farewell, watching her walk away meant I was that much closer to today. Kylie's trip may be finished, but my spring break fun is only half over.

I've arrived at McCarren early. My flight isn't even listed at its gate yet, but I preferred waiting here, with its crowds, shops, and noises, then in the silent void of my vacant apartment. Overcome with nervous excitement, I bolt from my seat at the gate and pace the store-lined hall, rolling my red suitcase along. My stomach twists and turns in a pleasant loop. It's a welcome feeling, a sign of my jubilation.

I think back to that phone call made eighty-four days ago, ringing him from the Planet Fitness parking lot, sweaty and flushed from my workout. I was flooded with endorphins, though my nervousness that he wouldn't pick up, that the call wouldn't go well, threatened my exercise high.

But he did pick up.

It was the first time I heard his voice, the first time we'd spoken since we parted ways on a midtown Manhattan Street on New Year's Day. Hearing his "hello" enhanced all my feelings: the exhilaration, the dread, and the hope.

We exchanged stiff pleasantries. My breath caught in my throat. This wasn't the start I wanted. *Hello. How are you? I'm fine.* All said with barely a hint of emotion. No. So I got right to it.

"I know you and I never talked about my marriage. That's my fault. I avoided talking with you about it when I should have been upfront from the start. The truth is, my marriage wasn't good. It was awful, and I was miserable. So fucking miserable. And then you randomly showed up and I started to see how happy I could be. I meant everything I said to you in New York. I would love to be with you. And I finally had the courage to end my marriage, so I'm hoping it's not too late and that there's still a chance with you. And if not, I still want to say thank you for helping me realize not just how unhappy I really was, but for helping push me in the right direction. For making me see what I truly wanted. So thank you."

I finished. Held my breath. Waited for him to respond. Would he hang up? Rebut me? Tell me how awful I was for cheating on my husband and making him a complicit partner to the cuckoldry?

He did none of those things.

"Rachael, I want to be with you too."

In the almost three months that passed since my parking lot (not bathroom) phone call, Faris and I were back to texting every day and had graduated to talking on the phone and an occasional Skype video call. The latter was always met with a scolding from Faris to "get an iPhone so we could Facetime."

I've yet to upgrade my phone and am unable to Google my flight status. It doesn't matter. My airport wandering brings me back to my gate and its information is updated.

Denver. 5:15. On Time.

Acknowledgements

At the end of my most recent trip "home," my mother presented me with an absolute treasure: all 230 handwritten pages of my first book, *The Nightmare Murders*. I thought I lost it, but she kept it safe for thirty years. The shock and awe that filled my body when she placed it in my hands acted like a time machine. Suddenly I was twelve years old again, writing my Christopher Pike-inspired horror novel late into the night during the summer of 1994, pushing myself to write one more page before going to sleep in the stifling heat of my bedroom, dreaming of getting it published the entire time.

I've wanted to be an author my entire life, and though that didn't happen with *The Nightmare Murders*, it's happened with *Second Set Chances*. I still can't believe it! Writing a book is so hard—algebra doesn't hurt my brain as much—and it takes commitment. I started the first draft in the weeks before Phish Dick's in 2019, and here I am in August 2024, the week before Dick's, "perfecting" the final iteration. Over the last five years, I've written and edited over a dozen drafts, participated in two writing workshops, tested it through two rounds of beta readers, and queried dozens of agents and publishers, hoping one would give me the green light to publication.

I'm forever grateful to Vine Leaves Press for saying yes. Thank you to Jessica Bell and Amie McCracken for taking a chance on both my story and Phish's community of music zealots (we're not a cult, I swear). You've made my dreams come true. An extra hug to Jessica for taking the time out of her hectic day to come meet me in-person when I was in Athens last summer. I felt like I was meeting a celebrity! I'm indebted to my editor, Melissa Slayton, for her numerous read-throughs of the manuscript and for giving *Second Set Chances* its own second chance.

At forty-two, I still can't decide whether the literary arts or musical arts are my preferred jam (and do I really need to pick one over the other), but my parents have always and continue to nurture both loves. Biweekly trips to the mall weren't complete without a stop at Walden Books, and Mom made sure we visited the library regularly. We've seen so much live music together, from Paula Abdul (my first concert at nine) to the Rolling Stones (twice), Billy Strings, and My Morning Jacket (you're welcome for that one, Mom). I truly hit the parent jackpot with the two of you.

Countless love and hugs to Tanya and Natalie, my forever show buddies for almost twenty-five years. Abby, you have been such a back-bone throughout my evolution. Life would be far different without your interventions! Meg, cheers for supporting me through every good and bad decision and for always helping me make sense of things. Ashley, you've become my sister. I'm glad we didn't have to fight over a boy. Monica, thanks for helping me navigate through such a heavy life period. I love you all so much!

I know everyone claims their Phish crew is the best, but my nuclear phamily really is. I must express my love and appreciation to the rest of my Cubes not named yet: Leigh, Lara, Dee, Teddy, and Ryan. Eternally grateful to share in these musical adventures across the continent with you.

To my Cour Four writing group, I may never have finished draft one without your feedback and collaboration. Joanna, our friendship is the shiniest silver lining to the world's worst job. That latter may be slightly hyperbolic, but you mean the world to me. Carm and Chris, thank goodness for the perfect timing when taking barre and writing classes. Carm, thanks for experimenting with book coaching with me. We both learned so much in that endeavor!

Second Set Chances

To all my beta readers: Grace, Laura, Amanda S, Amanda H, Meag, Mary, Jaclyn, Anne Marie, Diani, Meg, Nat, Leigh, Bonni, and Melisa. Thank you for helping morph *Clap Your Hands if You Think You're in the Right Place* into *Second Set Chances* and for shaping *Second Set Chances* into the best book it could be. I appreciate the time spent reading and reflecting on my words. I echo this sentiment toward my Lighthouse workshop writing group. Extra kudos to Alice Johnson and Christine Barbour for sticking with me and my writing long past the end of our class.

A special thank you to Chrisi French, for her creative vision and eye behind her camera. I'm obsessed with my author photos; no one has ever captured me looking like such a natural beauty. Kudos to Jason Gershunny, another Phish author, who so kindly took a moment from his day to speak with me about his publishing experience.

So much love to our Phish community. I honestly don't know where I would be if I hadn't been wrapped up in all the love and acceptance of our zany world. To all my friends made through this not-a-cult, I love you. Thanks for letting me be me and for reveling together in the magic of music.

To the music makers and authors of the world. I rely so much on these arts not just in my day-to-day, but in getting through dark periods when my mental health isn't cooperating. A concert is my church and one of the few places I feel most alive and connected to the unbreakable net. Getting lost in a book is my favorite means of escape, and the connections made through characters and their situations is pivotal in making me feel so less alone when dealing with my own life nonsense.

Mesh, I don't know if I believe in soul mates, but you make a strong case for their existence. You're the greatest second chance ever. There's no one else I'd rather dance through this real thing called life with than you. Thank you for forgoing your privacy this one (major) time. We're poster children, I tell you!

Vine Leaves Press

Enjoyed this book?
Go to *vineleavespress.com* to find more.
Subscribe to our newsletter:

BV - #0068 - 190625 - C0 - 229/152/14 - PB - 9783988321411 - Matt Lamination